Fashion Logistics

Fashion Logistics
Insights into the Fashion Retail Supply Chain

By
John Fernie
David B Grant

KoganPage

LONDON PHILADELPHIA NEW DELHI

First published in Great Britain and the United States in 2015 by Kogan Page Limited

2nd Floor, 45 Gee Street	1518 Walnut Street, Suite 1100	4737/23 Ansari Road
London	Philadelphia PA 19102	Daryaganj
EC1V 3RS	USA	New Delhi 110002
United Kingdom		India

© John Fernie and David B Grant, 2015

The right of John Fernie and David B Grant to be identified as the authors of this work has been asserted by them in accordance with the Copyright, Designs and Patents Act 1988.

ISBN   978 0 7494 7298 6
E-ISBN 978 0 7494 7297 9

British Library Cataloguing-in-Publication Data

A CIP record for this book is available from the British Library.

Library of Congress Cataloging-in-Publication Data

Fernie, John, 1948– author.
  Fashion logistics : insights into the fashion retail supply chain / John Fernie, David B. Grant.
      pages cm
   ISBN 978-0-7494-7298-6 (paperback) – ISBN 978-0-7494-7297-9 (ebk)   1. Retail trade—
Management.   2. Business logistics.   3. Inventory control.   I. Grant, David B., author.   II. Title.
   HF5429.25.F47 2015
   746.9'20687—dc23
                                                                            2015033997

Typeset by Amnet
Print production managed by Jellyfish
Printed and bound by CPI Group (UK) Ltd, Croydon, CR0 4YY

TABLE OF CONTENTS

Introduction to fashion logistics

T he overall objective of this book is to introduce the reader to the key challenges facing logisticians in managing an increasingly complex fashion retail supply chain. The authors have considerable experience of writing on supply chain management (SCM) issues, especially in retailing, and the fashion sector has become the focus of much of our current work. In the recent 4th edition of Fernie's co-edited book with Leigh Sparks, *Logistics and Retail Management*, there was considerably more debate around fashion issues rather than the more grocery-related content in earlier editions of the work.

Why is this the case? There is a range of mainly macro-environmental reasons for this change in focus. The phasing out of the Multi-Fibre Agreement in 2005 led to a more competitive global market for the supply of manufactured garments and offered retailers opportunities to source from a greater range of suppliers. This in turn resulted in more offshore sourcing and outsourcing, with the need to balance the benefits of cost savings with longer lead times. The controversies over the CSR issues around low-cost production, highlighted by the tragedy of the Rana Plaza building collapse in Bangladesh in 2013, drew media attention to the unacceptable aspects of offshore production. Closer to home, retailers also have to manage the supply chain consequences of the digital revolution, with consumers buying from a variety of channels and demanding more flexible options in the delivery, return or collection of their goods.

The structure of the book encapsulates many of the issues highlighted above and Figure 1.1 provides an overview of the chapters as they pertain to a wider discussion of the fashion retail sector or operational and supply chain issues regarding sourcing and distribution to consumers. The first three chapters discuss the main changes in the fashion retail environment and the supply chain consequences of such changes. This provides a backdrop to discussing the more operational aspects of offshore sourcing (international logistics), the digital revolution (online customer service) and in-store

FIGURE 1.1   Overview of this book's chapters

availability in the central chapters. The final two chapters focus upon the luxury sector, which has experienced much growth since the 1990s, and a topic that has warranted considerable discussion in the 2010s: sustainability in the fashion supply chain.

Chapter 2 is a scene-setting overview of trends in the fashion market and provides a review of supply chain changes that will then be discussed in more depth in subsequent chapters. It shows how the traditional fashion sector worked to a four-season planning model, but with the advent of fast fashion, consumers began to expect fresh new designs and innovative products to be constantly supplied to stores. The fastest growing sectors since the turn of the millennium have been in fast fashion and the luxury sector, but these sectors have been laggards in embracing online retailing. By contrast, middle-market retailers, many with a mail-order presence and well-developed store networks, have had the logistical infrastructure to capitalize on the shift to online retailing. The early movers online such as our case study company, Schuh, have been able to offer the customer a range of delivery and returns options including the increasingly popular 'click and collect/reserve' service. As competition increased in the fashion retail market, most companies followed the lead of fast-fashion retailers in sourcing products offshore. It will be shown that even Zara, Benetton and the luxury fashion retailers have followed this trend for non-core lines.

This theme is picked up in Chapter 3, with a more detailed discussion on offshore sourcing and outsourcing in the international fashion supply chain. The first part of the chapter provides a conceptual framework of types of sourcing and outsourcing strategies. This illustrates the different approaches taken by companies, from working through intermediaries to dealing directly with suppliers, with or without international hubs. Many retailers, including the case study company, Benetton, have preferred to use full-package suppliers from low-cost regions as their business has grown internationally. The nature of offshore sourcing has evolved as the costs of production change over time. We see in many of the examples cited that sourcing location is largely dependent on product category, cost and lead-time considerations. This has meant that basic, long lead-time products with low costs tend to be sourced in more distant markets such as China whereas the agile or leagile model is more relevant for seasonal basic products or fast-fashion items where flexibility and lead times are paramount. Markets closer to demand – Turkey and East Europe for West European retailers and Mexico and the Caribbean for US retailers – are more relevant here. Rising costs in China and other Asian markets have led to a slight move to 'reshoring' back to traditional textile markets. The example of Walmart and its attempt to source US $250 million of US goods by 2023 illustrates some of the difficulties in achieving 'reshoring'. The infrastructure in traditional markets has to be rebuilt and a new generation of workers has to be trained to produce competitively priced products.

The fourth chapter deals with major strategic issues revolving around the social and environmental consequences of offshore production. Much has been written about CSR, but numerous definitions exist from both the academic community and international organizations. Indeed, the chapter shows that some of the criticisms of CSR implementation emanate from a lack of clarity of the codes of conduct that companies have to adhere to. You can opt in or out of ISO 26000 as standards are voluntary not manda-tory. Many companies are accused of 'greenwashing' in that they produce PR 'spin' on aspects of CSR where they receive positive reviews. However, many reports do highlight companies that go beyond the basics of a stake-holder approach and are transparent in their reporting of audits and how they are monitoring social and environmental targets. Timberland is the case study example here showing how the company has embraced CSR initiatives since the 1980s when it developed a Path of Service programme that offered employees paid leave to perform community service activity. Since then it has incorporated three other pillars of CSR initiatives – climate, product and factories that establish quantifiable performance targets on *inter alia*

CO_2 emissions, recycling and social audits. The chapter also uses the example of Sri Lanka as a country that has positioned itself as an ethical producer of garments, notably added-value casual garments. While the so called 'race to the bottom' occurred in the 2000s and 2010s, with companies sourcing from cheaper and cheaper areas of production, Sri Lanka instead sought competitive advantage through its 'Garments without Guilt' campaign.

Chapter 5, International Logistics, is our first chapter that looks at the operational implications of the shift to offshore sourcing. After introducing the key concepts of supply chain management and in particular channels of distribution, the chapter discusses the impact of globalization on fashion retailers' international marketing entry strategy and the channels of distribution in specific regional markets. One of the most important concerns for fashion retailers is the risk of supply chain disruption when sourcing from distant, international markets. It is shown that risks take many forms, from man-made to natural disasters, and that supply chain risk management has risen in importance to mitigate risks and ensure an efficient recovery in supplying product when unforeseen events do occur. The chapter concludes by forecasting potential changes in international markets, with the need for greater collaboration among competitors, possibly through the use of 4PL intermediaries.

Chapters 6 and 7 consider the distribution, logistical and supply chain processes pertaining to national or domestic in-store and online retailing respectively. Each of these chapters begins with an introduction to the relevant processes, from port of entry into the national market in Chapter 6 or a retailer's national distribution centre in Chapter 7, through to the consumer, and then goes into important issues affecting retail performance and resulting consumer service. Key issues for in-store processes include the last 50 yards from the back of store to the shelf where on-shelf availability is a key problem for non-grocery retailers. Key issues for online retailers include a new, omnichannel environment where consumers can buy from multiple platforms such as mobile phones, tablets and laptops, and are very demanding, with high expectations for fulfilment and returns. As noted at the start of the introduction, recent work has focused less on the grocery sector – in particular because we have argued (Fernie and Grant, 2014) that the UK grocery supply chain may be considered to be the best in the world through its development from supplier-led inefficient supply in the 1980s to retailer-led, efficient and effective supply chains in the 21st century. Much of this achievement is down to the retailers taking control of supply chain matters during that time to improve product flows and service to consumers. However, some of it also rests with the fact that there is an oligopoly of grocery retailers in the UK aided and abetted by IGD and ECR UK. Recent problems in the grocery sector due to gains made by Aldi and Lidl may see further change. Nevertheless, there are many aspects in grocery supply chains that all retailers, including fashion retailers, might embrace and examples of some are provided in Chapters 6 and 7 where applicable.

In Chapter 8 we focus upon the luxury sector because of its spectacular growth since the late 1990s and the prominence of luxury brands as some of the world's most valuable brands. However, it was because of this growth into new product areas and international markets that companies began to face supply chain challenges. The chapter begins by defining the term 'luxury' and the key dimensions of the luxury brand, prior to discussing the factors responsible for the evolution and growth of the luxury brand. The democratization of luxury and the development of the pyramid model led to some companies, most notably Burberry and Gucci, losing control over their marketing channels through a flawed licensing strategy which then required a major repositioning of their iconic brands.

The degree of segmentation of the market by companies has determined the structure of their supply chain. So a company such as Hermès, which continues to focus on true luxury products, mainly manufactured in-house in French factories, contrasts with Burberry, which has grown through the expansion of diffusion lines, mostly produced by full-package suppliers in lower cost regions. Burberry is discussed in depth as a case study. The move to offshore sourcing has led to luxury companies receiving adverse criticism of their CSR policies, mainly in relation to sourcing of precious metals, leathers and furs. One criticism levelled at them was their lack of transparency at reporting CSR activities. It is noted, however, that the French Government implemented the Grenelle2 Act in 2012, which requires all large public companies in France to incorporate information on the social and environmental consequences of their activities in their annual reports. The world's largest luxury brands are primarily owned by French companies!

Our final chapter follows on the theme of CSR by discussing sustainability in fashion retailing. Unlike Chapter 4, much of this chapter focuses upon environmental sustainability rather than the social impacts of fashion retailers' operations. Initially concepts of sustainability are reviewed within the context of transaction cost economics, the resource-based view and the triple bottom line model of performance. Then the three main themes of environmental sustainability in logistics and SCM are addressed: reverse logistics, emissions assessment and the 'greening' of logistical and supply chain activities. Companies adopt a range of management tools such as life cycle analysis and environmental management systems to assess the feasibility of their sustainability strategies. Much of the research on the fashion sector suggests that retailers can only exercise direct influence over their own operations but, as indicated in other chapters (notably Chapter 3), companies have moved away from a vertically integrated supply chain model to an outsourcing/offshore production model. The onus on sustainability has now been placed on their suppliers. The main task at hand, however, is to change consumer perception of sustainability issues by influencing choice in the marketplace.

References

Fernie, J and Grant, D B (2014) On-shelf availability in UK retailing, in J Fernie and L Sparks (eds) *Logistics and Retail Management: Emerging issues and challenges in the retail supply chain* (4th edn), Kogan Page, London, pp 179–204

Fernie, J and Sparks, L (2014) *Logistics and Retail Management: Emerging issues and challenges in the retail supply chain* (4th edn), Kogan Page, London

The changing nature of fashion retailing:
implications for logistics

02

Introduction

The purpose of this chapter is to provide an overview of the evolution of fashion retailing in order to appreciate the challenges that logisticians have encountered, especially in recent times with the rise in offshore sourcing and online retailing. The chapter will also provide a context to chapters that follow in the remainder of the book. An initial historical perspective is taken to illustrate the role of culture in fashion prior to discussing the 'democratization' of fashion as globalization and technological advances have brought the latest trends to a wider consumer market. The rise of fast fashion challenged the traditional mindset of four seasons and long lead times to the market; however, slow fashion is now being advocated to bring a more ethical approach to the sourcing and distributing of fashion goods. The more recent advances in e- and m-commerce have necessitated radical changes in company organizational structures as retailers grapple with an omnichannel approach to satisfying consumer needs.

Fashion: its role in culture

Fashion is deemed a cyclical reflection of social, cultural and environmental characteristics that are unique to a certain point of time in a particular geographical setting, in addition to playing a crucial role in complementing one's self-image' (Azuma and Fernie, 2003, p 415).

It is therefore one of the arts of civilization and reflects the great cultures of the past. The social and political background of a given place can determine a particular dress code in a community (Yarwood, 1992). However, one of the greatest influences over fashion design is climate as clothes are worn to keep warm, preserve modesty with regard to moral codes and to protect the body. Thus designs were created with appropriate fabrics to not only reflect functionality but the latest styles of the time.

Fashion has always been dictated by countries that were rich and powerful at any moment in time. From the Roman Empire to the British Empire, the wealthy and influential members of society were trend-setters in wearing costumes that stood out from the crowd. It has been argued that the prominence of France as the world's foremost nation for fashion and style goes back to the extravagant lifestyle of the court of Louis XIV. Then the notion of fashion 'seasons' and changing styles were introduced. The French court, strongly influenced by Colbert, one of the king's key ministers, encouraged the exportation of luxury products stressing the excellence of craftsmanship (in 1954 the Committee Colbert was established to promote the values of French luxury goods around the world). While the Industrial Revolution led to the mass production of clothing goods, the French established their great couturier houses or *maisons* in the late 19th and early 20th centuries showcasing innovative designs and quality crafted French products.

Throughout the centuries fashions adopted by the rich were desired by the rest of society. This 'trickle down' effect has become even more significant in recent decades with the advent of fast fashion as the latest fashion designs are copied and made available to the mass market in a matter of weeks. We will now look at the impact of fast fashion and other trends in the market.

The changing fashion retail environment

By the 1970s and 1980s the industrial core of textile production remained in the traditional markets of Europe, the United States and latterly Japan; a reflection of the key centres for fashion shows and the origin of the main fashion houses. At that time the fashion design houses' main focus was on haute couture and ready to wear with the large textile firms undertaking mass production for the department store market. Fashion was still very traditional and dominated by relatively formal attire for the workplace until the 1970s when the counterculture of the era began to challenge the consumerism of the time. Fashion entrepreneurs anticipated lifestyle changes that were reflected in the casual clothes of the new generation. Indeed, Don and Doris Fisher saw a niche in the market for jeans sales and created Gap (the Generation Gap) in 1969 in San Francisco, the home of 'flower power' and hippy culture in the 1960s. Initially with strong support from Levi Strauss, another San Franciscan company, it later branched out into other casual products. Around the same time, in 1971 Phil Knight and Bill Bowerman had launched their first Nike trainer and the swoosh logo and were about to revolutionize the sports and casual footwear industry.

In Europe, companies that would have a profound influence on the fashion market were established; Luciano and Giuliana Benetton sold their initial colourful clothing through Italian department stores in 1965 and Amancio Ortega opened his first Zara store in La Corunna in 1975. Even earlier, Erling Persson had opened his first Hennes store in Sweden in 1947, changing the name to Hennes & Mauritz (H&M) on the acquisition of Mauritz Widforss in 1968, thereby also allowing the company to move into the menswear market.

The main drivers of change in the late 1980s and 1990s were the rise of the retail brand, the internationalization of the brand and the increased segmentation of the market. Those new US and European entrants to the fashion market stretched their brands into new segments but more significantly they took their retail concepts across the globe to influence the markets that they entered. In the UK for example, the traditional conglomerates such as Sears and Burton began to segment their offerings for different target markets. Many of these sub-brands later came under the ownership of Philip Green and the Arcadia group in the late 1990s. In response to consumer changes and new overseas competition, new concepts were introduced, such as George Davies' launch of Next in 1982, which initially targeted the working female consumer before moving into menswear and accessories. The demise of Sears in the 1990s can partly be attributed to their brands within their subsidiary, such as the British Shoe Corporation, coming under pressure from casual wear specialists (see the case study on Schuh later in the chapter).

The rise of fast fashion

By the late 1990s, more significant changes were affecting the fashion market. The vision of both Zara's and H&M's founders was to bring affordable style to the high street, since both had witnessed first-hand that it was only the rich who could afford well-made stylish clothes.

The phrase 'democratization of fashion' has been attributed to Zara's CEO in bringing style to the mass market (Tungate, 2008; Lopez and Fan, 2009). This fast-fashion phenomenon (Barnes and Lea-Greenwood, 2006, 2010; Divita and Yoo, 2013) was fuelled by celebrity culture so that consumers could wear copied styles seen in *Vogue* and celebrity magazines such as *Hello!* and *OK!* The 2000s saw the introduction of a slew of celebrity and fashion weekly magazines, such as *Heat, Grazia, Closer* and *Look*, which further fuelled the fast-fashion trend. Speed was of the essence and Zara could transform time to market (Christopher *et al*, 2004) from design concept to store in a matter of weeks, compared to the several month or even yearly cycle times of traditional retailers. In 2003, Crown Prince Felipe of Spain became engaged to Letizia Ortiz Rocasolano and for the official photos the bride wore a white trouser suit that would appear in Zara shops a few weeks later. On 16 November 2010, Prince William, the heir to the British throne, announced the date of his marriage to Kate Middleton. The £349 blue Issa creation she wore was replicated by Tesco and placed on its website one week later. The £16 dress sold out within an hour.

Fast-fashion retailers have transformed consumer behaviour in-store with their consumers aware that, unlike conventional retailers that are likely to hold stock for weeks, when a fast-fashion line is gone it is gone for good. They sell approximately 15 per cent of their merchandise on markdowns as opposed to 50 per cent for traditional apparel retailers (Shephard and Pookulangara, 2013). This is because fast-fashion retailers ship continuous small deliveries of a large number of designs so that new merchandise is always on the showroom floor. Zara makes 11,000 items in five to six colours and five to seven ranges annually (Divita and Yoo, 2013); H&M and Gap produce 2,000 to 4,000 items per annum. The net result has been that the fast-fashion retailers, especially the global players such as Zara, H&M and Mango, have grown faster than the clothing sector as a whole and have been gaining market share over traditional retailers.

The luxury sector

Considering that companies in the fast-fashion sector have achieved such growth through replicating styles of the famous fashion houses, it is ironic that the other sector to experience considerable global growth in the 2000s/2010s was the luxury market. Global sales grew from 77 billion Euros in 1995 to 223 billion Euros in 2014 despite a 10 per cent decline in 2009 after the onset of the global financial crisis (Bain and Company, 2014). The catalyst for growth has been the emergence of the Asian market, especially China which has become the leading market for luxury fashion goods as it has shifted from a production to a consumption economy. Luxury houses started in Europe in the 19th century, spread to America, and then to Japan in its post-war expansion. Now the emerging BRIC (Brazil, Russia, India and China) economies have created a new generation of millionaires who are demanding luxury brands. Yves Carcelle, the former CEO of Louis Vuitton, now represented in 64 countries, has called this the 'universalization' of the sector (Walsh, 2010).

The rapid growth of this sector can be attributed not only to demand from these emerging economies but also the changing structure of the luxury industry. The fashion design houses alluded to by Hollander (1970) in his seminal work focused mainly upon the couture and ready-to-wear market. By the 1990s many of these companies began to internationalize their businesses on a significant scale through the development of diffusion brands thereby splitting the market into good, better, best segments within family brand identities. For example, Armani has Giorgio Armani Privé (couture), Armani Collezioni (ready to wear), Emporio Armani (diffusion), and A/X Armani Exchange; the last for the mass market (Moore *et al*, 2000).

In order to make their market presence felt, fashion design houses developed flagship stores in the fashion capitals of the world. Fernie *et al* (1998) discussed the importance of specific streets in London (Bond Street and Sloane Street) and New York (Madison Avenue and Fifth Avenue). More recently Moore *et al* (2010) argued that the flagship store has become a key element of luxury companies' entry strategy to support and develop distribution strategies in foreign markets.

As these companies began to expand, they needed capital to fuel their growth. This resulted in many of these private, invariably family-owned companies becoming public companies; for example Donna Karan, Gucci, Tommy Hilfiger and Ralph Lauren achieved public listings in the 1990s. Other design houses merged to become part of stock market luxury goods conglomerates, most notably the French-based LVMH and Kering and Swiss-based Richemont. Moore and Birtwistle (2005) discussed the benefits of intra-business group synergies in giving companies within such large conglomerates 'parenting advantage' to achieve growth in the luxury sector, using the example of Gucci.

As the fast-fashion and luxury sectors have grown, there has become a degree of unexpected synergy between these diverse segments that has been classified as the 'Prada–Primark effect'. In recent years, in particular with a deteriorating financial situation, it is not uncommon to find celebrities taking the lead in mixing and matching their wardrobes between very expensive luxury items and their replica fast-fashion counterparts. The companies that have experienced most problems in the fashion market , because of the strength of these polarized sectors have been those caught in the middle lacking a differentiated offer. The difficulties experienced by department stores in particular highlight this problem with the bankruptcies of Karstadt in Germany, Mervyns in the United States and some smaller companies such as Lewis's in the UK. Although Karstadt was rescued from bankruptcy in 2010 it has failed to make a profit since then and speculation continues about its future in 2015.

The UK middle market has been most susceptible to competition because of the strong performance of the luxury and value sectors, as evidenced by the exit of C&A from the market in 2001 and the poor performance of Marks & Spencer and BHS for much of the 2000s and 2010s. However, these companies have since taken on board several of the supply chain innovations that have facilitated the growth of foreign market entrants to transform the British high street.

Fast fashion and CSR

One of the main concerns with regard to the shift to fast fashion has been the sustainability of such a method of production in terms of labour and material resources (Fletcher, 2010). As items purchased are so cheap, consumers are purchasing items more often but wearing them less frequently. This results in increasing amounts of textile waste ending up in landfill each year and fast fashion being associated with the term 'disposable fashion' (Birtwistle and Moore, 2007; Bhardwaj and Fairhurst, 2010; Morgan and Birtwistle, 2009). The shift to offshore production and the cheapness of products has led to further questions on the ethics and Corporate Social Responsibility (CSR) issues surrounding fast-fashion production, most notably the working conditions in factories and the use of child labour (see Chapter 4 on CSR for more detail). Although many consumers appear to champion socially responsible practices which impact upon their perceptions of fashion brands, fast fashion is the exception to the rule (Perry, 2012; Shephard and Pookulangara, 2013). This is confirmed by research by Joy *et al* (2012, p 286) which indicates that consumers are well aware of the ethical issues but are drawn to the trendier, price-driven offerings of these retailers thereby 'aesthetics trumps ethics'.

By the late 2000s the term 'slow fashion' began to be used as an alternative to fast fashion in much the same way as farmer's markets and organic food were a reaction to the fast-food revolution. Some of the earlier interpretations of slow fashion relate to local quality crafted products and/or through embracing CSR principles, especially environmental principles in production and recycling. Not surprisingly such a view with respect to quality and associated heritage craftsmanship led to associations with luxury retailers. Pookulangara and Shephard (2013), however, argue that slow fashion was not meant to be the antithesis of fast fashion or to slow down the supply chain. Instead the slow-fashion process embraces sustainable and socially responsible practices that are applied at the three levels of design, production and consumption.

To show that slow fashion can be applied to the fast-fashion sector, Shephard and Pookulangara (2013) illustrate how Zara and H&M have embraced some elements of slow fashion in their supply chains. In Figure 2.1 they show how H&M have developed initiatives at each stage of the supply chain. It shows the company's initiatives from encouraging designers to consider the long-term impacts of the products chosen for designs, to support for CSR practices in textile production, to finally educating consumers on disposal and recycling of clothing. For example, H&M encourages customers to bring in their discarded clothes to recycle in exchange for a discount on new merchandise.

Shephard and Pookulangara (2013) acknowledge that H&M has a long way to go to fully embrace the slow-fashion process. Nevertheless, the company has made an impressive start by producing an annual sustainability report and is relatively transparent in its sourcing strategy through the publication of a list of all factories and ratings of supplier compliance.

The online revolution

In the UK nearly 50 per cent of consumers go online to shop for clothes (*Retail Week*, 2014). The pace of change over the last decade has been accelerating to the extent that multichannel developments offer the main challenge to fashion retailers at the present time. In the same *Retail Week* report it was noted that half of consumers regularly use three or more channels to shop compared with ten years earlier in 2003 when consumers hardly used more than two channels.

Initial reticence by retailers was due to the lack of belief in selling clothes and shoes online, especially for low-cost items. However, new

FIGURE 2.1 The slow fashion process model applied to the H&M supply chain

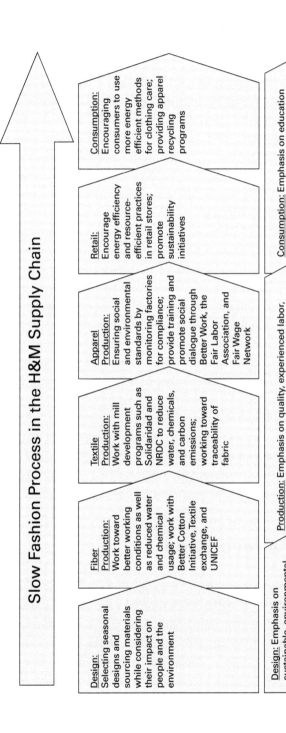

Slow Fashion Process in the H&M Supply Chain

Design: Selecting seasonal designs and sourcing materials while considering their impact on people and the environment

Fiber Production: Work toward better working conditions as well as reduced water and chemical usage; work with Better Cotton Initiative, Textile exchange, and UNICEF

Textile Production: Work with mill development programs such as Solidaridad and NRDC to reduce water, chemicals, and carbon emissions; working toward traceability of fabric

Apparel Production: Ensuring social and environmental standards by monitoring factories for compliance; provide training and promote social dialogue through Better Work, the Fair Labor Association, and Fair Wage Network

Retail: Encourage energy efficiency and resource-efficient practices in retail stores; promote sustainability initiatives

Consumption: Encouraging consumers to use more energy efficient methods for clothing care; providing apparel recycling programs

Design: Emphasis on sustainable, environmental, and ethical practices

Production: Emphasis on quality, experienced labor, and community

Consumption: Emphasis on education and product life cycle

SOURCE Shephard and Pookulangara (2013)

technologies have created virtual changing rooms and improvements in colour representation to remove some of the barriers for consumers to shop online. Also consumers have a range of e-fulfilment options available to them from delivery to the home to click and collect. The rise and success of online players with international operations such as ASOS from the UK, Zalando (Germany) and Alibabi (China) has meant that fashion retailers in all sectors have had to embrace the digital revolution. Not surprisingly, the traditional retailers with a mail order presence had the advantage of a logistical infrastructure already in place and some such as Next have migrated their business successfully online. Next Directory, launched in 1988, accounted for 37 per cent of overall sales in 2013 (Next, 2014).

Fast-fashion retailers were slow to recognize the potential of online sales primarily because their business models were geared to serving a store environment. Hence Zara's belated entrance to online retailing in 2010. However, like their competitors they quickly realized the benefits of a multichannel platform. Similarly the upscale luxury fashion companies were concerned that such expensive items could be sold online. But an online presence is more than selling and as Burberry has shown it provides a vehicle for engaging with the customer through podcasting fashion shows and receiving feedback from customers on Facebook and Twitter. After a slow start, online sales have grown from 1 per cent in 2003 to around 5 per cent of overall sales in the worldwide luxury fashion market in 2014 (Bain and Company, 2014).

All fashion sectors are now embracing omnichannel retailing in that consumers desire knowledge of products from a variety of sources and are willing to purchase and return goods through a variety of channels. The retailer now has the challenge to integrate the whole business to serve this customer so that stores are no longer just functional units selling product but are information centres, inspirational showcases and pick-up points for online purchases and returns. During the recession, store closures were documented in company reports as sales migrated online. This trend is now slowing down and indeed may be reversed in the future. Companies with a strong online presence are evaluating their store portfolios to maximize sales across channels so those with a strong click-and-collect offering will hope to enhance the brand and stimulate sales in store on pick up. In some cases it has been suggested that two different kinds of stores will be opened in the future: the flagship store which will be experiential, innovative and entertainment orientated, and multichannel hubs that focus more on functionality – click and collect and returns. Bearing in mind that 43 per cent of UK clothing and footwear customers returned items bought online in 2013, reverse logistics is as much of a challenge to fashion retailers as supplying the product in the first place (*Retail Week*, 2014).

Achieving the correct balance of utilizing store, e/m-commerce and social media will drive future sales for fashion retailers. Although mobile technology has become more important in many purchasing decisions, in relation to fashion purchases, screen size and resolution make smart phones less of an option than tablets and laptops. However, sales are the final outcome of a research process that customers make, having been influenced by family and friends, including Facebook and other social media. Retailers are becoming more proactive in communicating with their customers with the advent of Web 2.0 technology so that feedback on new ranges, store experiences, website designs etcetera can help companies improve their retail offer.

One area that has become important here is the role of the fashion blog because 'fashion and trends are mainly driven by inspiration between peers' (Halvorsen *et al*, 2013, p 211). While fashion companies produce corporate blogs to give insights to new developments in their business to inform stakeholders, independent fashion bloggers are competing with traditional fashion magazines as opinion formers and a source of PR for fashion retailers. Bloggers such as Chiara Ferragni (The Blonde Salad) and Susanna Lau (Style Bubble), based in the fashion capitals of Milan and London respectively, have a strong influence on purchase behaviour with their electronic word-of-mouth recommendations. This has resulted in retailers collaborating with key bloggers in much the same way as fashion journalists by giving prime seats in designer fashion shows and providing products to feature in blogs. As bloggers generate many more pages to view than fashion magazines, they have been targeted by fashion companies in order to promote their brands.

The supply chain response

As the conventional method of supply to retailers was transformed by the new international entrants to the market, retail logisticians were faced with the challenges of dealing with shorter product life cycles, more seasons and reduced lead times while sourcing a greater amount of product offshore. It should be noted that traditional supply chains continued to prevail in the 1980s. The headquarters of Next was relocated from Leeds to Leicester to be closer to suppliers. The Quick Response (QR) concept was introduced in 1985 in the United States as a response to inefficiencies in the domestic supply chain in the wake of Japanese textile imports and was part of the

'Pride with the USA' campaign to promote the purchase of US products. The QR model, however, is strongly dependent on relatively steady demand for basic fashion products, with strong relationships developed between retailers and apparel manufacturers in terms of sharing information on sales and inventory. Ironically, in the 1990s the Japanese began to implement QR in response to Chinese imports but Azuma (2002) pointed out that Japanese firms in fact forged their success on bridge fashion with flexible specialization through the use of a subcontracting network of process specialists in industrial clusters.

It can therefore be argued that these Japanese firms along with European innovators such as Benetton and Zara developed the network organization in fashion retailing. Indeed, both companies draw heavily upon the ideas developed by Toyota in implementing Just in Time (JIT) techniques in car manufacturing. Therefore the capital intensive parts of the operations (dyeing, weaving, knitting, cutting) that can benefit from economies of scale are conducted in-house while the labour-intensive parts of production (sewing, tailoring, finishing, pressing, quality control, packaging) are carried out by a network of sub-contractors (Camuffo et al, 2001; Tokatli, 2008; Christopher et al, 2004).

Although Zara and Benetton have often been heralded as the model to arrest the decline in domestic textile manufacturing in the industrial core areas, these companies are the exception to the rule. Tokatli (2008) questions Zara's low-wage policy towards Portuguese and Spanish sub-contractors and points out that with global expansion the company sources as much product outside of Spain as in the domestic market. The key decisions that companies have been faced with since the 1990s are where to source product and whether to manage the process of end-to-end supply chain coordination internally in-house or to outsource part or all of the logistics functions (see Chapter 3). In addition to Zara and Benetton, most domestic production in the industrial core areas centres around luxury and upscale textile products with a strong association to country-of-origin features: high-end luggage/handbags in France, shoes in Italy etc. The luxury fashion retailers exert strong control over the production and distribution of their products so their core product offering stresses craftsmanship, design and durability, made and quality controlled in the domestic market. As these companies move into other luxury areas they may outsource or partner with other luxury companies to work with their suppliers. Alternatively, they may work with specialist providers of manufacturing and distribution services such as Ittierre S.p.A, an Italian company that produces for several luxury brands including Dolce et Gabbana, John Galliano and Versace.

Global dispersion of fashion supply chains

The predominant trend, however, has been a move to mass offshore sourcing and outsourcing due to geopolitics and technological advancements (Azuma and Fernie, 2004). Furthermore, the model adopted for the international fashion supply chain has been the design, sourcing, distribution model rather than the vertically integrated model utilized by Benetton and Zara (see Chapter 3).

Due to the complexity and labour intensity of garment manufacture, the nature of offshore sourcing is dictated by the nature of the product, availability of raw materials and a large workforce, lead times and cost (Figure 2.2). The last two are the most important factors. The degree of outsourcing, however, relates to the retailers' perspective on the degree of control that it wishes to exert over the supply function and how it views sourcing within the organization. This links to Cox's (1996) contractual theory of the firm whereby a company that considers sourcing to be a core competence of the firm with high asset specificity will retain control of this function rather than use third-party specialists. The extent of the relationship with the third party will depend on the degree of asset specificity; high asset-specific skills will tend to be governed via long-term partnership arrangements while low asset-specific skills will be procured via arms-length market-based arrangements.

In terms of offshore sourcing, cost has been the main driver for change and the shift of garment production from the industrial core to newly emerging markets because of the large differential in labour costs. Hence, the processes remain labour intensive; for example sewing makes up around 30 per cent of the total garment cost (Jones, 2006). Commoditization of the core low-tech activities of garment manufacture means that labour-intensive CMT (cut, make and trim) operations can be located anywhere in the world where there is a readily available labour source, and can be moved from one low-cost country to another in a seamless manner according to business requirements (Sethi, 2003). Initially, Hong Kong, South Korea and Taiwan were the key countries for low-cost manufacturing but with rising domestic labour costs, they became uncompetitive on a cost basis. The influx of business from Western countries seeking lower labour costs enabled their economies to develop and their workers to become better trained. However, as a country's garment manufacturing industry matures, it becomes difficult to sustain competitive advantage based solely on cost. Firms therefore tend to move into niche markets, invest in more advanced technology or engage in subcontracting

FIGURE 2.2 The globally-dispersed garment supply chain

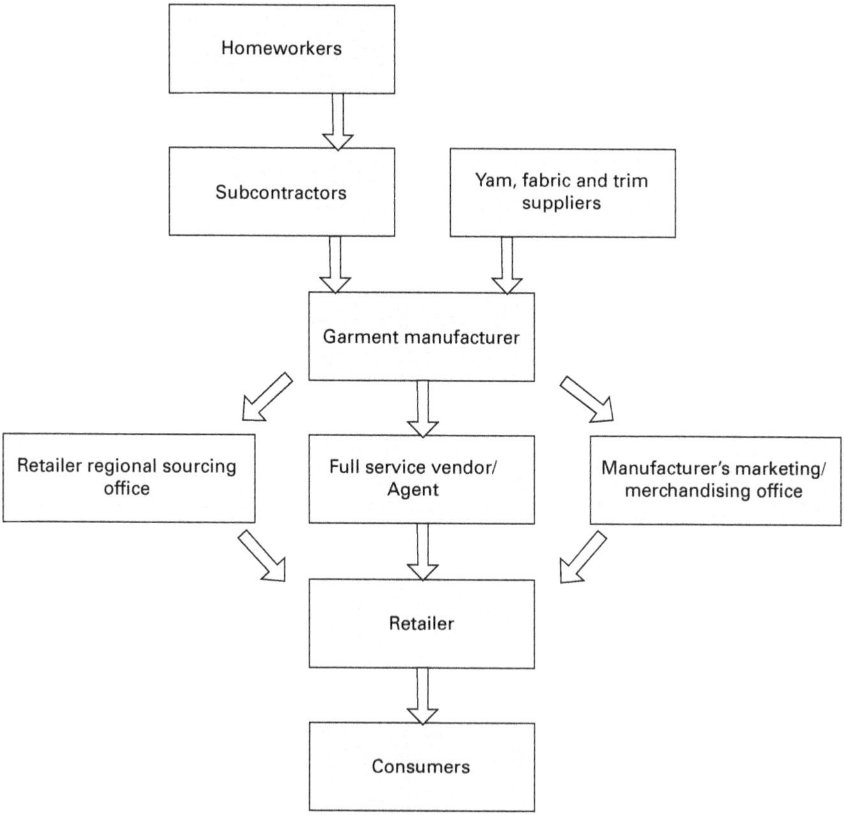

```
            ┌─────────────────────┐
            │     Homeworkers     │
            └─────────────────────┘
                      ↓
   ┌─────────────────────┐   ┌─────────────────────┐
   │   Subcontractors    │   │ Yarn, fabric and trim │
   │                     │   │     suppliers       │
   └─────────────────────┘   └─────────────────────┘
                ↓                   ↓
            ┌─────────────────────┐
            │ Garment manufacturer │
            └─────────────────────┘
        ↙             ↓             ↘
┌──────────────┐ ┌──────────────┐ ┌──────────────┐
│ Retailer     │ │ Full service │ │ Manufacturer's│
│ regional     │ │ vendor/      │ │ marketing/   │
│ sourcing     │ │ Agent        │ │ merchandising│
│ office       │ │              │ │ office       │
└──────────────┘ └──────────────┘ └──────────────┘
        ↘             ↓             ↙
            ┌─────────────────────┐
            │      Retailer       │
            └─────────────────────┘
                      ↓
            ┌─────────────────────┐
            │     Consumers       │
            └─────────────────────┘
```

SOURCE Fernie and Perry (2011)

arrangements to lower labour cost countries themselves (Singleton, 1997). The effect is that Hong Kong, South Korea and Taiwan have now moved away from labour-intensive garment manufacture into capital-intensive textile industries or production of higher value-added items which require skilled operators at a subsequently higher labour rate. Basic garment production has therefore migrated to lower-cost labour countries such as Vietnam, China and Indonesia (Sethi, 2003; Maitland, 1997; Elbehri, 2004).

As fashion product life cycles have sped up, and more so with the rise of fast fashion in the 2000s, retailers have faced increasing challenges of managing the trade-off between cost and lead time in offshore sourcing. Fast-fashion lines are often produced closer to the selling market to avoid missing the short window of the selling season. For UK retailers, fast fashion is often produced in Turkey or Eastern Europe, partly to avoid the long shipping times from Asia but also as they are locations that mediate between the demands of cost, quality and responsiveness/distance (Tokatli and Kizilgün, 2009, 2010). Similarly, for US retailers, the decision to source from Mexican, Caribbean or coastal Chinese suppliers is based on lead times of three, five and eleven weeks respectively (Abernathy *et al*, 2006).

In addition to fast-fashion retailers, the high street market segment also contains mid-market retailers that primarily sell seasonal or fashion basic products. The latter outsource most production to a small number of key suppliers with whom they have collaborative relationships. The former face greater pressure for both cost and lead time and therefore tend to rely on short-term, arm's-length trading relationships. Because of the short product life cycles of fast fashion, retail buyers tend not to place long-running orders, but rather small batches that may be easily moved from one supplier to another. For example, budget fast-fashion retailer Primark's business model has been based on sourcing products from the cheapest possible supplier, with short and variable trading relationships, sometimes even changing supplier mid-season (Newton Responsible Investment, 2005). The typology of fashion retailers in Table 2.1 summarizes the key differences in international supply chain relationships according to market segment.

In addition to cost and lead time pressure, a further SCM challenge in recent times has been the management of ethical issues in complex and fragmented global sourcing networks (Hughes *et al*, 2007) – something made more challenging during the economic downturn of the late 2000s and early 2010s (Hughes, 2012). Although worker exploitation may be found in a range of industry sectors, the fashion industry is particularly at risk as it is a high-profile consumer segment which attracts the scrutiny of the global media and the general public (Jones, 1999). For example, in 2010, following a media investigation into Indian garment suppliers, fashion retailers Gap, Next and Marks & Spencer faced strong media scrutiny of alleged inhumane working practices, such as long hours, wage violations and forced labour (Chamberlain, 2010). More recently, in 2013, a number of Western fashion retailers were implicated in the tragedy of the garment factory building collapse in Dhaka, Bangladesh, in which over 1,100 people were killed (Lund-Thomsen and Lindgreen, 2014). Implementation of SCM initiatives in fashion supply chains must therefore enable retail buyers and suppliers to reconcile ethical issues alongside the commercial pressures of cost and lead time. The case of H&M was discussed earlier in the chapter around how the company has embraced sustainability and CSR initiatives (Figure 2.1) and the topic is discussed fully in Chapter 4.

TABLE 2.1   Typology of fashion retailer supply chain
relationships

Vertically integrated or strong control of supply network

✓ Luxury fashion houses or those with a unique business model
(eg Zara/Benetton/American Apparel)

✓ But as these companies have developed a greater international store
network, more offshore sourcing has occurred

Mid-market retailers with collaborative relationships

✓ QR concepts applied offshore

✓ Development of international sourcing and distribution hubs

✓ Use of full-package intermediaries (eg Li & Fung)

Fast-fashion retailers

✓ Strong emphasis on sourcing from cheapest supplier

✓ Relationships can be short and variable

✓ Markets classified into short and long lead times

✓ For Western European retailers, a gradual shift from China to Vietnam;
Turkey to Egypt and Romania to Moldova in terms of sourcing patterns

---

SOURCE Fernie and Perry (2011)

Online logistical challenges

As online retailing has evolved during the last decade, the distribution networks to service the customer have become increasingly complex. Initially
the pure players such as ASOS and retailers with a mail order presence would
pick orders from a centralized distribution centre. Then a large proportion
of orders were channelled through the 'hub and spoke' networks of large
parcel carriers or mail-order companies to the home. The early challenges
for retailers were the 'last mile' problem and the large flow of returned product. The 'last mile' problem occurs when the customer is not at home and it
becomes expensive for both carrier and customer if there are repeated delivery failures. Returns were and still are a major challenge for retailers in that
product has to be retrieved, checked, repackaged and redistributed through

the logistics network. Much effort has been applied to provide solutions to these issues, and many have arisen with the entry of traditional store-based retailers to the online market.

The 'clicks and bricks' retailers had the steepest learning curve to overcome. Online customers were supplied from the same centralized distribution centre that served stores until demand increased sufficiently to build a dedicated online facility. However, the main advantage that these retailers have over their pure player competitors is their store portfolio. One way of addressing the 'last mile' problem was to offer customers alternative delivery options, including collection and delivery points. As many customers may find it more convenient to pick up items from a store near their workplace rather than to have home delivery, click and collect has proven to be a popular choice amongst customers. Next has 50 per cent of its online orders picked up in its stores. This is a win/win situation for retailer and customer. The latter is offered more delivery choices and the retailer reduces the high cost of delivering to the home. Furthermore, customers have several options available to them to return goods, including stores. Collection and delivery points (CDPs) have become the option of choice for online retailers. For example, Collect +, a joint venture between Yodel, a delivery company and PayPoint, a payment company, utilizes a network of 5,500 convenience stores and petrol stations in the UK where orders can be delivered, returned to and tracked. This has proven popular with both pure players such as ASOS and multi-channel retailers such as Schuh (see case study).

Schuh was an early adopter (2001) in selling footwear online when sceptics doubted if footwear could be sold without the customer trying on a pair of shoes in a store. In 2014 online accounted for 15 per cent of sales. It offers customers a range of options to buy: reserve or buy online, pick up in store, buy online for delivery to a local Collect + store or a timed delivery: free deliveries and free returns. Customers can enter a store and it may not be available in the right colour or size but to avoid a potential loss of sale, the company can offer a next-day delivery service to the customer's home of the required item.

CASE STUDY   Schuh's supply chain strategy

Schuh is a relatively new company in that it was founded in 1981 in Edinburgh, Scotland. Its growth and profitability in the late 1990s and 2000s made it an attractive target for the US listed footwear company,

Genesco, who paid £125 million for the business in 2011. Sales grew from £81 million in 2005 to £162 million in 2011. Genesco has allowed Schuh to operate independently but has given it sufficient capital injection to accelerate its growth plans in the UK. Since the takeover it had opened 35 new stores by 2013 with sales increasing to £233 million. Its 100th store was opened in January 2014.

Schuh's success can be attributed to its unique retail concept that is supported by a strong logistics infrastructure. Schuh retails key fashion brands such as UGG, Converse, Toms, Vans and Timberland targeted at a young (15–30-year-old) group. If it is fashionable, Schuh stock it. The hub of the operation is at its headquarters in Livingston, west of Edinburgh, and its new distribution centre at nearby Bathgate which opened in 2014. This new site at 245,000 square feet is five times larger than its Livingston site, which had already become too small even before the Genesco takeover. Stock from offshore suppliers is managed by Schuh's own proprietary warehouse management system (Shark) and stores then receive deliveries six days per week by 10 am each morning. Whilst Schuh has maintained strong control over its warehouse operations it contracts out the delivery to stores and online customers to parcel carriers. Schuh's efficient distribution system has given it the highest display densities of any of the main UK footwear retailer. It has at least 30 per cent more options per square foot than any of its peer group (Fernie and Temple, 2014).

Schuh has a straightforward merchandising strategy. It adopts a 'Best Store, Best Stock' philosophy in that stores are allocated stock according to local demand so when new lines are introduced slow movers are removed and returned to the warehouse for re-allocation to stores that perform better on these lines. At the distribution centre, a common stock base is used for all channels. The internet has allowed Schuh to carry 30 per cent more lines than any of the largest stores can stock. The online business has flourished since its introduction in 2001 and accounts for 15 per cent of sales. The customer base is young and digital savvy so Schuh has had to upgrade its website to accommodate the shift to m-commerce and embrace social media with live chat, Twitter and Facebook. Schuh was one of the first fashion retailers to use eBay to maximize the terminal price of distressed stock (odd sizes, tarnished items). This helps to maximize selling space within stores by clearing out this stock.

Because Schuh controls the whole network from a central hub, it can offer the customer a range of options with regard to delivery and return of items. For customers who still prefer to go to their most convenient store, they can check and reserve, one hour buy and collect or click and collect. Around a quarter of all orders are now picked up at stores. Alternatively they can use the Collect + service and pick up (and return) goods from a local convenience store. For online ordering and home delivery, a suite of options are available according to size of order and delivery time schedules; for example Schuh has teamed up with delivery company Shutl to offer a 90-minute, same-day service or a next-day time slot. This is free for orders over £75.

SOURCES Fernie and Temple (2014); Personal interview with the Managing Director, Colin Temple, 25 November, 2014.

A key challenge for fashion retailers will be the integration of systems so that a single view can be taken of stock availability across the supply chain. Now that the consumer can order, pick up and return to multiple locations, it is imperative that stock can be tracked from suppliers through to customers at these various destinations. These new omnichannel business models will also require a re-evaluation of organizational structures within companies. No longer can the online customer be separated from the store shopper. They are the same shopper and staff have to be trained across the organization to serve this customer. Web teams and store teams need to convey the same message to the customer. Store personnel in particular are not just sales people but have to advise customers of stock availability in different channels, including click and collect on site.

Conclusions

This chapter has shown how the fashion retail environment has changed over time and how the pace of change has quickened in the 21st century. The fast-fashion movement led by Zara revolutionized the business model for supplying fashion markets. No longer did we have a four-season planning cycle but one that constantly supplied the market with innovative new designs. At the same time the luxury market flourished as companies received capital injections, often through becoming part of one of the French conglomerates, and expanded into new product lines and new markets (mainly China). The traditional specialists and department store chains had to replicate the new business model to some degree but many were in a better position to capitalize on the changes brought about by the digital revolution. Fast-fashion and luxury retailers were slow to embrace online retailing, mainly because their appeal was an attraction to their store environments.

These changes in the market environment have produced many logistics challenges for fashion retailers. In order to compete with fast-fashion retailers, most companies have followed the lead of H&M and Primark in sourcing product offshore. This also includes luxury brand retailers that continue to produce iconic products in their home market but source offshore for other product lines. How to achieve the balance between cost savings, lead time to market and ethical considerations is a major challenge for fashion retailers and will be discussed in the following chapters. The most recent and rapid change has been the migration of sales from offline to online. The new generation of consumers, especially those in the most fashionable segments, are digitally savvy and expect to order from a variety of devices and have a range of delivery options available to them. The 'clicks and bricks' retailers that were early movers online such as Next and Schuh have been able to capitalize on the increasingly popular 'click and collect' option available to consumers in addition to providing a conventional delivery and returns service.

References

Abernathy, F H, Volpe, A and Weil, D (2006) The future of the apparel and textile industries: prospects and choices for public and private actors, *Environment and Planning A*, **38** (12), pp 2207–32

Azuma, N (2002) Pronto moda Tokyo style: emergence of collection-free street fashion and the Seoul-Tokyo fashion connection, *International Journal of Retail & Distribution Management*, **30** (3), pp 11–20

Azuma, N and Fernie, J (2003) Fashion in the globalised world and the role of virtual networks in intrinsic fashion design, *Journal of Fashion Marketing and Management*, **7** (4), pp 413–427

Azuma, N and Fernie, J (2004) The changing nature of Japanese fashion: can Quick Response improve supply chain efficiency? *European Journal of Marketing*, **38** (7), pp 790–808

Bain & Company (2014) 2014 Luxury Goods Worldwide Market Survey, 13th edn [online] http://www.bain.com/publications/articles/luxury-goods -worldwide-market-study-december-2014.aspx [accessed 28 November 2014]

Barnes, L and Lea-Greenwood, G (2006) Fast fashioning the supply chain: shaping the research agenda, *Journal of Fashion Marketing and Management*, **10** (3), pp 259–71

Barnes, L and Lea-Greenwood, G (2010) Fast fashion in the retail store environment, *International Journal of Retail & Distribution Management*, **38** (10), pp 760–72

Bhardwaj, V and Fairhurst, A (2010) Fast fashion: response to changes in the fashion industry, *The International Review of Retail, Distribution and Consumer Research,* **20** (1), pp 165–73

Birtwistle, G and Moore, C M (2007) Fashion clothing–where does it all end up? *International Journal of Retail & Distribution Management,* **25** (3), pp 210–16

Camuffo, A, Romano, P and Vinella, A (2001) Back to the future: Benetton transforms its global network, *Sloan Management Review,* Fall, pp 46–52

Chamberlain, G (2010) Gap, Next and M&S in new sweatshop scandal, *Observer,* 8 August

Christopher, M, Lowson, R and Peck, H (2004) Creating agile supply chains in the fashion industry, *International Journal of Retail & Distribution Management,* **24** (2), pp 50–61

Cox, A (1996) Relational competence and strategic procurement management: towards an entrepreneurial and contractual theory of the firm, *European Journal of Purchasing and Supply Management,* **2** (1), pp 57–70

Divita, L R and Yoo, J-J (2013) Examining global retailing's innovators: an overview of fast fashion supply chain research, in T-M Choi (ed) *Fast Fashion Systems: Theories and applications,* CRC Press, Leiden, The Netherlands, pp 23–34

Elbehri, A (2004) MFA quota removal and global textile and cotton trade: estimating quota trade restrictiveness and quantifying post-MFA trade patterns, paper presented at The 7th Annual Conference of Global Economic Analysis, Washington DC, June 17–19

Fernie, J, Moore, C M and Lawrie, A (1998) A tale of two cities: an examination of fashion designer retailing within London and New York, *Journal of Product and Brand Management,* **7** (5), pp 366–78

Fernie, J and Perry, P (2011) The international fashion retail supply chain, in J Zentes, B Swoboda and D Morschett, *Case Studies in International Management,* Gabler, Wiesbaden, pp 271–90

Fernie, J and Temple, C (2014) The footwear supply chain: the case of Schuh, in J Fernie and L Sparks (2014) *Logistics and Retail Management,* 4th edn, Kogan Page, London, pp 101–16

Fletcher, K (2010) Slow fashion: an invitation for systems change, *Fashion Practice,* **2** (2), pp 259–66

Halvorsen, K, Hoffman, J, Coste-Maniere, I and Stankeviciute, R (2013) Can fashion blogs function as a marketing tool to influence consumer behaviour? Evidence from Norway, *Journal of Global Fashion Marketing,* **4** (3), pp 211–24

Hollander, S (1970) *Multinational Retailing,* Michigan State University, MI

Hughes, A (2012) Corporate ethical trading in an economic downturn: recessionary pressures and refracted responsibilities, *Journal of Economic Geography,* **12** (1), pp 33–54

Hughes, A, Buttle, M and Wrigley, N (2007) Organisational geographies of corporate responsibility: a UK-US comparison of retailers' ethical trading initiatives, *Journal of Economic Geography*, 7 (4), pp 491–513

Jones, M T (1999) The institutional determinants of social responsibility, *Journal of Business Ethics*, 20 (2), pp 163–79

Jones, R M (2006) *The Apparel Industry*, Blackwell, Oxford

Joy, A, Sherry, J E, Venkatesh, A, Wang, J and Chan, R (2012) Fast fashion, sustainability and the ethical appeal of luxury brands, *Fashion Theory: The Journal of Dress, Body and Culture*, **16** (3) pp 273–96

Lopez, C and Fan, Y (2009) Internationalisation of the Spanish fashion brand Zara, *Journal of Fashion Marketing and Management*, **13** (2), pp 279–96

Lund-Thomsen, P and Lindgreen, A (2014) Corporate social responsibility in global value chains: where are we now and where are we going? *Journal of Business Ethics*, **123** (1), pp 11–22

Maitland, I (1997) The great non-debate over international sweatshops, *British Academy of Management Annual Conference Proceedings*, September, London, pp 240–65

Moore, C M and Birtwistle, G (2005) The nature of parenting advantage in luxury fashion retailing in the case of Gucci group NV, *International Journal of Retail & Distribution Management*, **33** (4), pp 256–70

Moore, C M, Doherty, A M and Doyle, S A (2010) Flagship stores as a market entry method: the perspective of luxury fashion retailing, *European Journal of Marketing*, **44** (1/2), pp 139–61

Moore, C M, Fernie, J and Burt, S L (2000) Brands without boundaries: the internationalization of the designer retailer's brand, *European Journal of Marketing*, **34** (8), pp 919–37

Morgan, L R and Birtwistle, G (2009) An investigation of young fashion consumers' disposal habits, *International Journal of Consumer Studies*, **33** (2), pp 190–98

Newton Responsible Investment (2005) *Corporate Governance and SRI – Q4 2005*, Newton Investment Management Ltd, London

Next (2014) Report and Results, July, *Next* [online] http://www.nextplc.co.uk /investors/reports-and-results/2014.aspx [accessed 15 July 2015]

Perry, P (2012) Exploring the influence of national cultural context on CSR implementation, *Journal of Fashion Marketing and Management*, **16** (2), pp 141–60

Pookulangara, S and Shephard, A (2013) Slow fashion movement: will it impact the retail industry – an exploratory study, *Journal of Retailing and Consumer Services*, **20** (2), pp 200–206

Retail Week (2014) Multichannel, *Retail Week*, 19 September [online] http://www. retail-week.com/multichannel/digital-edition-retail-week-multichannel -september-2014/5064356.article [accessed 15 July 2015]

Sethi, S P (2003) *Setting Global Standards: Guidelines for creating codes of conduct in multinational corporations*, Wiley, Hoboken, NJ

Shephard, A and Pookulangara, S (2013) The slow fashion process: rethinking strategy for fast fashion retailers, in T-M Choi (ed) *Fast Fashion Systems: Theories and applications*, CRC Press, Leiden, The Netherlands, pp 9–22

Singleton, J (1997) *The World Textile Industry*, Routledge, London

Tokatli, N (2008) Global sourcing: insights from the global clothing industry – the case of Zara, a fast fashion retailer, *Journal of Economic Geography*, 8 (1), pp 21–38

Tokatli, N and Kizilgün, Ö (2009) From manufacturing garments for ready-to-wear to designing collections for fast fashion: evidence from Turkey, *Environment and Planning A*, **41** (1), pp 146–62

Tokatli, N and Kizilgün, Ö (2010) Coping with the changing rules of the game in the global textiles and apparel industries: evidence from Turkey and Morocco, *Journal of Economic Geography*, **10** (2), pp 209–29

Tungate, M (2008) *Fashion Brands: Branding style from Armani to Zara*, Kogan Page, London

Walsh, K (2010) World too Small for Louis Vuitton, *Sunday Times*, 21 November

Yarwood, D (1992) *Fashion in the Western World*, Batsford, London

Offshore sourcing and outsourcing in the international fashion supply chain

03

Introduction

One of the key SCM trends within the mid-market high street sector has been the vertical disintegration and outsourcing of the production function to a global network of independent subcontractors. The expansion of free trade following the elimination of the Multi-Fibre Arrangement (MFA) – which governed the global trade in textiles and garments between 1974 and 2005, and imposed quotas on the amount developing countries could export to developed ones – resulted in a greater number of apparel producers across a wider variety of countries (Abernathy *et al*, 2006). It was shown in Chapter 2 that the extent of outsourcing is strongly related to the degree of control that a company wishes to exert across the supply chain and links to Cox's (1996) contractual theory of the firm. It is not surprising that luxury companies seek to retain control over the manufacturing and distribution of their brands to sustain a consistent brand image across international markets. Most companies, however, have moved to both the offshore sourcing and outsourcing options over the last 20 years. Despite recent indications that there will be 'reshoring' in the future because of the high cost of doing business in China it is unlikely that there will be a major upturn in traditional textile economies but more likely a boost to the economies of Eastern European suppliers to meet the demands of Western European retailers. To establish a context to these changing trends, it is first necessary to provide a background to the evolution of sourcing strategies, the nature of outsourcing relationships and the supply chain models that can be applied to different product groups.

Sourcing strategies

According to Zenz (1994, p 120) sourcing is 'the strategic philosophy of selecting vendors in a manner that makes them an integral part of the buying firm for a particular component or part they are to supply'. In other words, sourcing is more than just a business function of getting products at desired prices, but is an integral part of an organization's strategy (Zeng, 2000). Traditionally there were two main dimensions to sourcing strategy: supply markets (the geography of sourcing) and supply channels (whether or not to outsource the task of supplying products). Figure 3.1, however, shows two further dimensions, classified as 'organizational' and 'tactical'. The organizational dimension includes strategic or opportunistic sourcing. For example, sourcing from a large full-package supplier providing services from design and procurement to shipping leads to sustained retailer–supplier relations, which enhances reliability of supply as opposed to opportunistic sourcing of 'good deals' in the market. The tactical dimension includes single, double or hybrid/network sourcing. Much depends on the fashion sector so that multiple sourcing, for example, is more likely to be used where there are multiple suppliers of products that are low in price and where market conditions enable the buyer to switch suppliers easily and cheaply.

The early work on global sourcing emerged during the early 1970s with the shift of production to foreign (less developed) countries as a result of low labour costs and hence lower production costs (Leontiades (1971); Leff (1974); Matthyssens et al, 2006). This work was further developed by Swamidass (1993), Monczka and Trent (1991) and Trent and Monczka (2003, 2005). Initially Monczka and Trent (1991) suggested a four-phase development process that progressed from domestic purchasing to global sourcing but added a fifth phase in their later work (Trent and Monczka 2003, 2005) (see Figure 3.2). Smaller retailers will source domestically at Level 1. Level 2 is the use of international sourcing only when needed, ie the products cannot be sourced in the domestic market (reactive sourcing). Level 3 involves proactive international purchasing as part of an overall sourcing strategy. Level 4 is the first of two global sourcing strategies integrated across worldwide

FIGURE 3.1 The four dimensions of sourcing and their classifications

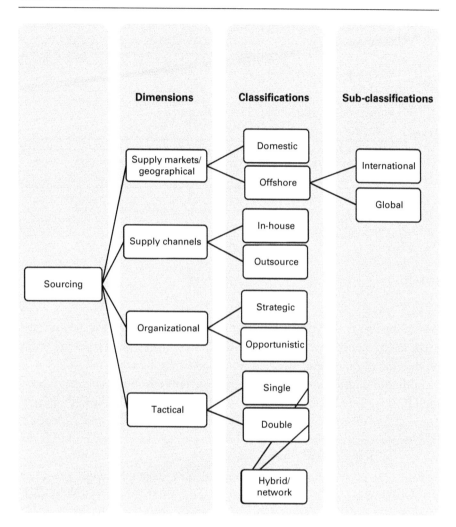

SOURCE Fernie *et al* (2009)

locations. Operating at this level requires executive leadership that endorses the global perspective.

It requires highly skilled personnel, advanced information systems and an organizational structure that enables coordination of global operations. In Level 5, global sourcing strategies are integrated not only across worldwide locations but also across functional groups such as product development or marketing. There is a horizontal link between sourcing and other functional

FIGURE 3.2 The five levels of sourcing

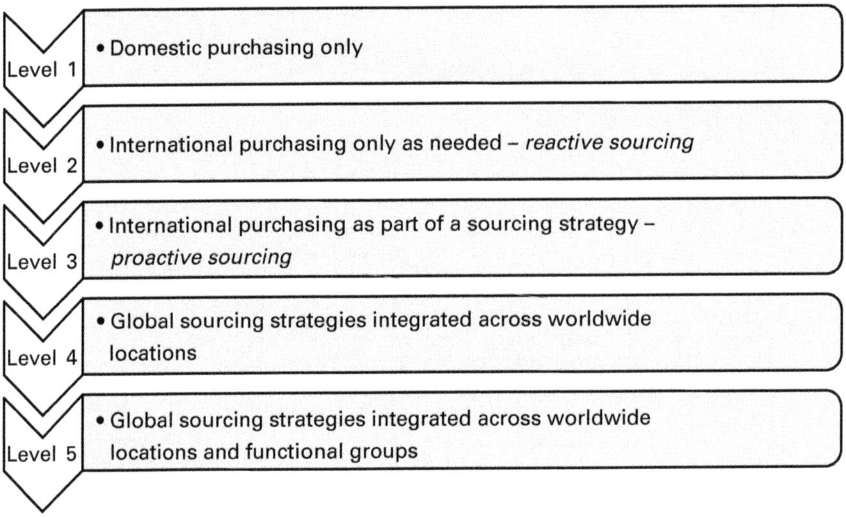

Level 1
• Domestic purchasing only

Level 2
• International purchasing only as needed – *reactive sourcing*

Level 3
• International purchasing as part of a sourcing strategy – *proactive sourcing*

Level 4
• Global sourcing strategies integrated across worldwide locations

Level 5
• Global sourcing strategies integrated across worldwide locations and functional groups

SOURCE Fernie *et al* (2009), after Trent and Monczka (2005)

areas. Activities such as design, product development and sourcing are assigned to the most competent units across the world. Worldwide capabilities in design, product development and sourcing are necessary to operate at this level.

Both sourcing overseas and outsourcing non-core functions have been used by large retailers in their quest to achieve profitability through driving down costs of product supply. Pyndt and Pedersen (2005) put forward a framework showing the different combinations of outsourcing and offshoring (Figure 3.3).

Fernie (2014) has shown how the evolution of the textile supply chain can be related to Figures 3.2 and 3.3 in that until the 1970s and early 1980s much sourcing was still at the early stages of the Trent and Monckza (2005) model and was domestic in nature. He used the examples of Zara, Benetton and Burton (in the UK) as companies that were vertically integrated and supplied their own stores. Marks & Spencer, by contrast, was always known as a manufacturer without factories as it sourced from UK suppliers and stressed its Buy British credentials in its marketing campaigns. Since the 1990s, however, the position has changed dramatically, with most fashion retailers (including M&S) acknowledging that offshore sourcing from external suppliers was the preferred model. As will be explained later, even the vertically integrated companies – Benetton, Zara and the luxury fashion houses – have moved production offshore with global expansion and increased competition.

FIGURE 3.3 Framework that addresses the different combinations of offshoring and outsourcing

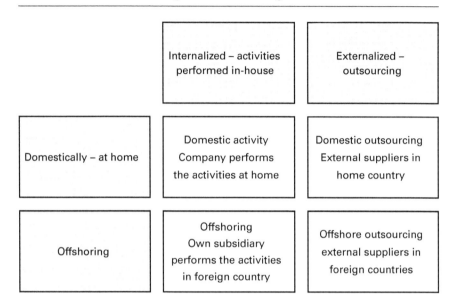

SOURCE   Fernie *et al* (2009) after Pyndt and Pedersen (2005)

The nature of outsourcing

Mass outsourcing was facilitated by a combination of geopolitical reasons (end of quotas), market needs (increased competition) and technological advancements (information technology and transport improvements) (Azuma and Fernie, 2004; Djelic and Ainamo, 1999). For example, in 2014, fast-fashion chain H&M used 872 suppliers from 1,964 factories worldwide (H&M, 2014). Walmart, the world's largest retailer, has over 100,000 suppliers (Walmart, 2014). Zara is no longer an exception to the globalization of production. While traditionally sourcing from Spain and Portugal, Zara has expanded its supplier base to include lower cost countries such as Morocco, Turkey and India, finding that suppliers are able to respond quickly and to the standard required (Tokatli, 2008).

In terms of the theoretical perspectives that underpin the outsourcing decision, most authors discuss transaction cost analysis, the resource-based view and network theory. (See Johnsen, Howard and Miemczyk, (2014) for a review and their addition of a natural resource-based view to incorporate ideas of sustainable resource development.) The resource-based perspective builds upon Porter's (1985) value chain model by focusing upon the various resources within the firm that will allow it to compete effectively. Resources, capabilities and core competences are key concepts in this theory. To gain competitive advantage in the supply chain the resource base extends across the boundary of the firm and therefore links to transaction cost analysis and network theory. Firms have therefore to make choices on the degree of vertical integration in their business, to 'make or buy' in production and the extent of outsourcing required in logistical support services. Building upon Williamson's (1979) seminal work, Cox (1996) has developed a contractual theory of the firm by revising his ideas on high-asset specificity and 'sunk costs' to the notion of core competences within the firm. Therefore, a company with core skills in either logistics or production would have internal contracts within the firm. Complementary skills of medium-asset specificity would be outsourced on a partnership basis, and low-asset specificity skills would be outsourced on an 'arm's-length' contract basis.

The nature of the multiplicity of relationships has created the so-called network organization. In order to be responsive to market changes and to have an agile supply chain, flexibility is essential. Extending the resource-based theory, the network perspective assumes that firms depend on resources controlled by other firms and can gain access to these resources only by interacting with these firms, forming value chain partnerships and subsequently networks. Network theory focuses on creating partnerships based on trust, cross-functional teamwork and inter-organizational cooperation.

It was shown in Chapter 2 that Benetton and Zara developed the network organization in fashion retailing. Furthermore, they kept in-house the capital-intensive parts of the operations such as dyeing and weaving and outsourced the labour-intensive parts of production such as sewing and tailoring to a network of sub-contractors (Camuffo *et al*, 2001; Tokatli, 2008; Christopher *et al*, 2004).

In terms of offshore sourcing these companies were viewed as the saviours of domestic textile production but global competition has forced them to increasingly source offshore. Tokatli (2008) notes that with global expansion Zara sources as much product outside of Spain as in the domestic market. Similarly Benetton (see case study) has developed a series of foreign production poles in order to reduce costs to compete in a global marketplace. Although designs are managed in Italy, around 40 per cent of production is now outsourced to suppliers in China, SE Asia and India while retaining offshore production in-house in closer markets to home, such as Tunisia, Hungary and Croatia.

CASE STUDY   The Benetton Group

The Benetton Group has around 6,500 shops in 120 countries, manufacturing plants in Europe, Asia, the Middle East and India, and revenues of more than €2 billion. It has divested its sportswear brands and now focuses its interests in fashion clothing, mainly casual wear, with the key brands of United Colors of Benetton, Undercolors of Benetton and Sisley.

Much of Benetton's success until the 1990s could be attributed to its innovative operations techniques and the strong network relationships that it has developed with both its suppliers and distributors. Benetton pioneered the 'principle of postponement', whereby garment dyeing was delayed for as long as possible in order that decisions on colour could be made to reflect market trends. At the same time, a network of subcontractors (small to medium-sized enterprises) supplied Benetton's factories with the labour-intensive phases of production (tailoring, finishing and ironing) while the company continued to manufacture the capital-intensive parts of the operation (weaving, cutting, dyeing, quality control) in Treviso in north-eastern Italy. In terms of distribution, Benetton sells its products through agents, each responsible for developing a market area. These agents set up a contract relationship, similar to a franchise, with the owners who sell the products.

Benetton is now beginning to transform its business by retaining its network structure but changing the nature of the network. Unlike most of its competitors, it increased vertical integration within the business in order to speed up the flow of materials from raw material suppliers through its production poles to ultimate distribution from Italy to its global retail network. Benetton's main production pole is at Castrette near its headquarters. To take advantage of lower labour costs, Benetton has located foreign production poles, based on the Castrette model, initially in Spain and Portugal (now closed), Hungary, Croatia, Tunisia, India, Turkey and more recently through its Asia Pacific subsidiary production in China, Bangladesh and SE Asia through Hong Kong. The Asia Pacific production is outsourced to full-package suppliers coordinated from Hong Kong, Bangkok and Bangalore. Castrette produces the designs for production in the regional poles. These foreign production centres often focus on particular types of product utilising the skills of the region.

The retail network and the products on offer have also experienced changes. Benetton had offered a standard range in most markets but allowed for 20 per cent of its range to be customized for country markets. Now, to communicate a single global image, Benetton is allowing only 5–10 per cent of differentiation in each collection. Furthermore, it has streamlined its brand range to focus on the United Colors of Benetton and Sisley brands.

The company also changed its store network to enable it to compete more effectively with its international competitors. It enlarged its existing stores, where possible, to accommodate its full range of these key brands. Where this is not possible, it will focus on a specific segment or product. Finally, it has opened more than 100 megastores worldwide to sell the full range, focusing on garments with a high styling content. These stores were initially owned and managed solely by Benetton to ensure that the company could maintain control downstream and be able to respond quickly to market changes.

In addition to Zara and Benetton with their unique business models, most domestic production in the industrial core areas centres around luxury and upscale textile products with a strong association to country of origin features: cashmere in Scotland, luggage/handbags in France, shoes in Italy, etc. Historically, the luxury segment of the market was structured in a vertically integrated manner to allow those luxury brands to retain control over merchandise quality and exclusivity, and thereby to demand premium prices for their products (Brun *et al*, 2008). French couture houses such as Chanel and Hermès therefore tend to internalize the production function in order to retain control over quality and to protect the artisan skills that underpin the production of bespoke luxury goods, which is paramount for protecting brand values. As they have moved into new luxury areas, they have also bought out suppliers; for example, Chanel bought its long-term cashmere supplier in Scotland and luxury groups, including Kering (formerly PPR) and LVMH have acquired a number of exotic skin suppliers and elite tanneries as part of a strategic move to secure a sustainable supply of high-quality raw materials (Socha, 2013).

Not all luxury companies, however, have a vertically integrated structure (Caniato *et al*, 2011). For example, in 2011, up to 20 per cent of Prada's collections across clothing, shoes and handbags were reported to have been made in China, with some manufacturing also taking place in Turkey and Romania (Sanderson, 2013), with a similar tendency toward using full-package overseas suppliers discussed in the case of Burberry (Tokatli, 2012). Indeed, with the demise of the Thomas Burberry line, only outerwear, including the iconic trench coat, is made in the UK. Globalization, heightened competition, advances in IT and the changing nature of the luxury consumer have resulted in a greater level of complexity and turbulence in the market; hence, flexible modular organizations are viewed as sometimes

FIGURE 3.4 Supply chain models in the fashion industry: vertical integration (VI) and design/source/distribute (DSD)

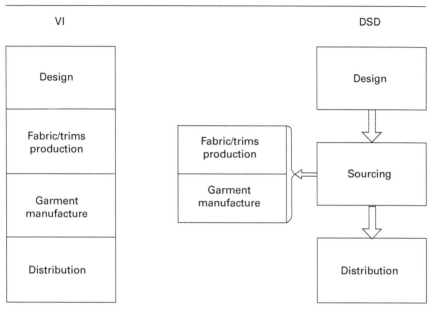

more effective than those with vertical integration (Djelic and Ainamo, 1999). This is discussed in more detail in Chapter 8 which includes a case study of Burberry (see Box 8.1).

It can therefore be argued that the vertical integration model is becoming rare even within the sectors that have been strong advocates of controlling the supply chain. With a predominant global shift of production to newly emerging markets, retailers across the fashion industry have moved to a design/source/distribute model by focusing on their core competences of design, branding and retailing, with the production function outsourced to global networks of independent suppliers, as shown in Figure 3.4.

Types of outsourcing

Fashion retailers source garments in three ways: (1) via third-party specialists; (2) directly from suppliers via their own headquarters; or (3) via overseas sourcing hubs (Fernie *et al*, 2009). If sourcing directly, retailers use:

- contract manufacturers ('cut-make-trim' – CMT) who cut, assemble and ship finished garments from imported inputs under the buyer's brand name; or

- Full-package suppliers who coordinate the entire production process on behalf of the buyer, from product development and procurement of raw materials through to manufacture and shipping (Neidik and Gereffi, 2006). Full-package supply requires pre-production capability in design and product development, as well as responsibility for sourcing fabric, including financing the procurement upfront.

As evidenced from Benetton earlier in the chapter, retailers generally prefer full-package supply rather than CMT (Lezama *et al*, 2004; Palpacuer *et al*, 2005), so that they can focus on their core competences in design, branding and retailing. In order to fulfil such demands, suppliers need to upgrade their capabilities to adapt to these retailer demands (Gereffi, 1999; Gereffi and Memedovic, 2003; Tewari, 2006; Palpacuer, 2006). By ensuring key capabilities, such as fabric production, are in-house, lead times can be reduced and extra duties payable on imported fabrics can be avoided. Tewari (2006, p 2327) noted an increasingly demanding situation for suppliers as 'market access... depends not only on low costs, or freer trade, but on the ability of local suppliers to meet increasingly stringent buyer demands for quality, customization, and full-package supply, in addition to low costs'. Indeed, some full-package manufacturers now have responsibility not only for procurement of fabric and trims but also for design and product development (Tokatli and Kizilgün, 2009), functions which would have previously been classified as core operations and therefore viewed as important to remain within the boundaries of the firm (Reve, 1990; Cox 1996). With the increasing demands of dominant retailers, it has become progressively more important for suppliers to develop upgraded networks of design and manufacturing, which offer a comprehensive and responsive service but from a low cost base.

With regard to sourcing from third-party specialists, the primary distinction of these intermediaries is whether they are based in the country of their customers (import intermediaries) or their suppliers (export intermediaries). Additionally, there are multinational trading companies that have offices in their customers' or more often suppliers' countries (or both). A typical example of a multinational trade intermediary is the Hong Kong-based Li & Fung, with 15,000 suppliers in 40 economies and offices in developed (customers' based) and developing (suppliers' based) countries (Magretta and Fung, 1998; Fung, 2010; Li & Fung, 2014). Their role is changing in order to meet the challenges of the market. For example, in the contemporary fashion environment, the need for supply chain efficiency and satisfaction of quick response strategies has led to the rapid development of 'full-package' intermediaries (Hines, 2007). These sourcing specialists can cover all operational pre-retail activities and deal with the problem of suppliers' co-ordination. The term 'full-package' identifies the range of their offered services: from the raw material selection to the labelling and packaging of the end product.

Some of the most common functions performed by intermediaries are the following (Fung *et al*, 2007; Ha-Brookshire and Dyer, 2008):

- product development and design;
- sourcing activities;
- identification and evaluation of new suppliers;
- supplier quality control for both products and processes through site visits and audits;
- shipping management and distribution.

They simultaneously negotiate with suppliers and customers, in order to finalize orders, reduce inventories and spread risks. Ha and Dyer (2005) add a number of other functions, traditionally related to the retailers' activities: market research, assortment planning and often customer service. Their overall scope is the development of a competitive supply chain that meets end-customers' needs. This scope is achieved by their in-depth knowledge and great experience of the market (Fung *et al*, 2007). Arguably, it is this knowledge and experience that drives their single existence.

Masson *et al* (2007) discuss how UK clothing retailers manage offshore production and distribution to the UK from two markets: China and Romania. In their research they 'found that the common norm, and of course, a practice that could eliminate complexities at a stroke, was simply for the retailers to make use of third-party indirect sourcing import/export agencies or what many choose to call intermediaries' (p 244–45). Masson *et al* (2007) also classify some of these companies as integrated service providers in that they provide in-house services from product design through manufacture to logistics provision to customers' (retailers') distribution centres.

The problem with intermediaries, however, is that the retailer pays an additional cost that they would not have incurred if they had sourced direct. Palpacuer (2006) states that in addition to these costs, other advantages are better customer service and more control over manufacturing and delivery time. The simplest way of performing direct sourcing is through the company's headquarters. In that way, the parent company has direct contact with its suppliers. However, the fragmented nature of the textile industry with numerous production stages, in addition to an extensive product range, requires the parent company to deal with a significant number of suppliers. In addition, disperse production across different countries, or even continents, creates a complex network that is difficult to manage by the headquarters of a single company.

Sourcing hubs can provide a solution to the aforementioned labyrinth of textile and clothing suppliers. Their operation allows the direct sourcing from suppliers, through cooperation between branches of the same organization. The role of international hubs includes identification and evaluation of suppliers, obtaining product samples, making site visits, dealing with operational issues and coordinating suppliers. Fundamentally, they carry out the critical functions of sourcing and can fully substitute for export intermediaries. Trent and Monczka's research identified the operation of international sourcing hubs as a potential critical success factor of global sourcing: 'organizations that are committed to global sourcing should seriously consider making international purchasing offices part of their structure' (Trent and Monczka, 2005, p 31).

Fernie *et al* (2009) analysed the role of international hubs in a UK fashion company's sourcing strategy in relation to the Pyndt and Pederson and Trent and Monczka taxonomies discussed in Figures 3.2 and 3.3. The case study company was committed to offshore sourcing but wished to retain control through a buying office and international hubs. In terms of Trent and Monczka's model the first two stages are not relevant and stage 4 is equivalent to that of the company's integrated international hub's structure.

There is a trend towards direct sourcing; according to Braithwaite (2007, p 334), 'the surge in growth of global trade is the result of more companies going into markets to deal direct – cutting out the middleman'. The effect of this trend is the increase of both margins and risk. In other words, it is preferable to source directly from manufacturers in financial terms, but the complexity of dealing with them increases the risk of supply chain disruption.

Offshore sourcing and reshoring?

The labour-intensive nature of apparel production and the large differential in labour rates have resulted in the global shift of production to developing countries. Garment manufacturing is not suited to extensive automation so labour-intensive sewing operations can be located where there is a readily available labour source, and can potentially be moved from one low-cost country to another according to business requirements (Sethi, 2003). As countries progressively develop their economies, labour rates increase and competitive advantage on the basis of cost moves successively to the next newly industrializing country where labour rates are even cheaper (Singleton, 1997). For example, Hong Kong, South Korea and Taiwan were initially popular sources of low-cost manufacturing labour in the 1970s and 1980s, but by the beginning of the 1990s, rising domestic labour costs meant they were no longer competitive on a purely cost basis. More recently, as labour rates in China's coastal areas have increased, garment manufacturing operations for longer lead-time products have relocated to cheaper inland regions (Zhu and Pickles, 2013). Likewise, as costs in Turkey have increased, some garment manufacturers have shifted production for shorter lead-time merchandise to nearby Egypt (Tokatli and Kizilgün, 2010). One response to this 'race to the bottom' has been for some individual supplier firms to move to more profitable and/or technologically sophisticated capital- and skill-intensive economic niches – something referred to in the research literature as 'industrial upgrading' (Gereffi, 1999, p 52; Neidik and Gereffi, 2006).

In certain cases, historic regional specializations give competitive advantage and result in certain countries becoming manufacturing centres for particular types of garment, based on the quality of the basic fabric (eg southern India for silks), proximity to fabric source (eg China for cotton), specialization in design and production (eg Italy for leatherwear and tailoring), and particular highly skilled sewing details (eg India for hand embroidery and embellishment) (Dunford, 2006; Fernie and Perry, 2011). In the case of East-Central Europe, the existence of skilled workers in the apparel industry enabled the region to develop a reputation for relatively high-value tailored garments, which complemented its cost and proximity advantages (Begg et al, 2003. See also Kalantaridis et al, 2008; Smith et al, 2008). However, despite the existence of regional pockets of specialization, suppliers continue to face price pressure from low-cost developing countries.

Much recent debate has focused upon the changes in the economic environment so that the competitive advantage once enjoyed by China is being eroded away by rising labour costs, long lead times and the need for flexibility in a digital age. Comparing China with Portugal and Turkey, a UK fashion supply chain director noted that labour rates fell by 11 per cent in Portugal and 8 per cent in Turkey in 2013 compared with Chinese labour inflation (depending on source) of 15–25 per cent, while lead times are up to three weeks better from European suppliers (DWF, 2014). In the same report the head of transport at another retailer focused upon ethical sourcing. Although happy with the cost and quality of the products, concern was expressed at the environmental footprint of sourcing from China.

In another UK consultancy report published in 2014, Pricewaterhouse-Coopers discusses how reshoring is picking up in the UK economy to the extent that the prime minister highlighted how some businesses such as call centres had been reshored from offshore service centres. The report does use the textile industry as a case study in addition to listing key points for reshoring, some of which are more relevant than others to the fashion sector. For example it is forecast that wage rates in China, Poland, Turkey and Mexico will be closer to yet still lower than the UK or US levels by 2030, supply chain risk is high in the event of political or natural disasters, and the cost of managing a distant operation is currently offset by lower production costs, an advantage that will diminish over time.

While this paints a bright prospect for a revival in traditional core industrial economies, this optimism has to be tempered by short-term realism. Although China is becoming more expensive, this does not mean a return to the scale of operations of 25 years ago. An initial reaction by retailers will be to source from 'new' low-cost centres. Siegel (2014) notes the interest of H&M in Ethiopia, Gap in Myanmar and Haiti for US retailers. Much of the reshoring in textiles is in the SME, niche sector or high-end, higher price elements of mainstream retailers. In the UK it is estimated that only 5,000 jobs are likely to be created in the short term with a figure of 20,000 projected for 2025 (PricewaterhouseCoopers, 2014).

The barriers to reshoring relate to operational scale and the skills required to produce domestically after decades of decline. The downside of outsourcing is that textile-related skills have been exported and workers with such skills are either retired or have been retrained to other sectors. Most firms that have production at home are small scale and much investment would be required in domestic infrastructure to compete in the mass market. Similar issues have been cited in the United States when Walmart pledged to buy an extra $250 billion of US goods from 2013–2023. Already the company is experiencing difficulties in finding suppliers that have to restart/rebuild a manufacturing capability with an inexperienced workforce. It can be argued that Walmart was a contributor to offshore sourcing in the first place. Its everyday low price (EDLP) proposition is predicated on a low-cost operation model that pressurizes suppliers to reduce costs. Many did and moved production offshore.

Supply chain relationships and responsiveness by product category

The increased importance of independent flexible supply chain networks has drawn attention to supply chain relationships. This approach can be traced back to the 1980s and the Quick Response (QR) concept which was a response to inefficiencies in the US domestic supply chain in the wake of Japanese textile imports and part of the 'Pride with the USA' campaign to promote the purchase of US products. QR performance relied upon a network of close alliances with supply chain partners, since such collaborative relationships are a precursor to responsiveness (Sheridan *et al*, 2006). By improving supply chain efficiency and promoting collaboration between retailers and suppliers, it was hoped to make the United States more competitive in the face of increasing imports. In the UK, QR techniques were used to develop collaborative working relationships, which enabled domestic manufacturers to compete with the offshore sourcing of garments from lower labour cost countries (Christopher *et al*, 2009; Emberson and Storey, 2006). QR was originally targeted at core fashion lines that had steady demand profiles and were sold in department stores (Wood, 2002). Nowadays, core fashion lines with relatively steady demand profiles are typified by good quality casual garments, such as chinos and plain jeans, which are fashionable but not as time-sensitive as fast fashion.

Although QR was unable to prevent the large-scale global shift of production to lower labour cost countries (Tokatli 2008), it laid the foundations for companies to adopt a 'fast fashion' strategy, whereby retailers such as Zara, Primark and ASOS replicate catwalk and celebrity trends quickly to provide budget versions for their customers. Progressively, traditional buyer-supplier relationships in the fashion industry that had been short-term and adversarial, characterized by multiple sourcing, price orientation and competitive bidding, have changed to exhibit greater degrees of vertical disintegration (Jones, 2006; Barnes and Lea-Greenwood, 2006; Hines and McGowan, 2005). These 'buyer-driven global sourcing networks' have seen the balance of power in the supply chain shift comprehensively to large retailers at the expense of manufacturers (Gereffi *et al*, 2005; Hines and McGowan, 2005). These global sourcing networks are led by powerful retail buyers who are able to exert control over all aspects of production, distribution and retail (Gereffi *et al*, 2005; Barrientos and Smith, 2007) by leveraging their dominant position in the network to dictate terms to manufacturers. Meanwhile, as discussed earlier, shorter product life cycles and rapidly changing consumer demands have led to a renewed focus on agility as a means of reducing lead times. The industry has therefore seen an increasing shift away from adversarial relationships to strategic partnerships based on commitment, trust and continuous improvement (Hines and McGowan, 2005; Bixenden and Abratt, 2007) and the development of long-term upgraded supplier capabilities (Tan, 2001).

Collaboration between supply chain partners can lead to significant business performance improvements, potentially creating a seamless, synchronized chain which results in better responsiveness and reduced inventory costs (Vereecke and Muylle, 2006; Holweg *et al*, 2005). Building supplier partnerships is therefore an important influencing condition of successful fashion supply chain management (Hines and McGowan, 2005). As such, many larger retailers are moving towards rationalization of their global supply networks, in order to reduce costs and develop closer partnerships with a fewer number of 'preferred' suppliers (Welford and Frost, 2006; Palpacuer *et al*, 2005).

Lean, agile or leagile?

The nature of trading relationships is strongly dependent upon the nature of the product in that the product influences the design and complexity of the supply chain (Fisher, 1997). Since Naylor *et al*'s 1999 work on supply chain configurations to meet the changing needs of the marketplace, numerous papers have discussed the merits of the lean, agile and leagile paradigms (see Purvis *et al*, 2014 for a review).

The fashion sector has been discussed in this context (Bruce *et al*, 2004; Towers and Bergvall-Forsberg, 2009; Purvis *et al*, 2014) because its products cover the distinguishing attributes that help to define each paradigm (See Table 3.1 and Figure 3.5). Fashion merchandise can be segmented into three major categories according to product life cycles, sensitivity/time/cost requirements and subsequent supply chain geographies (Lowson, 2003):

- Basic products: little variation in style, predictable demand profile eg plain black socks, plain white t-shirts.
- Seasonal (or fashion basic) products: greater variation in style, less predictable demand profile eg chino trousers, straight-leg jeans.
- Short season (or fast-fashion) products: great variation in style, unpredictable demand profile eg owl-print t-shirts, mullet-hem skirts or midi skirts.

TABLE 3.1 Comparisons of lean, agile and leagile supply chains

Distinguishing attributes	Lean supply chain	Agile supply chain	Leagile supply chain
Market demand	Predictable	Volatile	Volatile and unpredictable
Product variety	Low	High	Medium
Product life cycle	Long	Short	Short
Customer drivers	Cost	Lead time and availability	Service level
Profit margin	Low	High	Moderate
Dominant costs	Physical costs	Marketability costs	Both
Stock-out penalties	Long-term contractual	Immediate and volatile	No place for stock out
Purchasing policy	Buy goods	Assign capacity	Vendor-managed inventory
Information enrichment	Highly desirable	Obligatory	Essential
Forecast mechanism	Algorithmic	Consultative	Both/either
Typical products	Commodities	Fashion goods	Product as per customer demand
Lead time compression	Essential	Essential	Desirable
Rapid reconfiguration	Desirable	Essential	Essential
Quality	Market qualifier	Market qualifier	Market qualifier
Cost	Market winner	Market qualifier	Market winner
Lead time	Market qualifier	Market qualifier	Market qualifier
Service level	Market qualifier	Marker winner	Market winner

SOURCE After Agarawal *et al* (2006), p 212

FIGURE 3.5 Demand pyramid: basic vs. fashion items (based on Lowson, 2003)

While supply chains for basic products focus on cost reduction and prioritize lean supply, fast-fashion products require agility in order to match supply to demand (Childerhouse and Towill, 2000; Mason-Jones *et al*, 2000). For basic products, such as black socks or white t-shirts, which are typically low margin, have a long product life cycle and predictable demand, a highly efficient supply chain ensures physical costs, such as production and distribution, are minimized. Where there is stable, predictable demand, a lean manufacturing strategy can improve supply chain efficiency by eliminating waste, including time (Mason-Jones *et al*, 2000), resulting in lower labour costs, increased throughput and hence operating profit (Frohlich and Westbrook, 2001). Supply chains for these functional products are less complex than for fashion products and thus can be simplified in order to maximize efficiency and reduce transaction costs (Williams *et al*, 2002). Conversely, short-season or fast-fashion products are less price sensitive, but have a shorter product life cycle and unpredictable demand levels; therefore the supply chain must achieve a high level of effectiveness in terms of manufacturing flexibility and minimizing lead time (Fisher, 1997). It is interesting to note from our earlier discussion on Benetton that the Asian Pacific production poles produce basic products compared with the European poles' focus on fashion products with shorter product life cycles.

The different demand profiles for basic and fashion products are illustrated in Figure 3.5. The pyramid shape shows that fashion basic products with longer product life cycles, such as chinos or straight-leg jeans, have long-running orders of each particular style. Fashion products with short product life cycles are made in small amounts of frequently changing styles. Perry, Fernie and Wood (2014) used the examples of owl-print t-shirts and mullet-hem skirts that were in fashion at the time. The time-sensitive nature of seasonal (fashion basic) and short-season (fast-fashion) products prioritizes lead time over cost. The leagile model, however, is more applied to seasonal products because the selling season is much longer than for fast-fashion products. Benetton was the leader in championing the principle of postponement in that it produced small batches of product in the introduction stages of the life cycle and once a clearer picture of demand was known it moved to a lean production model for the growth and maturity stages.

As fashion product life cycles have speeded up, and more so with the rise of fast fashion in the 2000s, retailers have faced increasing challenges of managing the trade-off between cost and lead time in offshore sourcing. Fast-fashion lines are often produced closer to the selling market to avoid missing the short window of the selling season. For UK retailers, fast fashion is often produced in Turkey or Eastern Europe, partly to avoid the long shipping times from Asia but also as they are locations that mediate between the demands of cost, quality and responsiveness/distance (Tokatli and Kizilgün, 2009, 2010).

Earlier research on sourcing by UK fashion firms by Birtwistle *et al*, 2003 confirmed these trends by showing that basic lines from the Far East can be ordered three months in advance, seasonal lines are augmented by Eastern European and North African suppliers in three weeks and shorter runs of re-makes are manufactured by British companies. Through a series of case studies, Bruce *et al* (2004) also show how a combination of lean, agile and leagile approaches have been taken by UK companies to reduce production costs from offshore sourcing whilst at the same time retaining capacity closer to home in order to be able to respond flexibly to an increasingly volatile fashion market. In the research cited earlier by Fernie *et al* (2009) on international hubs, they show that each hub had a strategic role for the UK company: its Italian hub focused upon design and innovation for high-value items such as tailored jackets, the Turkish hub provided cost and agility advantages to react to trends whilst the Hong Kong hub represented the lean supply model of low-cost production of basic items such as t-shirts and vest tops.

Similarly trends are evident in the Americas; for US retailers, the decision to source from Mexican, Caribbean or coastal Chinese suppliers is based on lead times of three, five and eleven weeks respectively (Abernathy *et al*, 2006). Flexibility and responsiveness are crucial in fashion markets with unpredictable demand and high levels of uncertainty, since success is based on aligning garment delivery to emerging consumer demand in order to avoid the costs of excess inventory and obsolescence (de Treville *et al*, 2004; Weller, 2007).

Conclusions

This chapter has shown how retailers have increasingly outsourced products from offshore locations during the last 20–30 years. Even the advocates of a strong domestic business model (Zara, Benetton and some of the luxury houses) have turned to full-package suppliers in their quest to remain competitive in a global marketplace. It was shown, however, that outsourcing is evident in a variety of forms, from dealing directly with suppliers to using intermediaries or setting up international hubs to retain control of the sourcing function.

The prominent locations for offshore sourcing have evolved over time from the traditional centres of Hong Kong and Taiwan to more recent low-cost centres in China and South East Asia. The rising costs in China as that country's economy grows and it becomes as much a consumer society as a producer economy means increased scarcity of textile products. New markets such as Ethiopia, Myanmar and Haiti have been mooted as new textile centres of production in addition to a greater degree of reshoring back to traditional textile areas. But the case of Walmart's campaign to buy American goods and the UK's initial attempts at reshoring show a lack of infrastructure and relevant skills to make a short-term impact in the marketplace.

Until recently domestic markets were used mainly to supply luxury or niche products in addition to making changes to fast-fashion garments that were sourced offshore. Indeed the evidence from many case studies cited here is that offshore locations are largely determined according to product category, cost and lead time considerations. Thus more distant markets such as China were used for basic products where lead times were long and cost was the key consideration. The lean supply model was more appropriate here compared to the agile or leagile approaches to fast fashion or seasonal basic products. Here lead times are very important in addition to flexibility (hence adaptations in the local, consumer markets). Turkey, Eastern Europe and North African suppliers are more relevant for seasonal fashion products for the Western European market, and Mexico and the Caribbean are more relevant for the US market.

References

Abernathy, F H, Volpe, A and Weil, D (2006) The future of the apparel and textile industries: prospects and choices for public and private actors, *Environment and Planning A*, **38** (12), pp 2207–32

Agarawal, A, Shankar, R and Tiwari, M K (2006) Modelling the metrics of lean, agile and leagile supply chain: an ANP-based approach, *European Journal of Operational Research*, **173**, pp 211–25

Azuma, N and Fernie, J (2004) The changing nature of Japanese fashion: can quick response improve supply chain efficiency? *European Journal of Marketing*, **38** (7), pp 790–808

Barnes, L and Lea-Greenwood, G (2006) Fast fashioning the supply chain: shaping the research agenda, *Journal of Fashion Marketing and Management*, **10** (3), pp 259–71

Barrientos, S and Smith, S (2007) Do workers benefit from ethical trade? Assessing codes of labour practice in global production systems, *Third World Quarterly*, **28** (4), pp 713–29

Begg, R, Pickles, J and Smith, A (2003) Cutting it: European integration, trade regimes and the reconfiguration of East-Central European apparel production, *Environment and Planning A,* **35** (12), pp 2191–2207

Birtwistle, G, Siddiqui, N and Fiorito, S S (2003), Quick response: perceptions of UK fashion retailers, *International Journal of Retail & Distribution Management*, **31** (2), pp 118–28

Bixenden, M and Abratt, R (2007) Corporate identity, ethics and reputation in supplier-buyer relationships, *Journal of Business Ethics*, **76**, pp 69–82

Braithwaite, A (2007), Global sourcing and supply, in D Waters (ed) *Global Logistics: New directions in supply chain management,* 5th edn, Kogan Page, London

Bruce, M, Daly, L and Towers, N (2004) Lean or agile: a solution for supply chain management in the textiles and clothing industry? *International Journal of Operations and Production Management*, **24** (2), pp 151–70

Brun, A, Caniato, F, Caridi, M, Castelli, C, Miragliotta, G, Ronchi, S, Sianesi, A and Spina, G (2008) Logistics and supply chain management in luxury fashion retail: empirical investigation of Italian firms, *International Journal of Production Economics*, **114** (2), pp 554–70

Camuffo, A, Romano, P and Vinella, A (2001) Back to the future: Benetton transforms its global network, *Sloan Management Review*, Fall, pp 46–52

Caniato, F, Caridi, M, Castelli, C and Golini, R (2011) Supply chain management in the luxury industry: a first classification of companies and their strategies, *International Journal of Production Economics*, **133** (2), pp 622–33

Childerhouse, P and Towill, D (2000) Engineering supply chains to match customer requirements, *Logistics Information Management*, **13** (6), pp 337–45

Christopher, M, Lowson, R and Peck, H (2004) Creating agile supply chains in the fashion industry, *International Journal of Retail and Distribution Management*, **24** (2), pp 50–61

Christopher, M, Lowson, R and Peck, H (2009) Fashion logistics and quick response, in J Fernie and L Sparks (eds) *Logistics and Retail Management*, Kogan Page, London, pp 102–20

Cox, A (1996) Relational competence and strategic procurement management: towards an entrepreneurial and contractual theory of the firm, *European Journal of Purchasing and Supply Management*, **2** (1), pp 57–70

De Treville, S, Shapiro, R D and Hameri, A (2004) From supply chain to demand chain: the role of lead time reduction in improving demand chain performance, *Journal of Operations Management*, **21** (6), pp 613–27

Djelic, M L and Ainamo, A (1999) The coevolution of new organizational forms in the fashion industry: a historical and comparative study of France, Italy, and the United States, *Organization Science*, **10** (5), pp 622–37

Dunford, M (2006) Industrial districts, magic circles, and the restructuring of the Italian textiles and clothing chain, *Economic Geography*, **82** (1), pp 27–59

DWF (2014) Supply chain: trends and innovations in retail 2014–2015, Retail Week Reports, *Retail Week*, London

Dyer, B and Ha-Brookshire, J E (2006), Apparel import intermediaries' secrets to success: redefining success in a hyper-dynamic environment, *Journal of Fashion Marketing and Management*, **12** (1), pp 51–67

Emberson, C and Storey, J (2006) Buyer-supplier collaborative relationships: beyond the normative accounts, *Journal of Purchasing and Supply Management*, **12** (5), pp 236-245

Fernie, J (2014) The internationalization of the retail supply chain, Chapter 3 in J Fernie and L Sparks (eds) *Logistics and Retail Management* (4th edn), Kogan Page, London

Fernie, J, Maniatakis, P A and Moore, C M (2009) The role of international hubs in a fashion retailers' sourcing strategy, *International Review of Retail, Distribution and Consumer Research*, **19** (4), pp 421–36

Fernie, J and Perry, P (2011) The international fashion retail supply chain, in J Zentes, B Swoboda and D Morschett (eds) *Fallstudien zum Internationalen Management*, Gabler Verlag, Wiesbaden, pp 271–90

Fisher, M (1997) Which is the right supply chain for your product? *Harvard Business Review*, **75** (2), pp 105–17

Frohlich, M and Westbrook, R K (2001) Arcs of integration: an international study of supply chain strategies, *Journal of Operations Management*, **20** (2), pp 185–200

Fung, P K O, Chen, I S N and Yip, L S C (2007) Relationships and performance of trade intermediaries: an exploratory study, *European Journal of Marketing*, **41** (1/2), pp 159–80.

Fung, S (2010) An assessment of the changing world of manufacturing, Drapers Fashion Summit 2010, London, 16–17 November

Gereffi, G (1999) International trade and industrial upgrading in the apparel commodity chain, *Journal of International Economics*, **48** (1), pp 37–70

Gereffi, G, Humphrey, J and Sturgeon, T (2005) The governance of global value chains, *Review of International Political Economy*, **12** (1), pp 78–104

Gereffi, G and Memedovic, O (2003) *The Global Apparel Value Chain: What prospects for upgrading by developing countries?* United Nations Industrial Development Organization (UNIDO), Vienna

H&M (2014) Our Supply Chain [online] www.hm.com/supplychain [accessed 8 July 2014]

Ha, J E and Dyer, B (2005) New dynamics in the US apparel import trade: exploring the role of import intermediaries, International Textile and Apparel Association Proceedings [online] http://itaaonline.org/?page=139 [accessed 15 July 2015]

Ha-Brookshire, J E and Dyer, B (2008), Apparel import intermediaries: the impact of a hyperdynamic environment on US apparel firms, *Clothing & Textiles Research Journal,* **26** (1), pp 66–90

Hines, T (2007) Supply chain strategies, structures and relationships, in T Hines and M Bruce (eds) *Fashion Marketing: Contemporary issues,* 2nd edn, Butterworth-Heinemann, Oxford, pp 27–53

Hines, T and McGowan, P (2005) Supply chain strategies in the UK fashion industry: the rhetoric of partnership and power, *International Entrepreneurship and Management Journal*, **1**, pp 519–37

Holweg, M, Disney, S, Holmstrom, J and Smaros, J (2005) Supply chain collaboration: making sense of the strategy continuum, *European Management Journal*, **23** (2), pp 170–81

Johnsen, T E, Howard, M and Miemczyk, J (2014) *Purchasing and Supply Chain Management: A sustainability perspective*, Routledge, London and New York

Jones, R M (2006) *The Apparel Industry*, Blackwell, Oxford

Kalantaridis, C, Slava, S and Vassilev, I (2008) Globalisation and industrial change in the clothing industry of Transcarpathia, Western Ukraine: a microlevel view, *Environment and Planning A*, **40** (1), pp 235–53

Leff, N H (1974) International sourcing strategy, *Columbia Journal of World Business*, **6** (3), pp 71–79

Leontiades, J (1971) International sourcing in the LDCs, *Columbia Journal of World Business*, **6**, pp 19–26

Lezama, M, Webber, B and Dagher, C (2004) *Sourcing Practices in the Apparel Industry: Implications for garment exporters in commonwealth developing countries*, Commonwealth Secretariat, London

Li & Fung (2014) Our business [online] www.lifung.com/our-business [accessed 9 December 2014]

Lowson, R H (2003) Apparel sourcing: assessing the true operational cost, *International Journal of Clothing Science and Technology*, **15** (5), pp 335–45

Magretta, J and Fung, V (1998), Fast, global, and entrepreneurial: supply chain management, Hong Kong style, *Harvard Business Review*, September–October, pp 102–14

Mason-Jones, R, Naylor, B and Towill, D R (2000) Lean, agile or leagile? Matching your supply chain to the marketplace, *International Journal of Production Research*, **38** (17), pp 4061–070

Masson, R, Iosif, L, MacKerron, G and Fernie, J (2007) Managing complexity in agile global fashion industry supply chains, *International Journal of Logistics Management*, **18** (2), pp 238–54

Matthyssens, P, Pauwels, P and Quintens, L (2006), Guest editorial, *Journal of Purchasing and Supply Management,* **12** (4), pp 167–69.

Monczka, R M and Trent, R J (1991) Evolving sourcing strategies for the 1990s, *International Journal of Physical Distribution & Logistics,* **21** (5), pp 4–12

Naylor, J B, Naim, M M and Berry, D (1999) Leagility: integrating the lean and agile manufacturing paradigms in the total supply chain, *International Journal of Production Economics*, **62**, pp 107–18

Neidik, B and Gereffi, G (2006) Explaining Turkey's emergence and sustained competitiveness as a full-package supplier of apparel, *Environment and Planning A*, **38** (12), pp 2285–303

Palpacuer, F (2006) The global sourcing patterns of French clothing retailers: determinants and implications for suppliers' industrial upgrading, *Environment and Planning A*, **38** (12), pp 2271–83

Palpacuer, F, Gibbon, P and Thomsen, L (2005) New challenges for developing country suppliers in global clothing chains: a comparative European perspective, *World Development*, **33** (3), pp 409–30

Palpacuer, F and Parisotto, A (2003) Global production and local jobs: can global enterprise networks be used as levers for local development? *Global Networks*, **3** (2), pp 97–120

Perry, P, Fernie, J and Wood, S (2014) The international fashion supply chain and corporate social responsibility, in J Fernie and L Sparks (eds) *Logistics and Retail Management*, 4th edn, Kogan Page, London

Porter, M (1985) *Competitive Advantage: Creating and sustaining superior performance*, Free Press, New York

PricewaterhouseCoopers (2014) Reshoring: a new direction for the UK economy? *UK Economic Outlook,* March, pp 25–33

Purvis, L, Gosling, J and Nain, M M (2014) The development of a lean, agile and leagile supply network taxonomy on differing types of flexibility, *International Journal of Production Economics*, **151**, May, pp 100–11

Pyndt, J, Pedersen, T (2005) *Managing Global Offshoring Strategies: A case approach*, Copenhagen Business School Press, Copenhagen

Reve, T (1990) The firm as a means of internal and external contracts, in M Aoki *et al* (eds) *The Firm as a Nexus of Treaties*, Sage, London

Sanderson, R (2013) Manufacturing: consumers push big luxury names to account for supply chains, *Financial Times*, June 3, p 4

Sethi, S P (2003) *Setting Global Standards: Guidelines for creating codes of conduct in multinational corporations*, Wiley, Hoboken, NJ

Sheridan, M, Moore, C and Nobbs, K (2006) Fast fashion requires fast marketing: the role of category management in fast fashion positioning, *Journal of Fashion Marketing and Management*, **10** (3), pp 301–15

Siegel, N (2014) Not made in China, *Ozy* [online] www.ozy.com/fast-forward /not-made-in-china/36612 [accessed 9 December 2014]

Singleton, J (1997) *The World Textile Industry*, Routledge, London

Smith, A, Pickles, J, Buček, M, Begg, R and Roukova, P (2008) Reconfiguring 'post-socialist' regions: cross-border networks and regional competition in the Slovak and Ukrainian clothing industry, *Global Networks*, **8** (3), pp 281–307

Socha, M (2013) Kering acquires Tannery France Croco, *Women's Wear Daily*, 25 March, **205** (60), p 2

Swamidass, P M (1993), Import sourcing dynamics: an integrated perspective, *Journal of International Business Studies*, **24** (4), pp 671–91

Tan, K C (2001) A framework of supply chain management literature, *European Journal of Purchasing and Supply Management*, **7**, pp 39–48

Tewari, M (2006) Adjustment in India's textile and apparel industry: reworking historical legacies in a post-MFA world, *Environment and Planning A*, **38** (12), pp 2325–44

Tokatli, N (2008) Global sourcing: insights from the global clothing industry: the case of Zara, a fast fashion retailer, *Journal of Economic Geography*, **8** (1), pp 21–38

Tokatli, N (2012) Old firms, new tricks and the quest for profits: Burberry's journey from success to failure and back to success again, *Journal of Economic Geography* **12** (1), pp 55–77

Tokatli, N and Kizilgün, Ö (2009) From manufacturing garments for ready-to-wear to designing collections for fast fashion: evidence from Turkey, *Environment and Planning A*, **41** (1), pp 146–62

Tokatli, N and Kizilgün, Ö (2010) Coping with the changing rules of the game in the global textiles and apparel industries: evidence from Turkey and Morocco, *Journal of Economic Geography*, **10** (2), pp 209–29

Towers, N and Bergvall-Forsberg, J (2009) Agile merchandising in the European textile fashion industry, in J Fernie and L Sparks (eds) *Logistics and Retail Management*, Kogan Page, London, pp 121–40

Trent, R J and Monczka, R M (2003), Understanding integrated global sourcing, *International Journal of Physical Distribution & Logistics Management*, **33** (7), pp 607–29

Trent, R J and Monczka, R M (2005), Achieving excellence in global sourcing, *MIT Sloan Management Review*, **47** (1), pp 23–32

Vereecke, A and Muylle, S (2006) Performance improvement through supply chain collaboration in Europe, *International Journal of Operations and Production Management*, **26** (11), pp 1176–198

Walmart (2014) Suppliers, *Walmart* [online] http://corporate.walmart.com/suppliers [accessed 11 December 2014]

Welford, R and Frost, S (2006) Corporate social responsibility in Asian supply chains, *Corporate Social Responsibility and Environmental Management*, **13** (3), pp 166–76

Weller, S (2007) Fashion as viscous knowledge: fashion's role in shaping transnational garment production, *Journal of Economic Geography*, 7 (1), pp 39–66

Williams, T, Maull, R and Ellis, B (2002) Demand chain management theory: constraints and development from global aerospace supply webs, *Journal of Operations Management*, 20, pp. 691–706

Williamson, O E (1979) Transaction cost economics; the governance of contractual relations, *Journal of Law and Economics*, **22**, October, pp 223–61

Wood, S (2002) Organisational restructuring, knowledge and spatial scale: the case of the US department store industry, *Tijdschrift voor economische en sociale geografie*, **93** (1), pp 8–33

Zeng, A Z (2000) A synthetic study of sourcing strategies, *Industrial Management & Data Systems*, **100** (5), pp 219–26

Zenz, G J (1994) *Purchasing and the Management of Materials* 7th edn, John Wiley & Sons Inc., New York

Zhu, S and Pickles, J (2013) Bring in, go up, go west, go out: upgrading, regionalisation and delocalisation in China's apparel production networks, *Journal of Contemporary Asia*, **44** (1), pp 36–63

Corporate social responsibility (CSR) in international fashion supply chains

04

Introduction

The concept of corporate social responsibility (CSR) in the textile industry is not new. During the Industrial Revolution in the UK philanthropic mill owners such as Robert Owen and Titus Salt developed housing, recreational and educational facilities for their workforces. Now, New Lanark and Saltaire are UNESCO World Heritage sites bearing testament to the idea that a well-fed, educated and happy workforce are a productive source of labour. It can be argued that CSR only became prominent in terms of public debate during the 1960s with the advent of dissent at the misleading claims of marketers, the quality of products and the despoliation of the environment. This was embodied in John F Kennedy's speech to Congress in 1962 on consumers' four basic rights – the right to be informed, to be heard, to be safe and to have choice. These rights were to become the basis of environmental and consumer legislation in the 1970s. The concept of Societal Marketing was introduced by Kotler in 1972; CSR became the centre of debate between the free market shareholder approach of Friedman (1970) and that of the stakeholder model originally suggested by Coase in 1937 and developed by Freeman in 1984.

It is fair to say that the stakeholder model is the one that prevails today. However, there is much debate on the extent to which CSR is incorporated into fashion companies' business plans and the degree to which 'greenwashing' exists, whereby 40 years on, marketers continue to make extravagant claims of their 'green' or ethical credentials. This chapter begins by defining CSR and the institutional framework companies operate in, before discussing the role of CSR in international fashion supply chains. Examples will be given of initiatives to implement CSR, highlighting the positive approach of several companies, including Timberland and the efforts by Sri Lanka as a country to be the model of CSR implementation.

Defining CSR and its institutional context

> During the past 20 years CSR has emerged as the conflicted, paradigmatic compromise between the public demand for sustainable goods and services and investors' demands for business competitiveness (ie maximum profits) (Alves, 2009, p 3)

In essence Alves argues that the former is guided by environmentalists' concern for the planet, especially climate change, and the latter by the dominance of neo-liberal capitalism (for example see Greenspan, 2008).

The literature is therefore replete with definitions of CSR in relation to the perspective taken by the author or organization. In consequence, the oft-quoted definition by the World Business Council for Sustainable Development (WBCFSD) is:

> the continuing commitment by business to behave ethically and contribute to economic development while improving the quality of life of the workforce and their families as well as of the local community and society at large (WBCFSD, 1999, p 3).

WBCFSD is a forum of business leaders and was founded in 1992 on the eve of the Rio Earth summit. Its CSR definition includes economic growth because the Council's main aim is to combine environment protection with economic growth.

A decade after the WBCFSD definition, in November 2010 the International Organization for Standardization (ISO) produced its guidance on social responsibility to business and public sector organizations, ISO 26000. The creation of these guidelines was the result of five years of deliberations by a working group of 450 participating experts drawn from 99 ISO member countries (ISO Press Release 2 November 2014). The guidance does not give a direct definition of CSR but states that the objective is to 'contribute to sustained development' and 'to ensure healthy ecosystems, social equity and good organizational governance' (ISO, 2014, p 2).

A schematic overview of ISO 26000 is given in Figure 4.1. Here the clauses of ISO 26000 guidance are portrayed by identifying the scope and principles of social responsibility on the left, the key actions to be carried out in the centre with expected outcomes on the right. Clause 7 is fundamental to the successful implementation of CSR. A company would have to make 'social responsibility integral to its policies, organizational culture, strategies and operations; building internal competency for social responsibility; and regularly reviewing these actions and practices related to social responsibility (ISO, 2014, p 17).

All of these definitions are from international organizations yet there are numerous definitions in the academic literature (see Perry, 2011 for a discussion on these). As the later part of this chapter focuses upon Sri Lanka it is perhaps appropriate to draw upon the work of Wijayasiri and Dissanayake (2009), who discuss the impact of the ending of the Multi-Fibre Agreement (MFA) on Sri Lanka's textile and clothing industry. They state that 'CSR is a growing global phenomenon whereby organizations consider the interests of society by taking responsibility for the impact of their activities on customers, employees, communities and the environment in all aspects of their operations, often going above and beyond what is required by law' (p 166).

It is evident that the stakeholder model has been the dominant paradigm in the 21st century, reinforced with the rise of anti-consumerism, often related to what is seen as mindless consumption of fast fashion. This has led to consumer resistance, boycotts and counter-cultural movements (Shaw and Riach, 2011). During the aftermath of the financial crisis in the late 2000s, anti-capitalist marches often ended in violence at G8 summit conferences.

The problem with a stakeholder approach to CSR is the numerous conflicting interests among the large number of protagonists involved. This has meant that codes of conduct such as ISO 26000 are only voluntary guidance standards and cannot be used for accreditation or certification compared with their standards on quality (ISO 9001:2008) or environmental management (ISO 14001, 2004). Similarly the Ethical Trade Initiative (ETI) established in 1998 to improve working conditions around the world implemented a base code of labour practice drawn from the standards of the International Labour Organization (ILO). However, it is a voluntary organization and again no certification is granted.

FIGURE 4.1 Schematic overview of ISO 26000

Schematic overview of ISO 26000

The following graphic provides an overview of ISO 26000 outlining the relationship between the various clauses of the standard.

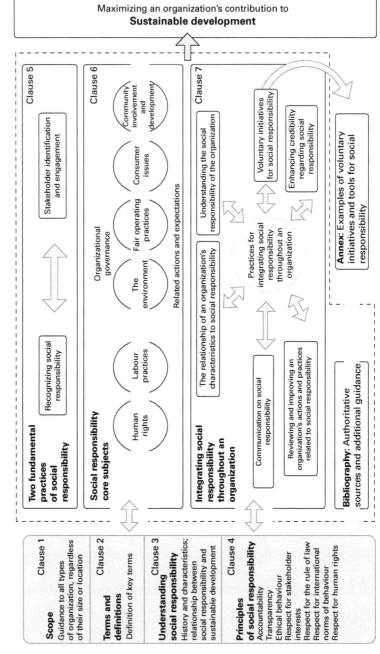

Source The diagram taken from the publication Discovering ISO 26000 is reproduced with the permission of the International Organization for Standardization, ISO. Copyright remains with ISO.

This leads us to question the broader issue of corporate behaviour with regard to what David Vogel (2005) calls the market for virtue. So is Walmart a responsible company for bringing low-priced goods to consumers in many markets of the world or an irresponsible company for paying low wages, being anti-union and for putting small companies out of business when it enters some of these markets? In the UK in 2014 many MPs including senior politicians wore t-shirts supporting women's rights. These t-shirts subsequently created a political and media storm when it was reported that the shirts, retailing at £45 (US $67), were being produced in sweatshop conditions in Mauritius. The retailer Whistles had claimed that the factory had met all of the social and ethical audited compliances but was it the 62 pence (91 cents) wages per hour figure that was quoted in the press that triggered such media reaction? This then begs the question of what are 'acceptable' conditions in the host country compared with home country standards. This issue was highlighted by Werther and Chandler (2005) who argued that the global media 'evaluate overseas operations through the lens of home country standards' (p 320).

Laudal (2010), when discussing the fashion industry, noted that as one of the most global industries in the world the retailer had to balance variations in government regulations, employment, environmental protection and wage levels. This resulted in a plethora of commercial, legal and moral standards to consider in the sourcing decision. Many countries with authoritative regimes have used forced labour in the textile industry and others have used 'cheap' labour or relaxed enforcement standards on pollution to attract foreign direct investment to their countries. For example, Perry (2011) discussed the use of forced and child labour in Myanmar and Uzbekistan and noted that Brazil's rapid industrial development was facilitated by lax pollution enforcement standards. Indeed, the avoidance of sourcing cotton from Uzbekistan is a key issue in fashion companies' CSR reports, and strong lobbying continues in 2015 to influence the Uzbekistan Government to end the practice of forced labour. Numerous studies have noted relaxed labour regulations in export processing zones which conflict with the ILO Core Convention for respecting workers' rights to freedom of association and collective bargaining (Miller, 2004; Arnold and Han Shih, 2010).

Strategic CSR

There is a distinction between strategic CSR and CSR as a mere business process in that strategic CSR must deliver clear benefits to the firm, shareholders and stakeholders through its core business activities. Porter and Kramer (2006) argue that CSR is 'a source of opportunity, innovation, and competitive advantage' (p 80), and that activities should be able to add value to both the firm and society as a whole. CSR initiatives can therefore extend beyond good corporate citizenship to confer competitive advantage to the firm (Garriga and Melé, 2004; Porter and Kramer, 2006). This is known as strategic CSR (Lantos, 2001). Increasingly, firms are using CSR benefits to serve their own commercial interests (Hanlon and Fleming, 2009). Hemingway and MacLagan (2004) concur and give examples of 'image and reputation management, the manipulation of stakeholders and the integration of the organization into its host community' (p 41) as benefits of CSR which also serve the firm's strategic commercial interest. In doing so 'firms build long-term loyalty, legitimacy, trust or brand equity that reinforces the corporation's other strategic objectives' (Godfrey and Hatch, 2007, p 88). Burke and Logsdon's (1996) five measures of strategic CSR help to determine the likelihood of CSR activity resulting in value creation for the firm (Table 4.1). Value creation for the firm is more likely if it is able to realize these five measures in its CSR activities.

Conceptualizing CSR as a strategic business initiative broadens understanding of the reality of corporate drivers and inhibitors of better working conditions in global production networks. Perry, Wood and Fernie (2014b) note that CSR initiatives in the agri-food sector evolved from technical and quality requirements to the inclusion of social and environmental criteria – mainly to protect reputation and enhance quality control rather than any

TABLE 4.1 Five dimensions of strategic CSR (after Burke and Logsdon, 1996)

Measure	Meaning
Centrality	Closeness of fit to a firm's mission
Specificity	The ability of a firm to internalize private benefits of CSR
Pro-activity	The degree of planning to anticipate emerging social trends
Voluntarism	Scope for discretionary decision making and lack of externally imposed compliance requirements
Visibility	Observable or recognizable credit by firm's stakeholders

explicit goal to improve supplier welfare (Tallontire, 2007). The under-standing of CSR in apparel production networks is an attempt therefore to reconcile CSR objectives alongside business ones. The next section will discuss the implementation of CSR objectives within the context of global fashion supply chains.

Implementation of CSR initiatives in global fashion supply chains

We discussed at some length in Chapter 3 on offshore sourcing/outsourc-ing how the apparel industry has globalized since the 1990s. This expand-ing geography of sourcing and manufacture of apparel has resulted in retailers trading off reduced manufacturing costs with spatial proximity/lead-time considerations (Abernathy *et al*, 2006; Masson *et al*, 2007). The trend towards vertical disintegration of retailers' supply chains increases the degree of global dispersal (Gereffi, 1999) and sees a shift of the gar-ment manufacturing function to lower labour cost countries (Pickles, 2006; Taplin, 2006; Pickles and Smith, 2011). Concomitantly, debate increasingly focuses on the socio-economic impact of global business operations on developing countries with respect to worker safety, exploitation, sweatshops and child labour (New, 1997; Smestad, 2009). While retailers retain higher order functions of distribution, marketing and brand management, manu-facturing activities are outsourced to a complex network of independent subcontractors. This shift may result in reduced visibility and control of the worker experience for the lead firm (Doorey, 2011).

The retailer codes of conduct and broader international multi-stakeholder schemes and accreditations discussed in this chapter seek to address the negative outcomes of globalization in terms of labour standards, by impos-ing various conditions upon the lead firm and its suppliers (Hale and Wills, 2007; Hughes *et al*, 2007, 2008; Ruwanpura and Wrigley, 2011). CSR may therefore be perceived as a form of privatized governance in the absence of necessarily tight national forms of regulation (Christopherson and Lillie, 2005; Tallontire, 2007; Mayer and Pickles, 2010), though its uneven imple-mentation remains a concern (Ruwanpura, 2013). Despite this, retailers are keen to publicize their commitments to worker conditions and wider CSR in communications with stakeholders (Mann *et al*, 2014).

In practice, the implementation of CSR within garment production networks commonly involves the application of guiding mechanisms and management tools such as codes of conduct and ethical audits to encourage socially responsible practices in the manufacturing process. Therefore, the rhetoric of CSR implementation may not always conform to the ideal of going beyond minimum legal or regulatory requirements. Welford and Frost (2006) note that CSR is often perceived as a compliance issue in Asian supply chains, while Hughes (2005) notes how the notion of ethical trade is commonly understood to mean the establishment of a minimum set of standards for suppliers – something that may be seen as conflicting with framing CSR as a voluntary activity (Dahlsrud, 2008; McWilliams and Siegel, 2001).

A rules-based approach to CSR governance does not necessarily lead to improvements on the factory floor or increased worker involvement in the governance process (Raj-Reichert, 2013; Ruwanpura, 2013). Indeed, active worker participation in corporate code implementation is seen as important in securing worker benefits (Yu, 2009). At its worst, the adoption and implementation of codes of conduct may be seen as little more than a PR exercise to deflect further criticism of lead firms, with the monitoring of codes a mere box-ticking exercise that fails to fully address exploitative working conditions for the workers' benefit. Plank *et al* (2012) note the limitations of apparel retailer codes of conduct in affecting the social upgrading of supplier facilities, given their focus on measurable standards such as wages, working conditions, and health and safety issues, rather than enabling rights which seek to provide voice and empowerment to workers, such as freedom of association and collective bargaining. More broadly, numerous researchers discuss widespread economic upgrading of the global apparel value network, while acknowledging that *social upgrading* remains somewhat more challenging to achieve (Barrientos *et al*, 2011; Bernhardt, 2013).

Barrientos (2013) explores how NGOs take up the cause of workers by adopting variegated strategies of engagement with lead retail firms in the production network – at times involving alliances and at others pursuing more adversarial campaigns which may threaten the former dominance of the lead firm in the network (Coe and Hess, 2013). In the process, Barrientos argues such initiatives involve strategies that emphasize the commercial (risk) or alternatively the social (caring) dimensions of corporate engagement. Retailers attempt to address working conditions in the supply chains that produce their merchandise, irrespective of whether or not they own the production facilities (Andersen and Skøtt-Larsen, 2009; Hughes, 2005; Hughes *et al*, 2007).

Compromises to CSR in global apparel production

The lead retailers that orchestrate global apparel production networks are conscious of their CSR vulnerabilities and keen to promote their CSR credentials. Achieving CSR brand leadership requires a shift from a view of the brand as tactical and reactive towards seeing it as strategic, multi-stakeholder and visionary (Lindgreen *et al*, 2012). CSR needs to be embedded throughout the entire value chain and within stakeholder relationships (Maon *et al*, 2009). Even when efforts have been made in this direction, with lead firms co-operating with workers, NGOs and trade unions, results often remain disappointing (eg Lund-Thomsen and Coe, 2015 in the case of Nike). Specifically in the highly competitive mid-market fashion retail sector, the realities of CSR demands may be compromised at the factory level by the need to balance the competing commercial realities of cost and lead time (Plank *et al*, 2012; Hearson, 2009; Barrientos and Smith, 2007). In particular, flexibility and responsiveness must be finely balanced against sourcing cost to achieve success (Hines and McGowan, 2005; Masson *et al*, 2007).

Given a backdrop of demanding buying practices of powerful Western retailers that require more frequent shipments of cheaper garments, a supplier's ability to fund and therefore adhere to ethical standards is challenged (Laudal, 2010; New, 1997). Tokatli *et al* (2008) note how retailers have demanded greater product variety from manufacturers as well as adding mid-season purchasing to the traditional two-season calendar.

Palpacuer *et al* (2005) found that UK retailers made increasing demands of their suppliers for production flexibility and risk transfer, in addition to imposing continuous price reductions. In particular, increased payment terms and cost reduction practices affect the supplier's ability to manage costs, especially for full-package suppliers that purchase fabric upfront. In 2013, UK fashion retailer Monsoon Accessorize requested a 4 per cent retrospective discount from all suppliers, as well as an increase in payment terms from 60 to 90 days (Hurley, 2013). Similarly, Laura Ashley requested a 10 per cent discount on cost price from suppliers with immediate effect, including on orders already placed (Cookson, 2013). Given these competing demands, Pickles (2006) notes that as order volumes and contract manufacturing prices declined in western Slovakia, compliance with codes of conduct became more tenuous for suppliers. Although open-book accounting allows buyers to facilitate cost management across the supply chain network by accessing suppliers' costing data, this practice may also be used opportunistically for inducing competitive bids from rival suppliers (Free, 2008).

Buying practices that have developed to address commercial pressures may jeopardize labour standards at the factory level and undermine CSR efforts, especially with the fast-fashion business model (Hearson, 2009). Industry evidence suggests that retail buyers are unwilling to increase prices paid to suppliers to reflect the increased cost of ethical production (Ruwanpura and Wrigley, 2011; Yu, 2008). Hughes' (2012) study of retail buyers during the Western recession found that as ethical trading budgets succumbed to growing financial pressure, there was greater focus on *strategic CSR* to deliver benefits to the business in terms of efficiency gains and reputation protection, as opposed to improvements to labour standards being pursued as a fundamental human right. Ruwanpura and Wrigley (2011) concluded that the compatibility of retailer sourcing strategies with the implementation of CSR in production sites was further challenged by the global recession, as suppliers lost orders to lower labour cost countries and buyers prioritized price over compliance. Similarly, in the Caribbean basin, Schrank (2004) noted how full-package suppliers sought to undercut each other in the race for greater market share during a period of economic recession, which resulted in downgraded conditions for workers.

Case studies of CSR in practice

It is clear from this general discussion that guiding mechanisms and management tools to encourage socially responsible practices invariably have questionable effectiveness in the apparel supply chain, given the complexity and the inherent focus on sourcing cost and lead time (Mamic, 2005; Welford and Frost, 2006; Mares, 2010). It is important to highlight positive examples where CSR has been the focus of management attention and a core element of corporate strategy rather than the rules-based, box-ticking approach of most companies in the sector.

Most companies have been accused of 'greenwashing' in that they highlight selective elements of the CSR agenda to support their green or ethical credentials. Some environment groups or brand consultancies such as Eco Age would argue that fast fashion and sustainability is an oxymoron in that volume production and consumerism do not go hand-in-hand with CSR. Such proponents do acknowledge that H&M (see Chapter 2, Figure 2.1) are doing much in tackling sustainability but note that money-off vouchers to bring in used clothing is a form of 'greenwashing' as it is a marketing tool to bring consumers back in store to spend more.

Doane (2005) is very critical of CSR initiatives because their voluntary nature can mean programmes fall prey to the vagaries of the market. Her paper is general in nature but has relevance to the fashion market. She claims that there are two main approaches to ethical business, that of the 'ethical minnows' and the 'multinational mammoths'. The former have emerged from the Fair Trade movement and are niche operators that have found difficulty in scaling up because of higher costs and therefore lower returns on investment. Examples of these ethical minnows are People Tree, a UK pioneer in sustainable, fair trade fashion and more recently Honest by, a Belgian fashion retailer formed in 2012, which claims to be the first company to have open transparency of its cost breakdown through every part of its supply chain. The mammoths, by contrast, are most of the multinational corporations that try to reduce their negative impacts instead of avoiding them. The implementation of such measures often occurs after scandals of ethical transgressions leading to shareholder and stakeholder pressure, classified as coercive social responsibility by Castka and Balzarova (2008). Doane (2005) uses Shell and Nike as two examples of 'mammoths' that serve as warnings to others because of scandals relating to reputational risk.

Rankings of socially responsible companies

While there is regular comment in the media of greenwashing and of scandals of one sort or another, some publications have produced their own ranking of company performance in relation to a range of criteria. For example Wrinkle *et al* (2012) produced a report for Not for Sale, a strong California-based lobbying group whose aim is to eradicate modern slavery. They used data from Free2Work – a project established by Not for Sale – to collect information on working conditions throughout the supply chain in addition to assessing management systems in three other categories:

- policies;
- traceability/transparency;
- monitoring and training.

In essence they analysed 50 companies operating in the United States on their CSR practices, including examples of model practices in specific categories. The rankings graded companies from A to F. In the overall ranking

Inditex (Zara) and Timberland were awarded As with Patagonia and H&M receiving a B grade. Inditex received a good practice commendation for policies pertaining to upholding workers' rights whereas Patagonia and Timberland (see case study) were singled out for the transparency and traceability of their supply chains.

In the UK the magazine *Ethical Consumer*, in a report produced in 2014, ranked 57 UK high street brands according to similar CSR criteria and ranked Zara, Marks & Spencer and H&M as their best-buy labels because of their policies on transparency of their supply chains, paying a living wage and their attitude to toxics in the production process. For the last factor these companies scored well in the Greenpeace scorecard on the reduction or removal of hazardous chemicals.

It is interesting that two fast-fashion companies and two companies that produce outdoor clothing and footwear products come at the top of most independent assessments of companies with sound CSR principles. Marks & Spencer is different in that it is involved in food and homeware in addition to the clothing business. Nevertheless, it has always had a sound reputation as a good company to work for and established its Plan A (there is no Plan B!) in 2007 with revisions in 2010 and 2014 (see Marks & Spencer, 2014). The initial Plan was very focused upon technical issues associated with climate change and waste whereas the new plan, Plan A 2020, focuses on customer, employee and supplier engagement. Plan A 2020 is divided into four key sections and includes 100 commitments that are monitored in relation to targets set. M&S scores particularly well on the climate change and waste targets that were initially established in 2007. For example, the company has carbon-neutral operations in the UK and Ireland and intends to extend this commitment to its international operations. It continues to maintain zero waste landfill for its UK and Ireland operations and is certified by the Carbon Trust's Waste, Carbon and Water standards.

On analyzing the data on companies with good practice on CSR initiatives, common themes emerge. All companies have a commitment from senior management to CSR; indeed in the case of Timberland and Patagonia their mission statements/values embrace social responsibility. As noted in the following case study with Timberland and H&M in Chapter 2 good companies are transparent in their reporting and establish targets to meet environmental and social justice initiatives. Companies that supply these brands have their factories publically listed and publish their audit performance. It is also important that employees 'buy in' to the CSR agenda, especially with regard to community service. Although this paints a rosy picture of CSR, the path to achieving some initiatives can be difficult. Patagonia, for example, is very frank in discussing its auditing of suppliers and conceding that it lost its way in the late 1990s. In the early days the company would not deal with suppliers if they could not audit the factories themselves. By the mid-1990s Patagonia began to employ third-party auditors but at the same time began to source new products from new factories, many of which subcontracted work out to other factories. The net result was a loss of control and knowledge of working conditions in parts of their supply chain. Throughout the 2000s Patagonia refocused their efforts on working closer with a smaller number of factories to around 70 suppliers, in addition to certifying subcontractors.

CASE STUDY Timberland and CSR

Our initiatives have proven that corporate responsibility doesn't need to be an add-on, but instead can be a powerful competitive advantage. We have saved money by reducing energy costs and greenhouse gas emissions and are creating top line growth by meeting consumers' growing desire for eco-friendly products. We also recognize our responsibility for preserving the outdoors we need for our industry to thrive (Stewart Whitney, President, Timberland LLC, 2014).[eq]

The Timberland story revolves around the entrepreneurial flair of the Swartz family. Nathan, the founder, was in the shoe business from 1918 when he was an apprentice in Boston, and he eventually bought a half interest in the Abington Shoe Company in Massachusetts in 1952, buying the remaining stock in 1955. By then his sons had joined the company and in 1965 the family had produced the revolutionary injection-moulding technology that fused soles to leather uppers to produce waterproof footwear. This enabled the Swartz family to develop a range of footwear, notably outdoor products, under the newly created brand name of Timberland in 1973. The company also changed its name to the Timberland Company by the end of the decade (1978).

It was after becoming a public company in 1987 that Timberland began to fully embrace CSR initiatives. In 1989 it partnered with the Boston-based City Year Inc. by donating 50 pairs of work boots for young adults (18–24-year-olds) who pledged to support youths in after-school programmes. City Year's aims were not only to provide community service but to encourage leadership skills and civic activism amongst young people. Jeffrey Swartz saw the benefits of such a scheme for his own company and in 1992 developed the Path of Service programme, which offers employees 16 hours' paid leave per annum to perform community service activities. In 1995 and 1997 the service time was raised from 16 to 32 hours, then to 40 hours.

Timberland has championed this engagement strategy and together with City Year has activated over 10,000 consumers and retail partners in 25 countries to embrace annual service days (Mirvis, 2012). The company claims that the team building and community betterment of such a strategy leads to greater productivity and corporate effectiveness. Mirvis (2012) argues, however, that Timberland's CSR agenda has shifted more to the environmental elements of CSR and away from social justice initiatives. This means that its historical link with City Year has given way to more 'greening' service programmes.

Timberland has consistently received awards and accolades for being one of the best companies for sustainable stocks, and one of the most admired and best companies to work for in the *Fortune* magazine list of top companies. In 1993 it signed up to the Coalition for Environmentally Responsible Economies' (CERES) set of principles that advocate ethical and environmentally sustainable business practices. CERES was created in 1989 in the wake of the Exxon Valdez oil spill of that year. Since then Timberland has maintained its high CSR standards, introducing CSR performance data in 2001, and in 2004 it named the company names and locations of their contract factories around the world. By 2008 Timberland was reporting its environmental and social performance on a quarterly basis, meaning that the company was treating CSR reporting with the same respect as financial reporting.

In 2011 Timberland created a new CSR portal which set out goals for each of its four pillars:

- Climate: protect the outdoors.

- Product: innovate cradle to cradle.

- Factories: improve workers' lives.

- Service: engage communities.

For each of these goals the company has established quantifiable performance metrics and it publishes progress on meeting these targets in its CSR reports. The website is peppered with examples of initiatives with its stakeholders to positively influence a range of social and environmental issues. The Service pillar has already been discussed but a milestone was reached in 2014 when Timberland employees had volunteered over one million service hours since the Path of Service programme began in 1992.

In terms of the Climate pillar, it is Timberland's aim to reduce carbon emissions by 50 per cent from 2006 to 2015 (from 29,293 to 14,645 metric tons). It was well on the way to meeting this target as the figure for 2013 was 14,691 metric tons. It should be noted, however, that Timberland was acquired by the VF Corporation in 2011 and figures are being revised post-2011 to account for variations in company methodologies and reporting conventions.

Timberland utilizes eco-conscious materials in its products so the product pillar is replete with initiatives to incorporate recycled, renewable or organic products so that 70 per cent of all footwear has such materials in manufacture. They have increased their use of Green Rubber (recycled rubber) and diverted 50 million plastic bottles from landfill by using recycled PET in their footwear lines.

In its factory portal, Timberland claims to have gone beyond compliance in its approach to social and environmental impacts in its supply chain. The company sources from over 300 factories and produces factory sustainability reports on all CSR issues. They began this process in 2006 with the Recreation Footwear Company (RFC) in the Dominican Republic. This factory employs 2,200 people and is the only factory in Timberland's supply chain that is wholly owned and operated by the company. The company can therefore set the baseline standards required of all of its suppliers from RFC. The company utilizes a series of indices to measure CSR initiatives; for example it has produced a Green Index to measure climate, resource and chemical impacts associated with the production of its footwear throughout the supply chain. It is also a co-founder of the Sustainable Apparel Coalition. With regard to social impacts, Timberland uses the Social Accountability International's Social Fingerprint tool for benchmarking factories to achieve best-in-class social and labour management systems.

It should be noted that Timberland has adopted their new parent company's (VF Corporation's) factory audit ratings and compliance procedures, which have replaced Timberland's Code of Conduct

Sri Lanka and CSR practices in garment manufacture

The examples given in the previous section illustrated the best practice principles utilized by some companies. In this section we take more of a country perspective in that Sri Lanka has laid the CSR foundation for its companies through government directives, labour union histories and societal norms. In 2006, Sri Lankan Apparel, the textile industry body, launched the 'Garments Without Guilt' campaign to promote the country's ethical credentials by assuring buyers that garments produced in Sri Lanka were made under ethical conditions. This initiative sought to enhance the reputation of the country for ethical production and to differentiate it from lower labour cost countries. With the phasing out of the quota-based global sourcing system under the Multi-Fibre Arrangement in 2005 and the global recession of the late 2000s, price competition intensified (Wijayasiri and Dissanayake (2009). The aim was therefore to establish a differentiated form of competitive advantage founded on ethical manufacturing and to become recognized as a leader in terms of lack of child labour, high health and safety standards and the ratification of ILO Core Conventions (Goger, 2013).

The performance of Sri Lankan garment manufacturers in certain aspects of CSR is not only explained in terms of industry voluntary standards (Dahlsrud, 2008; McWilliams and Siegel, 2001), but also by the supportive local conditions of strong labour laws and socio-development achievements (Ruwanpura, 2012; Hancock et al, 2010). Ethical practices in Sri Lankan garment manufacturers are reinforced by cultural norms, specifically the moral teachings of the predominant religious persuasion of Sinhalese Buddhism, which demands fairness, social justice and equity (Perry, 2012). Additionally, Sri Lanka's (British Victorian) colonial history put pressure on garment factory owners to protect the virtue of the largely female workforce (Goger, 2013). These cultural underpinnings manifested themselves in the personal values of factory managers, and meant that some of the worker welfare practices which would later become known as CSR had long been embedded within Sri Lankan value systems (Loker, 2011; Perry, 2012).

Supplier–retailer relationships and CSR in garment production networks

The nature of buyer–supplier relationships in Sri Lanka is defined by the nature of the product – predominantly mid-market, basic fashion – and this in turn supports CSR implementation, especially for large global brands such as Gap, Nike and Marks & Spencer. This means that Sri Lanka competes in higher-value apparel segments rather than low-cost fast fashion (Ruwanpura and Wrigley, 2011), leading to a reputation for producing quality fashion basics, such as men's casual woven chinos and technically complex items such as bras. For core basics, product life cycles were longer than for high fashion and garment construction was relatively straightforward. The long-running nature of certain styles improved forecasting of retail demand and reduced pressure for short lead times. Factory managers were therefore better able to plan ahead and workers could achieve a higher rate of efficiency and earn production bonuses. There was also less likelihood of last-minute changes to orders: with core basics, buyers were able to forecast more accurately and the consequences of under- or over-buying were less severe than for fast-fashion products that may have a product life cycle of only a few weeks.

This has meant that Sri Lankan garment suppliers have developed long-standing relationships of 10–20 years with US and EU retailers. The trust in such relationships has led to strong collaboration on product design and product development thereby mitigating risks of order changes later in the supply chain process. The main source of friction in the early 2010s related to retailers' desire for better payment terms with many retailers demanding up to 90 days. Most of the larger full-package suppliers have been able to negotiate to improve their cash flow and in one case a supplier refused to supply an internationally well-known Spanish retailer (Perry *et al*, 2014a). By contrast Perry *et al* (2014b) note that the shared benefits between buyers and suppliers were confirmed by the head of sustainable business for a leading UK apparel retailer who recognized the opportunity for shared learning and mutual benefit, which produced better results than a coercive, compliance-based approach that stifled innovation and creativity.

Factory management perspectives

In their work on Sri Lankan garment manufacturers' perspectives of CSR, Perry *et al* (2014b) note that managers framed CSR in terms of compliance rather than going beyond regulatory requirements. These managers claim that they have benefited from a unique set of circumstances as discussed above which have supported the establishment and maintenance of CSR practices. However, such CSR practices were underpinned by an enduring awareness of the strategic CSR outcomes that would inevitably lead to improved productivity, output and enhanced relations with the lead retail clients (see summary in Table 4.2).

Factory managers linked CSR with positive worker outcomes in terms of staff retention and productivity; but also in terms of reinforcing relationships with powerful Western retail customers that required responsiveness and product quality yet remained aware of the vulnerability of their brands to non-ethical practices at the factory level (see Table 4.3). They conceptualized CSR in strategic terms so that improved working conditions through

TABLE 4.2 Factory management narratives on the linking of CSR activities and outcomes

CSR activities	CSR outcomes
Philanthropic donations to community	Legitimacy within society
Human capital development (training)	Attract and retain better workers; lower labour turnover
Monthly paid bonus	Attract and retain better workers
Dedicated CSR department or champion	Better control and visibility of CSR
Diversity management	Image and reputation management; legitimacy within society
Rehabilitation of ex-LTTE soldiers	Image and reputation management; investment in labour force in remote areas
Higher than minimum wage salaries	Attract and retain better workers; attract better retail customers
Minimum worker age (18) higher than legal requirement (16)	Image and reputation management; attract better retail customers
Employee–employer councils	Promote harmonious working relationships; lower labour turnover

training and employee councils attracted better workers, lower labour turnover and improved productivity.

Although Tables 4.2 and 4.3 show how factory managers drive forward CSR initiatives, there is a tension between commercial operatives and ethical outcomes for workers. Sri Lanka's reputation for CSR has led to increased business and pressure on supplying companies. Ruwanpura (2012, 2014a and b, 2015) has been a major critic of CSR implementation by Sri Lankan suppliers, especially with regard to labour relations. In 2012, she reported on how investments in improved factory working conditions were perceived to have been made primarily for the benefit of

TABLE 4.3 Factory management narratives on the linking of CSR goals and outcomes for workers and retailers

Managers' perspective on workers	Managers' perspective on retailers
CSR as a means of attracting and retaining better workers	CSR as a means of cementing long-term trading relationship
Worker outcomes	**Retailer outcomes**
Human capital development (training)	Increased quality levels
Employee–employer councils	Brand assurance given ethical standards

the business. She notes that labour rights activists contend that such investments were to 'show off' to buyers and auditors and thereby present an image of caring for the labour force. In addition, she reports that while Sri Lanka has been positioned at the vanguard of ethical sourcing, ethical codes are inconsistently interpreted and applied, leading to tensions for labour (Ruwanpura, 2014a). She has criticized suppliers for their lack of trade union voice for workers indicating that employee councils are not independent of the employer. In a more recent work in 2015, Rawanpura acknowledges that the Sri Lankan apparel industry has invested wisely in creating a pleasant working environment for the labour force. However, she argues that Sri Lanka should provide an excellent case to show that economic upgrading to higher value-added production should lead to commensurate social upgrading and a greater labour voice (Barrientos *et al*, 2011). Her research, derived from workers' diaries of their experiences, shows that widening inequality has occurred in conjunction with the implementation of an ethical agenda so that a living wage is not provided in the garment industry. She concludes by stating that 'The failure of ethical initiatives to provide a living wage raises serious questions over its efficacy in improving labouring lives. It also brings to bear the partial labelling and makes moot the apparel industry's claim to produce "garments without guilt", especially with regards to freedom to associate, collective bargaining and living wages' (Rawanpura, 2015, p 20).

Conclusions

This chapter has attempted to disentangle the rhetoric from reality in the implementation of CSR. The difficulty in achieving this relates to the institutional standards that act as guidance for companies. And this is the problem. Unlike other international standards, ISO 26000 and other standards are voluntary and not mandatory. No accreditation or certification is given so codes of conduct provide a framework for ethical behaviour which companies can adhere to or not. Not surprisingly many commentators have been very cynical about the motives behind some CSR initiatives and accuse companies of 'greenwashing' whereby selective PR statements are made to endorse their CSR credentials.

For most proactive companies a strategic CSR approach is undertaken whereby attempts are made to go beyond being a good corporate citizen by embracing a stakeholder approach to gain loyalty and trust with customers because of an ethical reputation. However, some companies have become well known for their CSR ethos and tend to rank highly in surveys of the best socially responsible companies. The Timberland case study highlighted how the company has developed its CSR initiatives from service to the community to fully embracing three other pillars of CSR: climate, product and factories. All companies that rank highly on social responsibility embrace CSR from the top and are transparent in their reporting of suppliers, locations and all audit procedures from CO_2 emissions to community work. Targets are set and annual CSR reports discuss whether these have been achieved.

The reader is referred to Chapter 8 on luxury fashion brands and CSR where we discuss how most luxury companies received negative media reviews on their attitude to CSR primarily because of their secrecy. However, since 2012 large companies listed on the French stock exchange have been obligated by law (the Grenelle 2 Act) to report within their annual reports on the social and environmental impacts of their operations. As most of the world's well-known luxury brands are French or owned by French companies, a wealth of information is now available on these companies' CSR activities.

The final section discussed a company-within-country perspective by focusing upon Sri Lanka because of its ethical production initiatives promulgated by Sri Lankan Apparel's 'Garments without Guilt' campaign. It was shown that Sri Lankan garment suppliers already had well-established CSR practices because of the country's political, historical and cultural background that had introduced working welfare practices such as safe, clean working environments and non-child labour as the norm in their business. Sri Lanka has capitalized upon CSR to promote the country as an ethical producer of garments, notably value-added casual products with long product life cycles for well-known UK, US and EU retailers. The problem for suppliers, however, is that these retailers are very demanding and commercial pressures have led to compromises in implementing codes of conduct.

References

Abernathy, F H, Volpe, A and Weil, D (2006) The future of the apparel and textile industries: prospects and choices for public and private actors, *Environment and Planning A*, **38** (12), pp 2207–32

Alves, I M (2009) Green spin everywhere: how greenwashing reveals the limits of the CSR paradigm, *Journal of Global Change and Governance*, **1** (1) pp 1–26

Andersen, M and Skøtt-Larsen, T (2009) Corporate social responsibility in global supply chains, *Supply Chain Management: An International Journal*, **14** (2), pp 75–86

Arnold, D and Han Shih, T (2010) A fair model of globalisation? Labour and global production in Cambodia, *Journal of Contemporary Asia*, **40** (3), pp 401–24

Barrientos, S (2013) Corporate purchasing practices in global production networks: a socially contested terrain, *Geoforum*, **44** (1), pp 44–51

Barrientos, S, Gereffi, G and Rossi, A (2011) Economic and social upgrading in global production networks: a new paradigm for a changing world, *International Labour Review*, **150** (3–4), pp 319–40

Barrientos, S and Smith, S (2007) Do workers benefit from ethical trade? Assessing codes of labour practice in global production systems, *Third World Quarterly*, **28** (4), pp 713–29.

Bernhardt, T (2013) Developing countries in the global apparel value chain: a tale of upgrading and downgrading experiences, *Capturing the Gains Working Paper* 2013/22, University of Manchester

Burke, L and Logsdon, J M (1996) How corporate responsibility pays off, *Long Range Planning*, **29** (4), pp 495–502

Castka, P and Balzarova, M A (2008) ISO 26000 and supply chains: on the diffusion of the social responsibility standard, *International Journal of Production Economics*, **111** (2) pp 274–86

Christopherson, S and Lillie, N (2005) Neither global nor standard: corporate strategies in the new era of labor standards, *Environment and Planning A*, **37** (11), pp 1919–38

Coase, R (1937) The nature of the firm, *Economica* (New Series), **4**, pp 386–405

Coe, N M and Hess, M (2013) Global production networks, labour and development, *Geoforum*, **44** (1), pp 4–9

Cookson, R (2013) Laura Ashley seeks 10% supplier discount, *Financial Times* [online] http://www.ft.com/cms/s/0/356a251c-9479-11e2-b822-00144feabdc0 .html [accessed 24 March 2015]

Dahlsrud, A (2008) How corporate social responsibility is defined: an analysis of 37 definitions, *Corporate Social Responsibility and Environmental Management*, **15** (1), pp 1–13

Doane, D (2005) Beyond corporate social responsibility: minnows, mammoths and markets, *Futures*, **37**, pp 215–29

Doorey, D (2011) The transparent supply chain: from resistance to implementation at Nike and Levi-Strauss, *Journal of Business Ethics*, **103** (4), pp 587–603.

Ethical Consumer (2014) Shopping guide to high street clothes, *Ethical Consumer* [online] http://www.ethicalconsumer.org/ethicalreports/fashionindustry.aspx [accessed 12 March 2015]

Free, C (2008) Walking the talk? Supply chain accounting and trust among UK supermarkets and suppliers, *Accounting, Organizations and Society*, **33** (6), pp 629–62

Freeman, R E (1984) *Strategic Management: A stakeholder approach*, Pitman, Boston

Friedman, M (1970) The social responsibilty of business is to increase its profits, *New York Times Magazine*, 13 September

Garriga, E and Melé, D (2004) Corporate social responsibility theories: mapping the territory, *Journal of Business Ethics*, **53** (1), pp 51–71

Gereffi, G (1999) International trade and industrial upgrading in the apparel commodity chain, *Journal of International Economics*, **48** (1), pp 37–70

Godfrey, P C and Hatch, N W (2007) Researching corporate social responsibility: an agenda for the 21st century, *Journal of Business Ethics*, **70** (1), pp 87–98

Goger, A (2013) Ethical labelling in Sri Lanka: a case study of Garments Without Guilt, in J Bair, M Dickson and D Miller (eds) *Workers' Rights and Labor Compliance in Global Supply Chains*, Routledge, New York

Greenspan, A (2008) *The Age of Turbulence: Adventures in a new world*, Penguin, London

Hale, A and Wills, J (2007). Women working worldwide: transnational networks, corporate social responsibility and action research, *Global Networks*, **7** (4), pp 453–76

Hancock, P, Middleton, S and Moore, J (2010) Export Processing Zones (EPZs), globalisation, feminised labour markets and working conditions: a study of Sri Lankan EPZ workers, *National Library of Australia* [online] http://www.nla. gov.au/openpublish/index.php/lmd/article/view/1612/2004 [accessed 04 March 2015]

Hanlon, G and Fleming, P (2009) Updating the critical perspective on corporate social responsibility, *Sociology Compass*, **3** (6), pp 937–48

Hearson, M (2009) *Cashing In: Giant retailers, purchasing practices, and working conditions in the garment industry*, Clean Clothes Campaign, Amsterdam

Hemingway, CA and Maclagan, P W (2004) Managers' personal values as drivers of corporate social responsibility, *Journal of Business Ethics,* **50** (1), pp 33–44

Hines, T and McGowan, P (2005) Supply chain strategies in the UK fashion industry: the rhetoric of partnership and power, *International Entrepreneurship and Management Journal*, **1** (4), pp 519–37

Hughes, A. (2005) Corporate strategy and the management of ethical trade: the case of the UK food and clothing retailers, *Environment and Planning A,* **37** (7), pp 1145–63

Hughes, A (2012) Corporate ethical trading in an economic downturn: recessionary pressures and refracted responsibilities, *Journal of Economic Geography,* **12** (1), pp 33–45

Hughes, A, Buttle, M and Wrigley, N (2007). Organisational geographies of corporate responsibility: a UK–US comparison of retailers' ethical trading initiatives, *Journal of Economic Geography,* **7** (4), pp 491–513

Hughes, A, Wrigley, N and Buttle, M (2008) Global production networks, ethical campaigning, and the embeddedness of responsible governance, *Journal of Economic Geography*, **8** (3), pp 345–67

Hurley, J (2013) Monsoon accused of 'shameless squeeze on supply chain', *Telegraph* [online] http://www.telegraph.co.uk/finance/newsbysector /retailandconsumer/9890005/Monsoon-accused-of-shameless-squeeze-on -supply-chain.html [accessed 11 March 2015]

International Organization for Standardization (2014) *Discovering ISO 26000,* ISO, Geneva, Switzerland

Kotler, P (1972).What consumerism means for marketers, *Harvard Business Review*, **50** (3), pp 48–57

Lantos, G (2001) The boundaries of strategic corporate social responsibility, *Journal of Consumer Marketing*, **18** (7), pp 595–632

Laudal, T (2010) An attempt to determine the CSR potential of the international clothing business, *Journal of Business Ethics*, **96** (1), pp 63–77

Lindgreen, A, Xu, Y, Maon, F and Wilcock, J (2012) Corporate social responsibility brand leadership: a multiple case study, *European Journal of Marketing*, **46** (7/8), pp 965–93

Loker, S (2011) The (r)evolution of sustainable apparel business: from codes of conduct to partnership in Sri Lanka, *JAAFSL* [online]http://archive.jaafsl.com/images/stories/ apparel_buzz/2011_03/RevolutionofSustainablel.pdf [accessed 5 March 2015]

Lund-Thomsen, P and Coe, N M (2015) Corporate social responsibility and labour agency: the case of Nike in Pakistan. *Journal of Economic Geography*, **15** (2) pp 275–96

Mamic, I (2005) Managing global supply chain: the sports footwear, apparel and retail sectors. *Journal of Business Ethics*, **59** (1/2), pp 81–100

Mann, M, Byun, S-E, Kim, H and Hoggle, K (2014) Assessment of leading apparel specialty retailers' CSR practices as communicated on corporate websites: problems and opportunities. *Journal of Business Ethics,* **122** (4) pp 599–622

Maon, F, Lindgreen, A and Swaen, V (2009) Designing and implementing corporate social responsibility: an integrative framework grounded in theory and practice, *Journal of Business Ethics,* **87** (1), pp 71–89

Mares, R (2010) The limits of supply chain responsibility: a critical analysis of corporate responsibility instruments, *Nordic Journal of International Law,* **79** (2), pp 93–244

Marks & Spencer (2014) *Plan A Report, 2014,* M&S, London

Masson, R, Iosif, L, MacKerron, G and Fernie, J (2007). Managing complexity in agile global fashion industry supply chains, *International Journal of Logistics Management,* **18** (2), pp 238–54

Mayer, F and Pickles, J (2010) Re-embedding governance: global apparel value chains and decent work, *Capturing the Gains Working Paper* 2010/01, University of Manchester

Mirvis, P (2012) Employee engagement and CSR: transactional, relational and developmental approaches, *California Management Review,* **54** (4) pp 93–117

McWilliams, A and Siegel, A (2001) Corporate social responsibility: a theory of the firm perspective, *Academy of Management Review,* **26** (1), pp 117–27

Miller, D (2004) Preparing for the long haul: negotiating international framework agreements in the global textile, garment and footwear sector, *Global Social Policy,* **4** (2), pp 215–39

New, S J (1997). The scope of supply chain management research, *Supply Chain Management: An International Journal,* **2** (1), pp 15–22

Palpacuer, F, Gibbon, P and Thomsen, L (2005) New challenges for developing country suppliers in global clothing chains: a comparative European perspective, *World Development,* **33** (3), pp 409–30

Perry, P (2011) Garments without guilt? An exploration of Corporate Social Responsibility within the context of the fashion supply chain: case study of Sri Lanka, unpublished PhD thesis, Heriot-Watt University, UK

Perry, P (2012) Exploring the influence of national cultural context on CSR implementation, *Journal of Fashion Marketing and Management,* **16** (2), pp 141–60

Perry, P, Fernie, J and Wood, S (2014a) The international fashion supply chain and corporate social responsibility in J Fernie and L Sparks (eds) *Logistics and Retail Management,* 4th edn, Kogan Page, London

Perry, P, Wood, S and Fernie, J (2014b) Corporate social responsibility in garment sourcing networks: factory management perspectives on ethical trade in Sri Lanka, *Journal of Business Ethics,* DOI 10.1007/s10551-014-2252-2

Pickles, J (2006) Trade liberalization, industrial upgrading and regionalization in the global clothing industry, *Environment and Planning A,* **38** (12), pp 2201–06

Pickles, J and Smith, A (2011) Delocalization and persistence in the European clothing industry: the reconfiguration of trade and production networks, *Regional Studies,* **45** (2), pp 167–85

Plank, L, Rossi, A and Staritz, C (2012) Workers and social upgrading in 'fast fashion': the case of the apparel industry in Morocco and Romania, *Working Paper 33*, ÖFSE, Vienna

Porter, M E and Kramer, M R (2006) Strategy and society: the link between competitive advantage and corporate social responsibility, *Harvard Business Review*, **84** (12), pp 78–92

Raj-Reichert, G (2013) Safeguarding labour in distant factories: health and safety governance in an electronics global production network, *Geoforum*, **44** (1), pp 23–31

Ruwanpura, K N (2012) Ethical codes: reality and rhetoric – a study of Sri Lanka's apparel sector, *Working Paper,* School of Geography, University of Southampton, Hampshire, UK

Ruwanpura, K N (2013) Scripted performances? Local readings of 'global' health and safety standards (the apparel sector in Sri Lanka), *Global Labour Journal*, **4** (2), pp 88–108

Ruwanpura, K N (2014a) Metal-free factories: straddling worker rights and consumer safety? *Geoforum*, **51** (1) pp 224–32

Ruwanpura, K N (2014b) The weakest link? Unions, freedom of association and ethical codes: a case study from a factory setting in Sri Lanka, *Ethnography*, doi:10.1177/1466138113520373

Ruwanpuru, K N (2015) Garments without guilt? Uneven labour geographies and ethical trading: Sri Lankan labour perspectives, *Journal of Economic Geography*, February, pp 1–24, doi:10.1093/jeg/lbu059

Ruwanpura, K and Wrigley, N (2011) The costs of compliance? Views of Sri Lankan apparel manufacturers in times of global economic crisis, *Journal of Economic Geography*, **11** (6), pp 1031–49

Sadler, F and Chamberlain, P (2012) Approaches to sustainable factory improvements, Paper presented to Impact Conference: Finding the Sweet Spot: Smarter Ethical Trade that Delivers More for All, 24 May 2012, London

Schrank, A (2004) Ready-to-wear development? Foreign investment, technology transfer, and learning by watching in the apparel trade, *Social Forces*, **83** (1), pp 123–56

Shaw, D and Riach, K (2011) Embracing ethical fields: constructing consumption in the margins, *European Journal of Marketing*, **45** (7/8), pp 1051–67

Smestad, L (2009).The sweatshop, child labour, and exploitation issues in the garment industry, *Fashion Practice*, **1** (2), pp 147–62

Tallontire, A (2007) CSR and regulation: towards a framework for understanding private standards initiatives in the agri-food chain, *Third World Quarterly*, **28** (4), pp 775–91

Taplin, I M (2006) Restructuring and reconfiguration: the EU textile and clothing industry adapts to change, *European Business Review*, **18** (3), pp 172–86

Tokatli, N, Wrigley, N and Kizilgün, Ö (2008) Shifting global supply networks and fast fashion: made in Turkey for Marks & Spencer, *Global Networks*, **8** (3), pp 261–80

Vogel, D (2005) *The Market for Virtue: The potential and limits of corporate social responsibility*, The Brookings Institution, Washington DC

Welford, R and Frost, S (2006) Corporate social responsibility in Asian supply chains, *Corporate Social Responsibility and Environmental Management*, **13** (3), pp 166–76

Werther Jr, W B and Chandler, D (2005) Strategic corporate social responsibility as global brand insurance, *Business Horizons*, **48** (4), pp 317–24

Wijayasiri, J and Dissanayake, J (2009) The ending of the Multi-Fibre Agreement and innovation in the Sri Lankan textile and clothing industry, *OECD Journal: General Papers*, **8** (4) pp 157–88

Wrinkle, H, Erikson, E and Lee, A (2012) Apparel industry trends: from farm to factory, *Not for Sale* [online] [ttp://www.free2work.org/trends/apparel/Apparel-Industry-Trends-2012.pdf [accessed 15 July 2015]

World Business Council for Sustainable Development (1999) *Corporate Social Responsibility*, WBCSD Publications, Geneva

Yu, X (2008) Impacts of corporate code of conduct on labor standards: a case study of Reebok's athletic footwear supplier factory in China, *Journal of Business Ethics*, **81** (3), pp 513–29

Yu, X (2009) From passive beneficiary to active stakeholder: workers' participation in CSR movement against labor abuses, *Journal of Business Ethics*, **87** (1), pp 233–49

International logistics

05

Introduction

This chapter discusses the importance of international logistics and supply chain management (SCM) in bringing fashion goods to market in the UK and Europe, particularly from Asian and South American producers. The previous chapters have considered fashion retailing, international sourcing and corporate and social responsibility, but have not really discussed concepts of logistics and SCM. This chapter begins by discussing concepts underlying them, introducing channels of distribution which are related and important to fashion logistics, and examining the economic impact of global logistics and supply chain activity. Next, issues of retail logistics and SCM in a fashion context are presented ahead of a wider discussion of globalization and its effects on international logistics and SCM in general and fashion retailing in particular.

Definitions, impact and channels of distribution

Logistics is a broad, far-reaching function that has a major impact on a society's standard of living. We have come to expect excellent logistics services but tend to notice logistics only when there is a problem, such as goods not being on a store shelf when consumers want to buy them. Indeed, the Freight Transport Association (FTA) asked its members in 2011 to rate UK society's understanding of the logistics sector. The FTA argued that the logistics sector has an impact on everything in society, for example homes, clothes, food, schools and hospitals, and should be a highly prized national industry, viewed by all as an essential, valuable contribution to society (Grant, 2012a). However, the survey found that more than 80 per cent of members said that the public had either 'no understanding' (35 per cent) or only 'a slight understanding' (48 per cent) of the role of logistics in the economy. These findings were echoed in an Ipsos MORI research study that found that the public's current knowledge and understanding of the logistics industry was at best modest. Many people questioned as part of the study admitted that they took the benefits of freight for granted and had rarely, if ever, considered the mechanics of how the industry works.

Definitions are presented next in order to set the scene for this vast and all-encompassing domain that appears to be poorly understood by many outside of it. The US Council of Supply Chain Management Professionals (CSCMP), defines logistics management as 'that part of supply chain management that plans, implements, and controls the efficient, effective forward and reverse flow and storage of goods, services and related information between the point of origin and the point of consumption in order to meet customers' requirements' (Grant, 2012b, p 2). Logistics management activities are considered to be part of a firm's business activities and primarily include the management of transportation, inventory, warehousing or storage, information technology and production or operations. They are also considered only within the context of an individual firm; however, that consideration changes as regards supply chain management and international logistics operations.

Once a firm actively engages with suppliers, customers and other stakeholders its logistical activities go beyond its own doors into the wider supply chain. Such engagement 'necessitates' additional management, known as SCM, and the CSCMP defines SCM as encompassing 'the planning and management of all activities involved in sourcing and procurement, conversion, and all logistics management activities. Importantly, it also includes coordination and collaboration with channel partners, which can be suppliers, intermediaries, third-party service providers, and customers' (Grant, 2012b, p 3).

SCM is considered an integrating function with a primary responsibility for linking major business functions and processes within and across companies into a cohesive and high-performing business model that also spans national borders in an international context. It includes all of the logistics management activities noted above and drives the coordination of processes and activities with and across marketing, sales, product design, finance and information technology, therefore providing a more holistic view of a firm. This holistic view is important in fashion supply chains, particularly in fast-fashion environments when time to market and profitability are critical.

Figure 5.1 shows a generic supply chain for a fashion retailer that includes international elements. The assumption underlying this figure is that a domestic retailer sources and produces goods in foreign (or international) markets for distribution and sale in its domestic market. However, goods may also be partly finished in the domestic market or distributed in other foreign markets, and these nuances will be discussed further in this chapter.

The first step in this chain sees the retailer's design team create the design and specifications for the goods that it wishes to bring to market. That step is likely conducted in the retailer's home country but it may be done elsewhere and Chapters 2 and 8 discuss these aspects. The second step is to source the raw materials and foreign producers to make the goods; issues surrounding such sourcing were discussed in Chapter 3. The third step is to have the goods produced or manufactured in the foreign market(s). The fourth and fifth steps involve international distribution and importation, and related brokerage services to bring the goods to the domestic market. The sixth step is to distribute the goods within the domestic market to make them available for purchase by consumers, either in-store or online in the seventh step, which will be discussed in Chapters 6 and 7 respectively. Steps three through six are the main topics discussed in this chapter.

FIGURE 5.1 A generic fashion supply chain (authors)

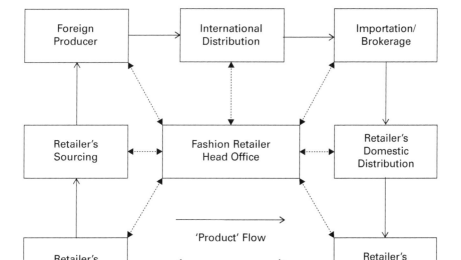

Economic impact of logistics and SCM on channels of distribution

Logistics and SCM activities have a significant economic impact on countries and their societies. These activities accounted for 8.2 per cent or US $1.39 trillion of US gross domestic product (GDP) in 2013 (Wilson, 2014). Across the 27 European Union (EU) countries in 2010 (Klaus, 2011) logistics markets comprised 7.2 per cent of GDP or €850 billion, with Germany leading the top five at €210 billion followed by France (€123 billion), the UK (€92 billion), Italy (€89 billion) and Spain (€80 billion).

Logistics activities embrace two basic concepts: movement or 'Go' and storage or 'Stop' (Grant, 2012b). 'Go' refers to goods being moved or transported to customers or back in a reverse logistics flow; this is a temporal or time concept. 'Stop' includes the storage of goods for processing and other operations or to await further movement to customers at a later time; this is a place or location concept. In Figure 5.1, the boxes represent 'Stop' locations while the solid lines and arrows represent the 'Go' flows – the dashed lines and arrows represent information flows from the retailer's head office to the various nodes in the international supply chain. These two concepts work together to meet the definitional objective of satisfying customers' requirements; that is, goods demanded by customers are provided in the right place at the right time. This objective provides time and place utility for customers and is also an important issue in fast-fashion logistics.

A corollary concept, particularly in the retail sector, is the channel of distribution. Channels comprise a collection of interdependent firms or intermediaries involved in the process of making goods available for use or consumption (Bucklin, 1965). Channels allow an exchange to occur between supplier and customer. Exchange takes place when there is a discrepancy between the amount, type, and timing of goods available, ie an assortment, and the goods demanded. A channel's activities can include buying, selling, transporting, storing, grading, financing, bearing market risk and providing marketing information. Hence, there is some overlap between channel and logistical or supply chain activities.

However, channels have traditionally been considered from the manufacturer or producer forward towards the final customer or consumer. In that context, channels facilitate the searching process by customers or consumers and enable the adjustment of the discrepancy of assortment by performing the functions of sorting and assorting. Bucklin (1965) first proposed a channel structure theory based on the ideas of postponement and speculation. Postponement is primarily a technique to decrease costs by reducing unwanted stocks of goods or inventory, and involves either postponing changes in the form and identity of a good to the last possible point in the marketing process or postponing inventory locations to the last possible point in time since risk and uncertainty costs increase as a good becomes more differentiated. On the other hand, speculation involves producing goods in advance to reduce costs through economies of large-scale production, reduced stock-outs and associated costs, and reduced uncertainty for retailers and consumers. The notions of postponement and speculation are akin to notions of lean and agile, which are discussed later in this chapter.

Since the 1960s the term 'channel of distribution' has fallen out of favour in logistics and SCM circles, and was considered to be primarily a marketing term or concept. However, it is interesting to note that the term has resurfaced in importance in recent years for multi-channel or omnichannel retailers in online environments.

Fashion retail logistics and SCM

A lot of retail logistics and SCM research has focused upon food/grocery retailing due to the dominance and power position of food retailers in the market (Fernie *et al*, 2010). For fashion retailers, the process has evolved differently mainly due to the different characteristics within fashion markets (Fernie and Sparks, 2014), such as:

1 short product life cycles – products are designed to represent a period in time (season) or trend, and these periods are getting shorter;

2 high volatility – trends gain and lose popularity due to forces outside the control of fashion retailers, for example the influence of celebrity;

3 low predictability – high volatility naturally decreases the ability to forecast sales; and

4 high level of impulse purchasing – consumers place high hedonic value on fashion goods and therefore there is an instant need to purchase it.

An additional characteristic in fashion retail is overseas sourcing which has contributed to the success of retailers such as Zara, H&M, New Look, Matalan as well as some of the grocery retailers, notably George at Asda, who emerged as strong entrants into the UK fashion market in the 1990s (Barnes and Lea-Greenwood, 2006). The increased level of threat from these retailers forced other UK retailers, for example previous market leader Marks & Spencer, to focus their attention on cost and find ways to decrease cost price. The case study in Chapter 6 provides a further discussion about Marks & Spencer's fashion supply chain trials and tribulations in recent years.

The natural reaction to these threats was for retailers to move production to countries with low labour costs (Bruce *et al*, 2004). This resulted in extensive and complex apparel supply chains, and consequentially to long lead times for fashion product due to large geographical distance between sourcing and selling markets (Barnes and Lea-Greenwood, 2006). However, fashion retailers considered the cost price benefits of offshore sourcing to be of greater concern than the negative impact on lead time (Fernie *et al*, 2010).

Quick response

A combination of the characteristics above have affected the way in which production and logistics processes have evolved for fashion retailers. One evolution was quick response (QR) also discussed in Chapter 3 that was developed in the United States in the mid-1980s partly as a result of inefficiencies in the US supply chain costing firms approximately $25 billion each year (Barnes and Lea-Greenwood, 2006). The factors underlying such losses included the amount of time between ordering a product and receiving it and the consequent disruptions between sales, order, receipts, restocking, etc (Birtwistle *et al*, 2003).

QR strategies are consumer-driven and look to speed up the time it takes for raw materials to be processed into finished goods through co-operative planning by supply chain partners and using IT and flexible manufacturing to eliminate inefficiencies from the entire supply chain. Simply put, QR is a process where suppliers and retailers develop mutually beneficial and long-term relationships to reduce lead times and forecasting errors (Fernie *et al*., 2010). The Spanish fashion retailer Zara is an often-used example of a vertically integrated retailer using QR methods (Ferdows *et al*, 2004). Zara only commits up to 20 per cent of their buying budget six months in advance of the season with commitment increasing to 50 per cent by the start of the season (Birtwistle *et al*, 2003). This affords Zara flexibility for its remaining 50 per cent budget and allows it to react to the latest fashion trends, with the result being the allocation of new stock to stores every two weeks and encouraging more frequent visits from customers. Zara's business is demand driven and its response time from design to product in store can be as little as 21 days (Birtwistle *et al*, 2003; Ferdows *et al*, 2004).

Information technology

Information technology (IT) is also an important factor in global supply chains that enables better, faster and more reliable communication. Logistics and SCM have interfaces with a wide array of functions and firms, and communication must occur between the focal firm, its suppliers and customers and various members of the supply chain who may not be directly linked to the firm, and the major functions within the firm such as logistics, design, accounting, marketing and production. Communications are a key to the efficient functioning of any integrated logistical or supply chain system.

The use of IT communications has increased remarkably since the 1970s due to increases in computing power and storage that have fostered the invention of the personal and laptop computers, global positioning systems, 'smart' mobile phones and tablets. Such technology has become increasingly automated, complex and rapid, and has enabled firms to develop longer but faster supply chains due to their ability to trace and track goods in production or storage and in transit.

Order processing is a key IT element for a firm to receive orders from customers, check their status, and communicate back, as well as actually filling the order and making it available to the customer. Increasingly, firms are turning to advanced order-processing methods and technologies such as:

1 electronic data interchange (EDI) and electronic funds transfer (EFT) to speed the process and improve accuracy and efficiency;

2 advanced electronic point-of-sale (EPOS) scanning in retail stores to track sales and generate inventory and replenishment records;

3 radio frequency identification (RFID) to track and trace products; and

4 cloud computing for storage and integrated data use by firms in the supply chain.

For example, Keyfort Limited, a cloud and IT supplier in Hull, England, has developed a logistics management information system in a cloud application called Keyfort Data Interchange Service (KDIS). KDIS takes data, stores it and then manipulates it to provide reports, analysis and on-demand enquiry responses. While the KDIS cloud system is for use by any firm, Keyfort has also developed a specific, optional application called KeyPOD to improve product traceability across a firm's delivery operations using a driver's smartphone. Using KeyPOD, distribution centres and carriers can work more efficiently together and provide a better service for firms by sharing real-time delivery information as and when it is required (Grant, 2012b).

Lean and agile supply chains

Time compression refers to reducing time in manufacturing and logistics operations. Longer lead times between ordering and receiving goods and longer processing times to produce them create inefficiencies such as requiring higher inventory levels and incurring greater handling, storage, transportation and monitoring. Advanced logistics and supply chain activities and technology help compress a firm's time by developing better relationships with suppliers and customers to share more real-time information and improve its accuracy. Many firms have initiated time-compression strategies to significantly reduce manufacturing time and inventory.

As a result, two different logistics and supply chain paradigms, lean and agile, emerged during the 1990s and which were also introduced in Chapter 3. The lean paradigm is based on the principles of lean production in the automotive sector where a value stream is developed to eliminate all waste, including time, and ensure a level production system (Jones *et al*, 1997). Firms make to order and therefore speculate on the number of products that will be demanded by forecasting. A firm assumes inventory risk through placing large orders that reduce the costs of order processing and transportation, adopting large-scale production in lower-cost developing economies, and reducing stock outs and uncertainty and their associated costs. Speculation very much fits a lean strategy. Conversely, the agile paradigm has its origins in principles of channel postponement and uses market knowledge and information in what is known as a virtual corporation to exploit profitable opportunities in a volatile marketplace inventory (Bruce *et al*, 2004). The final manufacturing of goods or their location in the supply chain may be delayed until the last possible moment before actual consumer demand is realized.

The lean approach seeks to minimize inventory of components and work-in-progress and to move towards a just-in-time (JIT) environment wherever possible. Firms using an agile approach are meant to respond in shorter time frames to changes in both volume and variety demanded by customers. Lean works best in high-volume, low-variety and predictable environments while agility is needed in less predictable environments where the demand for variety is high (Grant, 2012b). While the paradigms appear dichotomous, in reality most firms likely have a need for both lean and agile logistics and supply chain solutions, suggesting a hybrid strategy. Such a strategy has been called leagile (Naylor *et al*, 1999) and has two main features. A material decoupling point represents the point in a supply chain where goods production changes from a lean or forecasting push strategy to an agile or demand pull strategy. This point should be as far as possible downstream in the supply chain towards the consumer. Additionally, an information decoupling point represents the point where market sales or actual order information can assist forecasting efforts within the lean approach of this hybrid solution. This point should be as far as possible upstream in the supply chain towards production. Zara's use of IT to send trend information upstream for product design and rapid manufacture and then gauge consumer reaction before final product configuration shipping to certain retail store locations is a good example of a leagile strategy (Ferdows *et al*, 2004).

Outsourcing

In complex and disparate global markets there is a need for greater collaboration and mutually advantageous relationships among customers, suppliers, competitors and other stakeholders in an increasingly inter-connected and global environment, which can have positive benefits for sustainability. For example, two competitors could share transportation and warehousing facilities in an effort to avoid the empty running of trucks and also provide return or reverse logistics opportunities.

Outsourcing has been an area of growing interest and activity in business since the early 1990s and has its origins in transactional cost economics and the concept of core competencies (Williamson, 1975; Hamel and Prahalad, 1990). The latter activities are those that are unique to a firm, define its pre-eminence and provide unique value for customers. Such competencies should be retained while other firm activities can be undertaken by others.

Many firms have outsourced their logistics and SCM activities to third-party logistics (3PL) specialists, such as DHL or Norbert Dentressangle, to perform activities that are not considered part of their core competencies. As a result, the logistics and SCM outsourcing/3PL market across the globe is over US $616 billion, with the United States leading at US $160 billion, followed by US $191 billion in the Asia-Pacific region and US $160 billion in Europe (Langley and Capgemini Consulting, 2014). Across the globe, 81 per cent of domestic and 78 per cent of international transportation or 'Go' and 73 per cent of warehousing or 'Stop' activities are outsourced, followed by freight forwarding at 62 per cent and customer brokerage at 57 per cent.

Outsourcing can be very cost effective for firms to reduce capital expenditures and fixed assets related to transportation and storage infrastructure, reduce labour and internal operating costs, and enjoy the expertise and economies of scale provided by the 3PL service provider. However, firms lose control of those operations that they outsource, despite service level agreements and contracts, and may not have control over sustainability efforts of 3PLs or their sub-contractors.

Globalization

Globalization has increased tremendously since the 1970s due in large part to various developments in logistics and SCM. Factors influencing this growth include the widespread adoption of the standard shipping container, the expansion of transport infrastructure in ports, improved roadways and railroads, and trade liberalization. These factors helped to provide production and cost differentials between developed and developing countries. New markets are opening and existing markets are expanding worldwide. Economies in developed countries have matured, that is their economic growth rates have slowed, and firms in those countries have sought market opportunities abroad from both a sales and supply perspective. A global financial network has also developed that allows multinational firms to expand their operations. In addition, firms have increased new material and component acquisitions from other countries, ie global sourcing, as discussed in Chapter 3.

Global trade has increased significantly since the end of World War II as the world economy has become more interdependent. Total world merchandise exports were US $59 billion in 1948 and grew almost ten-fold to US $579 billion by 1973. However, total world merchandise exports in 2013 were US $18,301 billion, a 33 per cent increase in 40 years (WTO, 2014). The top 10 exporting and importing countries are shown in Table 5.1 and the EU leads on both counts by significant amounts.

To support its non-domestic or international markets, a firm must have a logistics or supply chain system or network that satisfies the particular requirements of those markets. For example, developing countries in Africa, South America or Asia are characterized by large numbers of channel intermediaries supplying an even larger number of small retailers. The systems in these nations are marked by inadequate transportation and storage facilities, a large unskilled labour force and an absence of logistics and SCM support systems. Developed countries, eg most of Europe, Japan, Canada, and the United States, have highly sophisticated logistics and SCM systems including good transportation systems, high-technology warehousing and skilled labour markets.

Many factors can influence a company's decision to enter international markets including:

- the international market's growth potential;
- geographic diversification;
- excess production capacity;

TABLE 5.1 Top ten exporters and importers of intermediate goods in 2012 (compiled from WTO, 2014)

Exporters	US $Billions
European Union (28)	3,595
People's Republic of China	819
United States	764
Japan	437
Hong Kong, China (including 295 re-exports)	314
Republic of Korea	293
Singapore	219
Chinese Taipei	203
Canada	201
Brazil	155
Total	**7,000**
Importers	
European Union (28)	3,309
People's Republic of China	1,063
United States	806
Hong Kong, China (including 34 retained imports)	329
Japan	296
Republic of Korea	234
India	228
Mexico	220
Canada	199
Singapore	171
Total	**6,855**

- products near the end of their product life cycle in the domestic market;
- a source of new goods and ideas; and
- reduced competition in the international market.

Firms can enter international markets incrementally through exporting, licensing or franchising, joint ventures, and ownership through foreign direct investment (FDI) in order of investment and financial commitment (Paliwoda and Thomas, 1998).

The most common form of distribution for firms entering international markets is exporting, which is selling products in another country, or importing, which is buying products produced in another country. Exporting requires the least amount of knowledge about foreign markets because domestic firms can engage an international freight forwarder, distributor, trading company or other organizations to carry out the logistics and marketing functions. Advantages include not having to invest in additional production facilities or logistics assets, not risking political uncertainties in the host market, and it is relative easy to withdraw from the host market. Importing allows a firm to source and buy internationally, usually at lower cost than from its own domestic market. Chapter 3 discussed more deeply the issues of sourcing and importing. Disadvantages of exporting and importing include having to pay import quotas and tariffs and facing unfavourable or fluctuating currency exchange rates in the international or domestic markets respectively.

Licensing or franchising involves agreements that allow a firm in the foreign or host country (the licensee or franchisee) to use the manufacturing, processing, trademark, know-how, technical assistance, merchandising knowledge or other skills provided by a firm in the domestic or home country (the licenser or franchiser). The primary difference between licensing and franchising is that the former usually involves local production and semi-autonomy from the licenser, while franchisers maintain an active role by providing production and other items required for the franchisee to follow the franchise 'formula'. For a licenser a royalty may be payable to the licensee for each product sold, while considerations for a franchisee may include an up-front franchisee fee, continuing sales royalties, commitments to purchase various supplies and co-operative advertising.

A joint venture allows the home firm to exercise more control over the host firm than is available in a licensing or franchising agreement, while at the same time stopping short of establishing a freestanding production plant or other facility in the host market. The risk is higher and the flexibility is lower for the home firm because an equity position is established in the host firm. The financial partnership, however, enables the home firm to provide substantial management input into the channel and distribution strategies of the host firm.

Complete ownership of a foreign subsidiary offers the domestic firm the highest degree of control over its international marketing and logistics strategies. Foreign direct investment (FDI) takes place through acquisition or expansion. Acquisition of a foreign facility minimizes start-up costs, which can include locating and building facilities, hiring employees and establishing distribution channel relationships. Compared with other forms of market entry, FDI requires the most knowledge of a particular international market. Disadvantages include a loss of flexibility because the home firm has a long-term commitment to the host market. Fixed facilities and equipment cannot be disposed of quickly if sales or profits decline, levels of competition increase or other adversities occur. The possibility of government nationalization of foreign-owned businesses is another drawback of FDI, especially in politically unstable countries, while exchange rate fluctuations change the relative value of foreign investments as they are valued in host or foreign currency instead of the currency of the home country. As an example, the following case study discusses how the Portuguese fashion accessories firm Parfois has engaged internationally by rapidly expanding selling opportunities through a combination of franchising and FDI while sourcing and importing its goods.

CASE STUDY   Parfois: Expanding internationally through franchising and FDI

Parfois is a Portuguese fashion accessory brand established in 1994 which designs and sells a wide range of products including shoes, hats, jewellery, handbags and purses. It opened its first store in Oporto and followed with more stores located in shopping centres, which was the Portuguese commercial trend in the 1990s.

Parfois' main goal is to offer consumers high-fashion products at low prices. Pursuit of this goal has seen Parfois grow substantially in international markets as it pursues a position as a world leader in what it terms the Specialized Retail Fashion Accessories sector. In 20 years since inception Parfois now has more than 550 stores all over the world. The main countries where Parfois is present include Portugal, Spain, France, Italy, Germany, Poland, Saudi Arabia, United Arab Emirates, Bahrain, Colombia, Brazil, Georgia, Russia, Romania, Ukraine, the Philippines, the UK and Ireland.

Its international supply chain is very simple in structure. Parfois is headquartered in Rio Tinto, Portugal and maintains one large warehouse there. It has three principal supply bases: one in India, one near Beijing in China, and one in Hong Kong. Parfois' designers and buyers deal with their suppliers and import all products or supplies to the Rio Tinto warehouse before deconsolidating shipments and assorting them into shipments for their retail stores.

The Rio Tinto warehouse is the central point of the supply chain, receiving and processing all merchandise to be sent to its stores, and is the link between them and suppliers. The warehouse is therefore a mirror of Parfois' logistical activities and in 2008–09 Parfois re-engineered its warehouse, adopting a lean-thinking throughput process to reduce waste and create better flow throughout the logistics system. The introduction of this philosophy in the operational side of the business was even more relevant given the economic crisis at that point as it was considered vital to be efficient and to have a competitive cost structure. Simple and low-cost ideas significantly changed the warehouse of Parfois and visibly contributed to reducing the waste of the system, and improving the environment and the safety of the workplace, the motivation and commitment of the staff and the efficiency of the process.

Additionally, Parfois undertook an optimization project of the stores' supply model focusing mainly on the international stores. The aim was to manage stocks better and improve management decisions. An innovative stock management model was also developed based on weekly collection plans that anticipate the quantities necessary to be shipped in each product range and family to each store. These initiatives have resulted in helping the commercial team to undertake more assertive decisions regarding product selection and shortening lead times.

Inbound transportation from international suppliers is either by sea shipping or air depending upon either time or cost factors for customers. Outbound logistics to Western and Eastern European stores is by trucks while sea shipping is used for stores in the Middle East and elsewhere in the world. All transportation is outsourced to third-party logistics service providers.

Parfois started franchising in 1996 with franchise Parfois stores in Portugal, which gave them the necessary experience to manage international franchisees more easily. It started its internationalization efforts in 2003 by opening own stores in Spain and establishing franchises in Saudi Arabia with the Azadea Group. This was followed by franchises in the United Arab Emirates and Kuwait in 2004, again in conjunction with the Azadea Group. Since then it has expanded rapidly, opening its own stores in several EU countries and continuing its franchising in other Middle East countries, Africa and the Philippines. The region that has attracted Parfois' attention in recent years has been Eastern Europe and Russia.

Two-thirds of Parfois stores around the world are franchises. Parfois shows a willingness to enter non-preferential markets under franchising agreements to minimize their risk and investment. This has proved prudent as there was a difficult moment with its Russian franchisee. The first partner had serious disagreements with Parfois during the first few years over not following the expansion agreed between the partners and payment issues. This led to a cancellation of the contract and the closure of stores in that country. In spite of this setback, Parfois' strategy remains valid and it has been able to get another partner in the region, which has allowed it to re-enter the Russian market. As a result, Parfois has changed its franchisee selection criteria and is now more selective, only having agreements with well-established companies in distant countries.

The first international 'own store' movement made by Parfois in 2003 was the expansion to Portugal's only neighbour, Spain. The expansion to Spain is considered natural due to geographic and psychic proximity, as well as similar retail structural development. The homogeneity of tastes, laws, cultural rituals, as well as the similarity of climate, trends and collections also facilitated the expansion with little or no change in the product line. Parfois also opened own stores in France in 2005. This was a continuation of its natural expansion but was also based on visibility. Parfois considers that owning a store in one of the international capitals of fashion, Paris, represents an important aspect of its image.

This expansion with its own stores saw an interesting development in 2009, with Poland added to Parfois' portfolio. This was a gamble for Parfois; opening eight company-owned stores (rather than lower risk franchises) in the country, a growing market, was a change to its usual strategy of focusing on mature markets with lower growth. However, it has been successful in Poland and so the gamble has appeared to pay off.

Notwithstanding this anomaly, there is a clear pattern in the internationalization strategy of Parfois. It is willing to open its own stores in the Western European market, where it feels comfortable, and lets franchise partners assume the investment risk in other regions, which is of particular relevance for the Middle East and Eastern Europe, regions with aggressive market growth over recent years due to their increasing openness to the 'western world' and their brands and companies.

Four main factors can be identified regarding Parfois' internationalization path over the last 20 years. The company's size seems to be the most important organizational factor to the internationalization process. Due to its small size it has been agile enough to adapt to new countries rapidly. This factor is correlated with one motivational factor: management's interest in this entire process. The third-party contacts were one of the main drivers in proceeding with the internationalization process, particularly in distant markets. The final factor, the environmental one, is clearly the geographic and cultural distance between the company's Portuguese base and the target countries where it is now present, with the already analysed differences of entry strategy.

SOURCES Castro, (2009); Forte and Carvalho, (2013); Parfois, (2015); Rocha, (2010).

A recent research study (Childs and Jin, 2015) investigated how fashion retailers internationalized and found they used incremental approaches to gain market knowledge and reduce uncertainty or perceived risk. The study included over 100 international fashion retailers categorized in four distinct types:

1 product specialists that focus on a specific product range (eg Nike) and have a clearly defined target group based on demographics or psychographics (eg sports);

2 fashion designer retailers that distribute their merchandise bearing the designer's name (eg Calvin Klein);

3 general merchandise retailers that offer a mix of fashion and non-fashion merchandise (eg department stores); and

4 general fashion retailers that offer a broad range of fashion and accessories merchandise (eg The Gap).

The study found that fashion retailers who offered athletic/sport products were able to provide their services in significantly more countries and continents compared with clothing retailers. This suggests that more functional products may be more universally accepted, whereas fashion items such as clothing may be slower to internationalize because acceptance of fashion can vary greatly by culture. Retailers offering functional products may be more flexible in their internationalization scale and scope whereas retailers offering fashion products may be cautious in their expansion and seek to first understand subtle cultural differences in consumer fashion tastes before entering international markets.

This study also provided promising implications for new and small and medium-sized enterprises (SMEs) as it found that a lack of firm experience or size does not inhibit internationalization of services, market choice, or financial performance. Such retailers may be audacious regarding international activity and should consider being more active in international markets.

Terms of trade across international borders have become highly standardized since the mid-1930s. The terms of trade provide important information on the actual export documents that state who is responsible for the various stages of delivery, who bears what risks, and who pays for the various elements of transportation. Payment continues to be by a letter of credit, which is a document issued by a bank on behalf of the buyer which authorizes payment for goods received. Once the buyer is satisfied that the terms of the agreement have been met by the seller, payment is made to the seller by the bank instead of the buyer.

First published in 1936, the Incoterms (2015) rules have been developed and maintained by experts and practitioners and provide internationally accepted definitions and rules of interpretation for most common commercial terms. They help companies trading internationally to avoid costly misunderstandings by clarifying the tasks, costs and risks involved in the delivery of goods from sellers to buyers. The latest version, Incoterms 2010, came into effect at the beginning of 2011 and a few of the more familiar and popular Incoterms include:

1 EXW stands for Ex-Works (... named origin). The origin should be identified as factory, plant, etc. and the seller's only responsibility is to make the goods available at their premises. The seller bears the costs and risks until the buyer is obligated to take delivery. The buyer pays for the documents, must take delivery of the shipment when specified, and must pay any export taxes.

2 CPT stands for Carriage Paid To (... named destination). The seller pays the freight for the carriage of the goods to the named destination. However, the risk of loss, damage to the goods or cost increases transfers from the seller to the buyer when the goods have been delivered to the custody of the first carrier.

3 DDP stands for Delivered Duty Paid (... named place of destination). DDP represents the seller's maximum obligation and notes that the seller bears all risks and all costs until the goods are delivered. This term can be used irrespective of the mode of transport.

4 FOB stands for Free on Board (... named port of shipment). The goods are placed on board a ship by the seller at a port of shipment named in the sales agreement. The risk of loss of or damage to the goods is transferred to the buyer when the goods pass over the ship's rail and the seller pays the cost of loading the goods.

Logistics and SCM in a global economy

The impact of globalization on logistics and SCM has been significant since the 1970s. Global container trade has increased on average by 5 per cent each year and at its peak in the mid-2000s comprised 350 million 20-foot equivalent units (TEU) a year (Grant, 2012b). However, the impact of globalization doesn't only affect sea-borne containers. Worldwide demand for and subsequent fulfilment of smart phones and tablets has led to an increase in air freight volumes and prices. For example, Apple sold a record 74.5 million iPhone 6 and 6Plus units in the last quarter of 2014, which helped Apple post the largest quarterly profit ever of any publicly traded firm in the world: US $18 billion (Apple, 2015). Air freight rates, which were at their lowest in 2009 during the depths of the recession, rose almost 12 per cent by October 2014 to US $3.75 per kilogramme (Lennae, 2014).

Managing a global logistics and SCM system is much more complex than a purely domestic network. Managers must properly analyse the international environment, plan for it, and develop the correct control procedures to monitor the success or failure of the foreign system. Concepts of corporate strategy provide tools and techniques for analysing the firm's external and internal environments, such as PEST and SWOT respectively (Grant, 2012b). Elements in a firm's external environment are mostly uncontrollable or exogenous, and include political and legal systems in foreign markets, economic conditions, technology that is available, and social and cultural norms.

Firms involved in international business and logistics and SCM will try to minimize costs for the latter components while providing acceptable service levels to customers. Usually, international logistics is generally more expensive than domestic logistics due to increased shipping distances, documentation costs, larger levels of inventory, extra packaging and containerization, and longer order cycle times. However, a firm's cost–service mix will vary in international markets.

It has been argued that logistics performance measured by delivery reliability has deteriorated due to increasing customer requirements, greater volatility and problems with infrastructure, which may be a problem in emerging countries (Handfield *et al*, 2013). One way of determining the logistics capability of any country is the value of exports and imports as discussed above. A second way is the World Bank's Logistics Performance Index (LPI), which is a weighted average of individual country scores on six key dimensions with a maximum score of 5.0: the efficiency of clearance processes, quality

TABLE 5.2 World Bank logistics performance index 2014 (compiled from Arvis *et al*, 2014)

Country	Rank	LPI Score
Germany	1	4.12
Netherlands	2	4.05
Belgium	3	4.04
United Kingdom	4	4.01
Singapore	5	4.00
Sweden	6	3.96
Norway	7	3.96
Luxembourg	8	3.95
United States	9	3.92
Japan	10	3.91

of trade and transport-related infrastructure, the ease of arranging competitively priced shipments, the competence and quality of logistics services, the ability to track and trace consignments and the timeliness of shipments in reaching destination within a scheduled or expected delivery time (Arvis *et al*, 2014). Table 5.2 shows the 2014 top 10 performers in the LPI; the country at the top of the 2014 Index is Germany with a score of 4.12.

A third way to consider a country's logistics capabilities is the size of their total gross domestic product (GDP), which is an indicator of total economic activity. Table 5.3 reports that total global GDP in 2013 was estimated at US $74.3 trillion at official exchange rates (CIA, 2014). The three major geographic regions that account for the bulk of this economic activity are the 28 member states of the EU with 23.2 per cent, the United States with 22.5 per cent, and the two Western Pacific Rim countries of China and Japan with 19.3 per cent collectively. Those countries that have high values of imports and exports, LPI scores and GDP may be considered highly efficient in terms of production and logistics and SCM and hence offer less uncertainty or risk.

TABLE 5.3 Estimated 2013 gross domestic product (compiled from CIA, 2014)

Country	GDP US $trillion	Percentage World GDP
World	74.31	100.0
European Union 28	17.20	23.2
United States	16.72	22.5
People's Republic of China	9.33	12.6
Japan	5.01	6.7

Global risk, disruption and supply chain security

However, there are many other types of risk in international markets. Risk can be defined as the probability that a particular adverse event will occur during a stated period of time, or will result from a particular challenge (Adams, 1995). The notion of an adverse event connotes a detrimental consequence, and as a probability in a statistical theory sense, risk obeys all formal laws of combining probabilities and can be calculated. Outsourcing, globalization, improved infrastructure and information technology, and cheap labour and raw materials have extended supply chains into longer and complex networks (Manuj and Mentzer, 2008). This has consequently increased supply chain vulnerability, fragility and operational disruptions. There are also other factors such as shorter product life cycles, reduced suppliers, buffers and inventories, increased demand for on-time deliveries, change in consumer tastes and preferences, technology shifts or supplier priorities.

A heightened interest in supply chain risk management (SCRM) is attributed to the recent increase in high-profile man-made and natural incidents such as terrorist attacks, wars, earthquakes and the recent economic crisis. However, it is difficult to predict risks or assign probabilities due to the changing profile of risky events. Recent examples in 2013–14 include the Bangladeshi factory collapse, issues for Malaysian Airlines, and the European horse meat scandal (Rafi-Ul-Shan *et al*, 2014).

The aim of SCRM is to avoid delays, reduce costs, improve customer service, avoid major disasters and operational disruptions, increase the chances of quick recovery and enhance resilience. Usual risk management approaches largely depend upon the nature of market, industry, organizational structure and attitude, strategy, culture, leadership and geographic area in which a firm is operating and SCRM should also take these factors into account.

One useful model for considering risk was proposed by Peck (2005). Her model comprises four 'levels in a landscape' that require different considerations of risk at each level. These levels, from micro- to macro-focus, are:

1   a firm's value stream, products and processes that can be evaluated through operations management and business process engineering;

2   a firm's assets and infrastructure dependencies including logistics, information technology and human resources;

3   a firm's organizational relationship and inter-organizational networks determined by business strategy, production networks, and/or strategic purchasing; and

4   a firm's wider environment, eg the natural and social environment, which can be tracked using environmental scanning.

The essence of Peck's model is that risk is present at all levels of a firm's activities and therefore an SCRM strategy needs to encompass all these levels. Thus firms need to be aware of their place in a customer's 'landscape level,' most likely at level 3, so they can respond to increased demands to ensure risk can be mitigated throughout the entire supply chain. However, endemic in Peck's model are relationship management, cooperation and collaboration between supply chain partners, data exchange, inventory sharing and collaborative inventory planning, information sharing and trust-building measures enabling greater visibility to manage risks and enhance a supply chain's resiliency (Rafi-Ul-Shan *et al*, 2014). This is a challenge in international markets where outsourcing of activities has been the norm for several decades.

International logistics and SCM implications for fashion retailers

Recent research of European fashion and lifestyle firms such as Levi's, Foot Locker, Adidas, Polo Ralph Lauren and Urban Outfitters found they need to migrate to omnichannel, high-speed, end-to-end value chains to stay competitive in today's dynamic environment (BCI Global, 2014). This research identified several key developments according to current trends and they are presented next to help guide fashion retailers and their logistics and supply chain partners.

Overall retailing growth will come more from online retailing and less from physical stores alone. Omnichannel retailing, a hybrid between online and physical stores where consumers can buy from many different platforms such as in-store, computers, mobile phones, tablets or kiosk screens, will require greater and more cost-effective SCM (Rigby, 2011). Chapter 7 will consider the impact of online and omnichannel retailing.

Strong growth opportunities in new geographic markets such as Russia or Turkey will require a different supply chain strategy to that of more developed Western Europe markets. The lack of western infrastructure and technical systems may be inhibitors in these new markets and hence retailers will need to investigate their own strengths and weaknesses as well as risks in the external environment to exploit such opportunities. Peck's (2005) model, as well as usual SWOT and PEST techniques, can assist here.

Greater visibility within the supply chain is required to enable firms to make more informed business decisions related to routing, pick/pack and postponement decisions for key customers and markets. The use of appropriate IT should increase such visibility and may require vertical IT integration with suppliers to achieve it.

Firms will have to develop the ability to take new products to market faster than the competition, which requires speed and flexibility. Here again issues of time compression and lean, agile or leagile supply chains become important, especially in fast-fashion supply chains. But in reducing time to market it is equally important to look at the total time to market cycle, which includes the design and manufacturing phase. Nearsourcing closer to key markets, ie returning production from international markets, is increasingly being explored as traditional production sources in Asia become more expensive (Meyer, 2006). Using a better combination of transportation modes, for example multi-modal, is another option to explore with regards to improving time to market and will be discussed further in Chapter 6.

Moving the pick and pack process upstream to the point of origin allows orders to be picked/packed and shipped directly from source to key markets and/or customers, bypassing European distribution centres. BCI Global (2014) suggested that the hanging garment business in Europe seems to be on the decline from a logistics service offer perspective, but there is evidence to the contrary and these issues will be considered in Chapter 6.

Having an excellent firm open to innovation and change is key to migrating to a high-speed end-to-end value chain and horizontal and vertical collaboration may be vital elements. Vertical collaboration with suppliers and customers is easily understood, but horizontal collaboration among competitors represents a challenge as regards data/information security and competitive market advantage. To mitigate against such risks 3PL service providers might act as true intermediaries in their own right to provide that collaboration in what is termed fourth-party logistics or 4PL (Hingley *et al*, 2011).

Conclusions

The rapid growth in globalization has seen many firms expand their operations into the international sector to both sell and source products. As retail firms locate and service markets in various countries, they must establish logistics systems to provide the products and services demanded by consumers. While components of a global logistics system may be similar to those in a domestic system, the management and administration of the international network can be vastly different. To be an international player, a retailer's management must be able to coordinate a complex set of activities – marketing, production, financing and procurement – so that the least total cost logistics and supply chain costs are realized to maintain competitive advantage. This will allow a firm to achieve maximum market impact and competitive advantage in its international target markets.

This chapter has examined the context of logistics and SCM, its economic impact and various issues in a global context that affect fashion retail supply chains. The next chapter considers logistics and supply chain challenges in providing products in-store in a domestic retail setting in order to provide the right products in the right place at the right time for the right price.

References

Adams, J (1995) *Risk*, University College London Press, London

Apple (2015) Apple reports record first quarter results *Hot News* [online] https://www.apple.com/uk/hotnews/ [accessed 15 July 2015]

Arvis, J-F, Saslavsky, D, Ojala, L, Shepherd, B, Busch, C and Raj, A (2014) Connecting to compete 2014: trade logistics in the global economy; the logistics performance index and its indicators, *World Bank* [online] http://www.worldbank.org/content/dam/Worldbank/document/Trade/LPI2014.pdf [accessed 20 July 2015]

Barnes, L and Lea-Greenwood, G (2006) Fast fashioning the supply chain: shaping the research agenda, *Journal of Fashion Marketing and Management*, **10** (3), pp 259–71

BCI Global (2014) Fashion and lifestyle companies need a new business model, *BCI* [online] http://cs.bciglobal.com/news_detail.asp?cat=5002&dc=12081 [accessed 15 July 2015]

Birtwistle, G, Siddiqui, N and Fiorito, S (2003) Quick response: perceptions of UK fashion retailers, *International Journal of Retail & Distribution Management*, **31** (2), pp 118–28

Bruce, M, Daly, L and Towers, N (2004) Lean or agile: a solution for supply chain management in the textiles and clothing industry? *International Journal of Operations and Production Management*, **24** (2), pp 151–70

Bucklin, L P (1965) Postponement, speculation and the structure of distribution channels, *Journal of Marketing Research*, **2** (1), pp 26–31

Castro, M A O (2009) Optimização do Modelo de Abastecimento às Lojas na Parfois, *Relatório do Projecto de Dissertação da MIEIG 2008/2009*, Faculdade de Engenharia da Universidade do Porto

Childs, M L and Jin, B (2015) Firm factors that influence internalisation and subsequent financial performance of fashion retailers, *Journal of Service Theory and Practice*, **25** (1), pp 95–114

CIA (2014) World Factbook, *CIA* [online] https://www.cia.gov/library/publications/the-world-factbook/index.html [accessed 15 July 2015]

Ferdows, K, Lewis, M A and Machuca, J A D (2004) Rapid-fire fulfilment, *Harvard Business Review*, **82** (11), pp 104–10

Fernie, J and Sparks, L (2014) *Logistics and Retail Management: Emerging issues and new challenges in the retail supply chain* (4th edn), Kogan Page, London

Fernie, J, Sparks, L and McKinnon, A C (2010) Retail logistics in the UK: past, present and future, *International Journal of Retail & Distribution Management*, **38**, (11/12), pp 894–914

Forte, R and Carvalho, J (2013) Internationalisation through franchising: the Parfois case study, *International Journal of Retail & Distribution Management*, **41** (5), pp 380–95

Grant, D B (2012a) *Global Perspectives: United Kingdom*, Council of Supply Chain Management, Lombard, IL

Grant, D B (2012b) *Logistics Management*, Pearson Education Limited, Harlow, UK

Hamel, G and Prahalad, C K (1990) The core competence of the corporation, *Harvard Business Review*, **68** (3), pp 79–91

Handfield, R, Straube, F, Pfohl, H-Chr and Wieland, A (2013) *Trends and Strategies in Logistics and Supply Chain Management: Embracing global logistics complexity to drive market advantage*, BVL International, Bremen

Hingley, M, Lindgreen, A, Grant, D B and Kane, C (2011) Using fourth-party logistics management to improve horizontal collaboration among grocery retailers, *Supply Chain Management: An International Journal*, **16** (5), pp 316–27

Incoterms (2015), The New Incoterms 2010 Rules, *International Chamber of Commerce* [online] http://www.iccwbo.org/products-and-services/trade-facilitation/incoterms-2010/ [accessed 15 July 2015]

Jones, D T, Hines, P and Rich, N (1997) Lean logistics, *International Journal of Physical Distribution & Logistics Management*, 27 (3/4), pp 153–73

Klaus, P (2011) The assessment of competitive intensity in logistics markets, *Logistics Research*, 3, pp. 49–65

Langley, C J and Capgemini Consulting (2014) 18th Annual Third-party Logistics Study [online] http://www.3plstudy.com/ [accessed 15 July 2015]

Lennae, A (2014) Black Friday peak for air freight rates, but port congestion may bring a Xmas bonus *The Loadstar* [online] http://theloadstar.co.uk/air-freight-rates-2/ [accessed 15 July 2015]

Manuj, I and Mentzer, J T (2008) Global supply chain risk management strategies, *International Journal of Physical Distribution & Logistics Management*, 38 (3), pp 192–223

Meyer, (2006) Nearshoring to Central and Eastern Europe, *Deutsche Bank Research* [online] http://www.dbresearch.com [accessed15 July 2015]

Naylor, J B, Naim, M M and Berry, D (1999) Leagility: integrating the lean and agile manufacturing paradigms in the total supply chain, *International Journal of Production Economics*, 62, pp 107–18

Paliwoda, S and Thomas, M (1998) *International Marketing* (3rd edn), Butterworth-Heinemann, Oxford

Parfois (2015) http://www.parfois.com/en/

Peck, H (2005) Drivers of supply chain vulnerability: an integrated framework, *International Journal of Physical Distribution & Logistics Management*, 35 (4), pp 210–32

Rafi-Ul-Shan, P M, Grant, D B and Perry, P (2014) Managing sustainability risks in fashion supply chains, *Proceedings of the 19th Annual Logistics Research Network (LRN) Conference*, University of Huddersfield, Huddersfield UK, e-proceedings

Rigby, D (2011) The future of shopping, *Harvard Business Review*, December, pp 65–76

Rocha, T C (2010) Melhoria da Eficiência Operacional da Cadeia de Abastecimento na Parfois, *Dissertação de Mestrado*, Faculdade de Engenharia da Universidade do Porto

Williamson, O E (1975) *Markets and Hierarchies: Analysis and antitrust implications*, The Free Press, New York

Wilson, R (2014) *25th Annual State of Logistics Report: Ready for a new route*, CSCMP, http://www.cscmp.org/

WTO (2014) World Trade Organization International Trade Statistics 2014 [online] www.wto.org/statistics [accessed 15 July 2015]

In-store consumer service

06

Introduction

This chapter discusses in-store logistics, supply chain and service issues pertaining to fashion goods and fashion retailers. While Chapter 5 discussed issues in logistics and supply chain management (SCM) from an international perspective, this chapter looks at logistics and SCM issues that affect national or domestic supply chains, ie after the goods reach the port of entry of the country in which they will be sold, and the resulting in-store service that consumers expect and indeed demand. The chapter begins with an overview of a fashion retailer's national supply chain including ports of entry of land, sea and air, distribution centres (DCs) and distribution system types, retail store types, strategic decisions required for retail logistics systems, and information technology (IT) as an enabler for retail logistics and SCM. Next, matters regarding store replenishment, in-store on-shelf availability (OSA) and out-of-stock (OOS) issues that affect merchandising, are discussed. Finally, we look at the effect that a fashion retailer's logistics and SCM activities have on meeting consumer service needs. The issue of online or internet sales and service will be addressed in the next chapter and, consequently, will not be touched on here unless germane to the discussion.

The national fashion retail supply chain

Figure 5.1 presented a figure showing a generic fashion supply chain that was international in scope. Figure 6.1 shows a generic national supply chain for fashion goods.

FIGURE 6.1 A generic national fashion supply chain

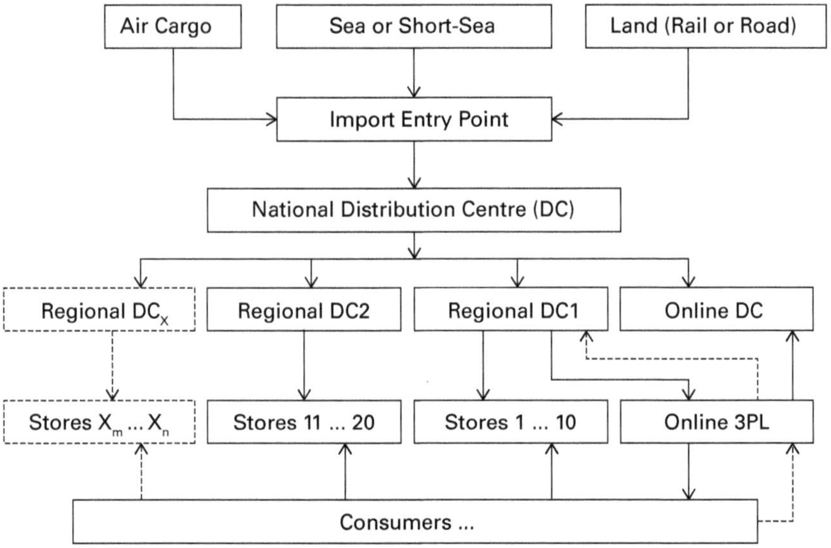

As noted in Chapter 5, goods that are sourced outside the domestic or home country require international distribution to the domestic or home market. That is the case for the vast majority of fashion retailers operating in Europe. The process is that their goods arrive at a port of entry by one of three transportation methods: air cargo, sea or short-sea container shipping, or land-based rail service or road freight. The goods are cleared through customs and the appropriate duties and taxes are paid before they are then transported to the retailer's national distribution centre (NDC) and stored. From there the retailer will transport and distribute stocks of goods to its various regional distribution centres (RDCs) to supply a number of stores. The retailer may use its own transport fleet or may outsource transport (and even the warehousing or NDC/RDC function) to a third-party logistics (3PL) service provider. Customers will then visit the stores to buy the goods they need; however, they may not choose to go the one closest to them. Alternatively, customers can order online from the retailer and the retailer will despatch the goods to them using an online 3PL company. The retailer may use their own transport systems to distribute and also handle returns, as shown by the dotted lines in Figure 6.1. The issues related to online purchasing, delivery and returns will be discussed in Chapter 7.

Naturally, this is a simplified and generic representation of how a retailer's national supply chain may look and many retailers may have different arrangements. For example, the UK fashion retailer Next, founded in Leeds, Yorkshire during the mid-1860s (under a different name), has eight RDCs in Great Britain but no NDC (Next, 2015). Three of these RDCs are located in Yorkshire with the remaining five at Motherwell in Scotland, Bristol, Warrington in Cheshire, Hemel Hempstead near London and Thurrock in Essex. NEXT has over 500 stores across the UK and Eire but also offers online and catalogue shopping, and operates its own transport fleet. Conversely, Matalan plc, a UK-based discount fashion retailer founded in 1985, has four RDCs servicing its network of over 200 UK stores. Matalan outsources its warehousing and transportation distribution to Advanced Supply Chain and its material handling systems to SDI Group Ltd (Matalan, 2015).

Mehrjoo and Pasek (2014) noted the apparel industry is essentially divided into three market segments based on competitive strategies to reach them: speed, brand equity and cost advantage. They argued that a key to success for the 'speed' or fast-fashion market segment is to provide customers with the most fashionable clothes in the shortest amount of time with prices that are not unreasonable. Mehrjoo and Pasek summarized the overall characteristics of this segment as 'cutting-edge fashion at an affordable price for Zara or similarly as fashion and quality at the best price for H&M' (2014, p 296). There has been much discussion about the fast-fashion sector since 2000, for example by Bruce *et al* (2004), Ferdows *et al* (2004), Tyler *et al* (2006), Caniato *et al* (2014) and Macchion *et al* (2015). However, it has focused on either consumer behaviour and branding for firms such as Zara and H&M, or on the lean and agile production systems used to compress time spent getting products to market. Both of these topics have already been discussed in Chapters 2 and 5 respectively.

Brun and Castelli (2008) argue that the brand equity market segment has derived from brand values that help 'consumers in retrieving and processing information, provide a basis for differentiation and positioning of a product, involve product attributes and... benefits that give consumers a reason to buy and use the brand, create mental associations that produce positive attitudes and feelings that are transferred to the brands, and provide the basis for product extensions [... that] can even justify a premium price due to their reputation and [... the fact] they provide psychological satisfaction' for consumers (2008, p 170). For example, Gucci maximized its brand equity through internal controls of product sourcing, brand communications and distribution as a way to successfully reposition itself as a luxury brand (Moore and Fernie, 2004).

The cost advantage market segment in fashion has two contexts. One is slow fashion, defined by Watson and Yan (2013, p 145) as products 'not produced under the ideals of a fast-fashion business model, and are generally not in response to quickly changing fashion trends … as designers begin to forgo the high-frequency fashion industry and adopt flexible, seasonless designs'. There is also a sustainability aspect where slow fashion is based on product designs incorporating high quality, small production lines, regional productions and fair labour conditions (Pookulangara and Shephard, 2013). Slow-fashion products will normally be less costly to produce and distribute than fast-fashion products, but this does not mean they are cheap to purchase.

The other context is that of the discount retailer such as TK Maxx or Primark. Primark is a wholly owned subsidiary of Associated British Foods and offers consumers 'value for money' through low prices. It achieves this by incurring no advertising costs and instead relying on consumer word of mouth regarding its products, buying stock in vast quantities and passing on the cost savings to consumers, keeping overheads to a minimum but investing in state-of-the-art logistics to enable its stores to replenish stocks quickly, and by not compromising its high quality standards and rigorous testing of products at various production stages (ABF, 2015). Primark also has a strong culture of corporate and social responsibility (CSR). For example, it reserves the right to cease trading with any suppliers who either consistently or severely violate its code of conduct (Perry and Towers, 2009), and made 2,058 factory inspections in 2013 after the collapse of the Rana Plaza factory complex in Bangladesh (Primark, 2015).

In consequence, these three market segments may have very different distribution strategies depending on the desired outcome, ie time to market or speed for a fast-fashion retailer, low cost and also low price if a discount retailer and exclusivity to protect brand image and equity if a premium brand retailer.

Retail logistical systems strategy and design

Retail and logistics managers need to understand strategy in order to make the decisions about logistical systems given their strategic objectives. Such managers can use a systems approach to analyse cost and other trade-offs to make informed business decisions; however, without a good understanding of corporate strategy and a corresponding logistical systems strategy, they may not be able to make the best decisions. For example, if a retailer's strategic objective is to achieve differentiation from competitors by offering timely and consistent service to consumers, ie if it is a fast-fashion retailer, it will likely make a trade-off between distribution costs versus delivery speed and reliability and so choose road freight or perhaps air cargo over rail freight or shipping by sea.

In a research study Sandberg (2013) used a business model technique to capture not only logistics issues, but also marketing and other strategic issues within a do-it-yourself (DIY) retailer. He called for a holistic or systemic approach and argued that, without proper understanding and description of events outside the logistics function, a retailer will not be able to design a suitable logistics system that can contribute to overall corporate objectives. Sandberg concluded, quoting one of his research respondents, that 'retailing does not have logistics, retailing is logistics' (2013, p 186).

A full discussion about corporate strategy is beyond the scope of this book and the reader is referred to a strategy text such as Johnson *et al* (2007). However, this section will briefly consider the various trade-offs among the logistical activities of transportation, warehousing in DCs, inventory management, and information technology (IT) management and order processing as the main components of a national retail supply chain. Purchasing and procurement, or sourcing, is not considered here as it was previously discussed in Chapter 3. Table 6.1 provides a strategy matrix detailing different decisions required for the four logistical activities above and the three different strategic levels: strategic or long-term ie greater than three years, tactical or medium-term ie greater than one year but less than three years and operational or short-term ie less than one year.

Again, a complete discussion about these four logistical activities is beyond the scope of this book and the reader is referred to a logistics management text such as Grant *et al* (2006) and Grant (2012). Here, however, are brief discussions about the important points for each of them as they affect the national retail supply chain drawn from both texts.

Modes of transportation

Administration of retail transportation activities or transport management includes major issues such as inbound and outbound transportation, contracts with 3PL service providers, strategic partnerships and alliances, private carriage/leasing, mode/3PL selection, routing and scheduling, service specifications and information technology. An understanding of the characteristics of each transport mode is essential for the effective design and management of transportation. This understanding assists a retailer in selecting

TABLE 6.1 Retail logistics activity strategic matrix (adapted from Grant, 2012, p 254)

Logistical activity	Strategic (>3 years)	Tactical (1–3 years)	Operational (<1 year)
Transport	Changing transport modes, eg road versus rail	Redrawing retail distribution centre delivery patterns	Altering weekly load planning of shipments to stores
Warehousing	Changing the number, size and location of warehouses or distribution centres	Redesigning internal warehouse layout configurations or adding cross-docking	Determining order picking and packing protocols for stores
Inventory management	Replacing suppliers or inventory tracking technology systems	Adjusting safety or buffer stock levels based on sales history	Fulfilling weekly store order and dealing with back-orders
Information technology management and order processing	Moving to a sales-based ordering (SBO) system using radio frequency identification (RFID)	Install temporary ordering channel for specific promotional offers	Processing incoming and outgoing orders and dealing with supplier invoices

and evaluating various mode and transport trade-offs and is important due to transportation's impact on customer service levels provided by the retailer.

Air cargo offers high levels of service relative to other modes. Service advantages include fast time-in-transit, low damage/loss rates, high consistency and frequent schedules. Disadvantages include limited weight (known as lift) or dimensional displacement (known as cube) capacity, limited market coverage and high cost. Often it is viewed as a premium, emergency service. Primary market coverage is limited to movements between major points, although reduced service is available to smaller cities. Products transported by air are generally of high value and low density or weight, making air cargo a useful option for fast-fashion clothing products in some circumstances.

Road freight using trucks is the dominant form of freight transport in Europe. Road freight offers more flexibility and versatility than other modes as it offers point-to-point service to any location reached by roads and highways. Time-in-transit is fast, although not as rapid as air, and reliable with relatively low levels of damage or loss. No other mode can provide the market coverage offered by road freight. Road freight is moderately priced compared to air, but is usually more costly than rail and water transport. It is the most widely available mode and transports products of all shapes, sizes and densities. From the standpoint of products transported, road freight moves a greater variety of items than any other mode.

Rail service is generally low in cost relative to air cargo and road freight. Loss and/or damage ratios are moderate, but are typically above those of air and road. Rail is at a service disadvantage relative to its major competitor, road freight, in terms of transit time and frequency of service. Market coverage is extensive because of the availability of track facilities, but not nearly as extensive as the highway network. The bulk of rail traffic is low-value, high-density products such as paper, chemicals and plastics, lumber, iron and steel, canned foods and motor vehicles. Rail service also lacks the versatility and flexibility of road freight since it is limited to fixed-track facilities, although multimodal service using containers on ships, rail flat cars and low-bed truck trailers has helped overcome some of these problems.

International sea or short-sea container shipping (ie between close port complexes such as Rotterdam in the Netherlands and Teesport in the UK) is perhaps the most inexpensive method of shipping. Sea shipping is also used for high-bulk, low-value commodities such as iron ore, grains, coal and petroleum. Transit times are lengthy, but this may not be a severe deficiency for fashion products that are not time sensitive. Inland water service is limited in most countries because of the availability of navigable waterways, but Europe does have an extensive canal and river system that is very well-used. For example, since 2012 the French-based 3PL service provider Norbert Dentressangle (ND) acquired in mid-2015 by the US firm XPO Logistics Inc., has been transporting products along the River Seine and delivering them to around 100 Franprix outlets. In partnership with Port Autonome de Paris and Voies Navigables de France, 26 containers, containing 450 pallets, will be transported by barge every day – from the port in Bonneuil-sur-Marne to the port Bourdonnais in the heart of Paris (7th arrondissement). ND estimates that the 26 containers delivered each day represent a saving of 450,000 km per year, reduce the number of trucks on the road by 3,874 and also save 37 per cent in CO_2 emissions annually (ND, 2013).

Warehousing

The three functions of warehousing include movement, storage and information transfer. While movement within a warehouse or DC is minimal in terms of distance, it is significant when examined in light of the activities of receiving, transfer, order picking/selection, cross-docking and shipping. Each element incurs costs and when performed inefficiently can erode profit margins for the retailer and also affect customer service levels. Storage is simply maintaining products in inventory prior to their sale or use. It involves physically maintaining one or more items in a designated facility or area. Storage may be temporary or semi-permanent. Information transfer should occur simultaneously with the movement and storage functions. Timely and accurate information is always required to efficiently administer warehousing activities. Information about inventory levels, throughput/turnover levels, stock-keeping locations, number and status of inbound and outbound shipments, customer data, facility space utilization and personnel are the main pieces required for effective warehouse management. However, the role of warehousing has changed since the late 1990s as warehouses or DCs are increasingly being used in the supply chain as 'flow-through points' rather than 'storage points' to meet customer demands in time-sensitive global supply chains. For example, the concept of cross-docking, where in-bound goods are placed in a nearby area for immediate out-bound despatch and never get put away into storage, was developed by Walmart in the 1990s and is commonplace today.

There are three basic warehouse location decision strategies for retailers. A market-positioned strategy locates warehouses nearest to the final consumer, ie to the retail stores, to help maximize consumer service levels and permit transportation economies from production or source locations. Factors that influence this strategy include transportation costs, order cycle time, the time sensitivity of the product, order size, local transportation availability, population density and service levels required by customers. A production-positioned strategy locates warehouses in close proximity to sources of supply or production facilities. Although these warehouses generally cannot provide the same level of customer service offered by market-positioned warehouses, they serve as collection points or mixing facilities for products manufactured at a number of different sites. Factors that influence the placement of warehouses close to the point of production include perishability of products, the number of products in the retailer's product mix, assortment of products ordered by customers and transportation consolidation rates. The final location strategy locates warehouses at an intermediate position between the final consumer and producer. This strategy is often followed when a retailer must offer reasonably high customer service levels but cost or other factors may affect operations. For example, many UK retailers have located warehouses or DCs in Northampton, about 50 miles north of London, due to cheaper land costs and a lack of suitable site space in London.

Various analytical models have existed for many years for locating and determining the optimal number of warehouses. A lot of these models were developed in the geography discipline, which is concerned about spatial dispersion and allocation, and use mathematical or linear programming, simulation and algorithms such as the centre of gravity, heuristic methods using experience and the Keuhn-Hamburger model (see for example Scott, 1970).

Inventory management

An inventory is simply a list of all products in stock at both the retailer's DCs and stores, and inventory management is the management of these stocks. Stocks are important to the efficient and effective management of a retailer as they:

1 enable the retailer to achieve economies of scale in purchasing, transportation and/or production;

2 balance supply and consumer demand to address seasonal variations or raw material availability;

3 provide protection from uncertainties between the order cycle and consumer demand; and

4 act as a buffer between critical interfaces internal to the retailer and externally within the retail supply chain.

Important factors for inventory management include customer service levels required, size of market(s) served, number of products, size of products, materials handling systems used, throughput rate or inventory turnover, production lead times, stock layout in the SC or retail store (ie merchandising), aisle requirements in the DC and retail stores, types of racks and shelves used and, finally, the level and pattern of consumer demand. In general, as the demands on the retail marketing, logistical and production systems increase, or as uncertainty becomes greater, larger or more numerous DCs are often required as in the case of mass retailers such as Primark or Marks & Spencer. Alternatively, if highly consistent transportation making more frequent deliveries is utilized, inventory levels can often be reduced which should result in fewer warehouses or DCs and/or smaller sized ones. The following case study on Marks & Spencer demonstrates how difficult such decision-making management is in a competitive fast-fashion marketplace.

CASE STUDY Marks & Spencer: Struggling with its UK domestic fashion supply chain

Despite best efforts within the entire organization, Marks & Spencer (M&S) continues to struggle to find its way in the fashion clothing sector. Chief executive Marc Bolland presided over the worst trading in general merchandise for three years in mid-2012, which included clothing, with the weakest performance in women's wear. He blamed the weather and stock shortages which meant it did not have enough bestselling lines, such as lightweight sweaters and bold-print tops. However, at the time analysts and rivals questioned whether M&S had got its styles wrong. At the same time, M&S was grappling with modernizing its supply chain, having too many stores on marginal high streets, and shops that looked shabby despite the previous CEO, Sir Stuart Rose, spending more than £2billion (about US $3billion) on them.

Retail analyst Tony Shiret believed Mr Bolland was doing the right things for M&S in the long term, such as repositioning its clothing away from the bottom of the market. But another retail analyst Nick Bubb believed M&S needed to recognize it was doomed to slow decline. Yet another independent voice, retail consultant Neil Saunders of Conlumino, believed M&S had two other options: muddle along in the middle or, more preferably, rip up the rule book and start again with its clothing lines.

In May 2014, M&S issued a press release announcing the opening of a new distribution centre (DC) in Castle Donington, England to assist M&S in multi-channel environments, including delivery abroad. The facility is 900,000 square feet, or about 90,000 square metres, and is capable of processing one million products every day, with around a third of these coming through the online channel Marksandspencer.com. Some 16 million products will be held at the centre with 1,200 people employed during peak periods such as at Christmas and during seasonal sales. The DC is one of the most modern, fully-automated distribution centres in the UK and its construction is part of the retailer's transformation programme which has a fast, agile and flexible supply chain at its heart.

First launched in 2009, the programme should be completed by 2015/16 with a new multi-channel platform to host the firm's website. The new and modern e-commerce distribution facility at the Castle Donington DC will benefit consumers with better product availability and the ability to order products later in the day and receive them less than 24 hours later. There was also investment placed in better buying and management systems for clothing, home and gift products, and M&S was hoping to source more goods direct from suppliers.

In order to rebuild its new supply chain, M&S removed 110 small warehouses, which stored clothing, home and gift products, from its network and consolidated into a number of larger, modern DCs, in essence adopting a decentralization strategy. Such a strategy means that the time it takes to move products from a port to different stores will be dramatically reduced. Castle Donington operates 24 hours a day, seven days a week, and 50 vehicles will come in and out every day. There was also going to be a reduction in relying on full-service vendors by migrating suppliers to a direct sourcing model, which should bypass the need for them to handle the distribution and storage of any given products.

In addition to all of this, M&S is transforming its IT and business management systems, which it accepted were outdated and complex, with new, modern and simple processes and software. These improved systems are due to come to the clothing, home and gifts sections, helping to mark down costs and provide a better view of stock availability.

However, after the re-launch of the firm's clothing range in 2013–14, the autumn 2014 trading season, which was supposed to be the season when benefits of the changes started to become clear, has not borne fruit. Andrew Hughes, analyst at UBS, noted that it is hard to ascertain what progress is being made at the front end of the business. However, despite M&S's numbers looking pretty shocking at face value, in general analysts and investors seem sanguine about the continued slump in sales. This is partly because the warm autumn weather created problems for all retailers on the high street and was further evidence that no one buys their winter wardrobe until they need it, according to Lord Wolfson, CEO of Next.

Thus, there is an acceptance that the performance of M&S's clothing business will not improve substantially for some time and some still argue that their problems are not rooted in the quality of its fashion and products, but the network behind it. The revamp of the company's clothing range – led by the head of general merchandise, John Dixon, and style director Belinda Earl – has won strong reviews from the fashion press. However, the company's still-cumbersome supply chain means that it has too often failed to get the right products in the right place at the right time. Shoppers outside London have complained about their stores running out of popular items and not stocking outfits that M&S promotes in its 'Leading Ladies' campaign.

By comparison, Inditex, the owner of Zara and the biggest fashion retailer in the world, sends new clothes to all of its stores twice a week, meaning it is able to adapt to unpredictable weather conditions. It is able to do this because more than half of its clothing is produced in Europe or North Africa, which the company describes as proximity markets. M&S meanwhile still relies heavily on its initial seasonal deliveries and it can take weeks for new orders to reach stores as the company still sources most of its clothing from the Far East. Bolland and the senior M&S team continue to make changes such as decentralizing its storage operations, re-launching its website and hiring the Hong Kong-based brothers Neal and Mark Lindsey as joint sourcing directors. Both worked for Next on its 'virtual manufacturing' initiative and it appears M&S is adopting the Next supply chain model. The first garments sourced by the Lindsey brothers came into stores for the 2015 spring and summer season. A bigger proportion of orders will be left 'open to buy' depending on demand and M&S is moving to deliver new products in 12 phases a year, up from six to eight, with some coming on a three-weekly basis – closer to a Zara-style 'fast-fashion' offering.

And yet clothing sales continue to fall due in part to disruption from the changes Bolland has made; for example online sales were down 8 per cent after the company switched to the new website. Bolland has pledged to increase the margin on the clothing M&S sells by 100 basis points or 1 per cent during the year and hopes to deliver this performance through improving the efficiency of its supply chain and selling more clothing at full price. However, it is difficult to determine the impact of interactions between consumer demand and M&S's international and national supply chains to see where, when and how these improvements will take place.

SOURCES Felsted, (2012); Marks & Spencer, (2014); Ruddick, (2014); Davey and Thomasson, (2015).

Information technology and order processing

The order processing system (OPS) is the nerve centre of any retail logistics system. An OPS is driven by a consumer order or in-store purchase – these are the primary and most important communications messages, and they set the logistics process in motion. The speed and quality of information flows have a direct impact on the cost and efficiency of the entire retail operation. Slow and erratic communications can lead to lost sales or consumers, excessive transportation or trans-shipments, increased levels of inventory, additional warehousing utilization and possible production inefficiencies caused by frequent line changes – all of which increases costs. Systems such as electronic point-of-sale (EPOS) and electronic data interchange (EDI) are commonplace for larger retailers today and support the high speed and accuracy necessary (in order entry and order transmittal in particular) to provide effective and efficient OPS. However, such systems require substantial initial investment in equipment hardware and software.

To support time-based competition, ie fast fashion, retailers are increasingly using information technology (IT) as a source of competitive advantage. The systems utilized vary according to the requirements of the different business areas: for example enterprise resources planning (ERP) and just-in-time (JIT) are found in upstream production and fulfilment, efficient consumer response (ECR) in grocery retail or quick response (QR) in non-grocery retail replenishment and customer relationship management (CRM) at the consumer interface. CRM integrates a number of information-based technologies to reduce order cycle times, increase speed responsiveness and lower supply chain inventories. ECR and QR were discussed in Chapter 5 but will also be revisited in this chapter in the section covering in-store consumer service.

IT and accompanying decision support systems (DSS) encompass a wide variety of models, simulations and applications that are designed to ease and improve decision making. These systems use information from a retailer's database in an analytical framework to represent relationships among data, simulate different operating environments, and conduct uncertainty and 'what-if' analysis prior to calculating and recommending a feasible decision. Artificial intelligence tools can be incorporated into the DSS and may contain decision analysis frameworks such as data envelope analysis (DEA) or the analytical hierarchy process (AHP), as well as forecasting, simulation and linear programming models. Direct IT applications for logistics activities include automating repetitive transactions, creating customer orders, making payments through EDI and EPOS, creating operations planning systems such as ERP, operating computerized routing and vehicle scheduling (CRVS) and transport management systems (TMS), performing load and item tracking and tracing using barcodes or radio frequency identification (RFID) systems, as well as automating warehouse operations and monitoring performance using warehouse management systems (WMS).

Retail logistical system cost trade-offs

In summary, a retailer can design its logistical systems in a number of ways, depending on the parameters it selects for each of the logistical activities. The US Department of Transport (2015) considers there are four factors that influence that decision:

1   The cost of lost sales is the most difficult factor to quantify. It generally decreases with the number of warehouses and varies by industry, company, product and customer. Other cost components are more consistent across retailers.

2   Inventory costs increase with the number of warehouses, as retailers maintain a safety stock of most or all products at each facility.

3   More warehouses means higher warehouse costs. Fixed costs across many facilities are larger than the marginal variable costs of fewer locations.

4   Transportation costs initially decline as the number of facilities increase due to proximity. Costs can increase if a retailer maintains too many warehouses however, due to the combination of inbound and outbound transport costs.

FIGURE 6.2   Total logistics cost curve (adapted from US Department of Transport, 2015)

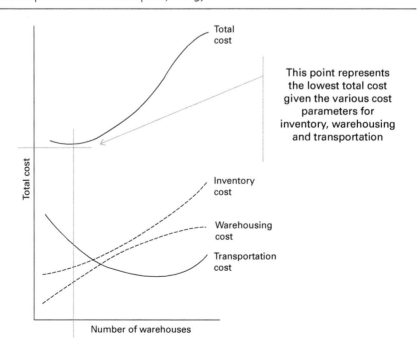

A retailer seeking to minimize total costs, which is the sum of the above components, could balance all cost components using IT and DSS techniques discussed previously and as depicted graphically in Figure 6.2. As transportation costs decline due to possible transport infrastructure investment such as more highway construction, a minimum total cost should be realized; however, after that point costs will rise. The nature and timing of such costs will occur at different points for different retailers depending on their overall organizational structure and geographic reach.

In-store consumer service

Retail stores are the final logistical link to the consumer in bricks-and-mortar retail supply chains. Good product availability at this penultimate supply chain node where consumers are the final node in the logistics definition of 'point-of-origin to point-of-consumption' (Grant, 2012). Availability is important to provide consumer satisfaction and ongoing loyal relationships (Grant, 2014). Notwithstanding, retailers often focus logistics activities on bringing products to the store and pay less attention to logistics processes inside the store. Ignoring the logistics required at this last node in the chain, ie the 'last 50 yards', can result in less than optimal availability (Fernie and Grant, 2014b). In-store processes not only involve physical on-shelf replenishment but also require attention to managerial tasks such as ordering, shelf space planning and in-store consumer service (Kotzab and Teller, 2005).

In-store consumer service consists of both marketing elements such as assortment, merchandising, promotions and store environment or ambience, as well as logistical elements in support of the marketing elements, such as shelf replenishment to maintain on-shelf availability (OSA) of products, IT, and delivery and possibly assembly for larger products. OSA remains an important challenge for all retailers as items being out of stock (OOS) results in consumer dissatisfaction, which manifests in reactions ranging from product substitution to customers 'voting with their feet' and seeking products elsewhere, (Corsten and Gruen, 2003). Further, the fashion apparel sector tends to have short life cycles, high volatility, low predictability and a high level of impulse purchasing, particularly in fast fashion, all affecting retailers' decisions on what and how much product to stock on-shelf. Too much stock will increase inventory and storage costs while too little stock will result in OOS and possible consumer dissatisfaction.

Many UK fashion retailers have also focused on decreasing costs and one popular response has been to move or outsource production to developing countries that have lower labour costs, as discussed in Chapter 5, in order to remain competitive with increasing competition from fast-fashion retailers such as Zara and H&M, and low-cost national discount retailers such as Primark and TK Maxx (Fernie and Sparks, 2014). However, geographically long supply chains can also exacerbate stock availability in the national market. OSA therefore remains the primary logistical issue for in-store consumer service.

Most research on this topic has focused upon the retail grocery sector but, despite some extant studies (see for example Grant and Fernie, 2008; Zinn and Liu, 2008; Meng *et al*, 2012), there has been limited OSA research undertaken in the non-food sector generally and the fashion sector in particular. Many researchers (for example Birtwistle *et al*, 2003; Fiorito *et al*, 1995, 1998) and retailers and their 3PL partners (for example Davenport and O'Dwyer, 2011; Logistics Manager, 2011) have considered that the implementation of QR and other systems techniques such as RFID and 'big data' analytics should alleviate issues of OSA. And yet, these strategies have provided mixed fortunes, as discussed in the following case study.

CASE STUDY   RFID: Panacea or predicament?

Radio frequency identification or RFID has not lived up to its initial hype, and Walmart's intention to have all its top 100 suppliers providing products with RFID tags by 1 July 2005 failed. Notwithstanding, some retailers have found RFID to be useful. Macy's started piloting it in 2009 at its Bloomingdale SoHo location by tagging virtually everything in the store and then scanning and doing cycle counts. The tags, which contain a simple chip and antenna, are embedded into product pricing labels such as those that hang from apparel, and are powered by a radio signal emitted from hand-held or fixed-in-place readers. The readers allow store employees to check the inventory of an entire rack of hanging clothing by simply walking around the display with a handheld reader. The software then displays a list of sizes or styles that need to be replenished and the employee can narrow in on needed items in the stockroom by turning the reader to a 'Geiger counter' setting. Bill Connell, Macy's senior VP of logistics and operations, said that attempting this kind of replenishment by visually inspecting items or scanning bar codes would take an untenable amount of time. 'You can count [inventory] once or twice a year with bar codes with limited accuracy, because the person can be distracted, or scan the same code twice. We can count up to 24 times a year using RFID. It just enables us to keep inventory accuracy in the high 90s [percentage].' Based on early pilot success, Macy's began installing RFID infrastructure in all its 850 stores. Starting in early 2014 Macy's expanded the number of vendors it has asked to ship items that are pre-tagged with RFID. By the end of the year Macy's had planned to have half of all replenishment vendors sending RFID-tagged merchandise.

It appears RFID helps retailers more significantly on the sales floor than in their supply chains. This is especially important with apparel where multiple size and colour combinations can be troublesome to keep properly stocked. Bill Hardgrave, Dean of Auburn University's College of Business noted that 'a warehouse can be Six Sigma, but [inside] a store is No Sigma. Stores are chaotic. The processes are not repetitive, customers don't behave the same way every day, the weather isn't the same every day and that impacts buying patterns. So this is where RFID has the most value.'

SOURCES Attaran, (2012); O'Connor, (2014).

Some empirical studies

The first reported piece of research on clothing OSA was presented at an ECR UK conference in 2007 by Carey and Staniforth (2007). Their firm, the large UK department store chain House of Fraser was experiencing poor OSA due to inefficient location of products in crowded stock rooms and the valuable staff time being taken to get products ready for sale in-store. House of Fraser commissioned a consumer exit survey that discovered that 36 per cent of customers visiting House of Fraser who planned to purchase in fact did not do so. The main reason for this behaviour was the non-availability of size and/or colour of clothing products.

In-store shelf replenishment issues, in addition to DC replenishment and inventory accuracy, account for a high percentage of retail OOS situations (Corsten and Gruen, 2003, Fernie and Grant, 2008). In the clothing and fashion sector these in-store replenishment problems are aggravated by reprocessing or 'repro' stock which is not accounted for in the re-ordering process. Repro stock is merchandise that is left in other locations in-store such as in changing rooms or on other displays. This is more of a problem in the clothing sector due to the usual behaviour of consumers trying on clothing and then discarding those items they do not wish to purchase wherever they see fit. House of Fraser found that all these factors contributed to an overall OSA level of 71 per cent across the stores they investigated, compared to OSA levels in the mid-90 per cent range in the food and grocery sector. The company determined that if half of their consumers who could not find stock were able to do so and make a purchase their sales would increase by £63 million (Carey and Staniforth, 2007).

Fernie and Grant (2014a) investigated OSA and OOS in the UK clothing retail sector through an in-depth case study of two independent OSA improvement initiatives undertaken by one major retailer. The first initiative related to the retailer's objective to increase market share in a specific children's wear category, namely a summertime 'back to school' promotion. This category was chosen because of the short time window for such a promotional campaign in which stores were asked to achieve 100 per cent availability on the top 20 lines in the retailer's school wear range. The second initiative focused on the product category of women's jeans as the retailer likes to have a constant state of availability due to this product usually being planned into product catalogues for up to six months.

The results for the first initiative saw the retailer fail to achieve its ambitious targets. The average sales floor availability across the 12 stores in the region during this initiative was 73 per cent with the best store achieving 80 per cent and the poorest achieving 63 per cent. Although two of the smaller stores achieved the poorest availability, there was no clear pattern of stock availability at store or DC level across the region and indeed the best performers tended to be the medium-sized stores. Semi-structured interviews revealed numerous reasons for this performance. The key issue related to poor housekeeping; customer assistants commented that there was too much stock in the stockroom and a need for greater reprocessing of stock in the store. It also became clear that the objectives of the back-to-school campaign had not been properly articulated to customer assistants on the floor – the stock control assistants were more familiar with these availability targets than the store operations staff. Staff also did not feel supported by management and therefore it was no surprise that they felt that 100 per cent availability of the top 20 lines was an unachievable goal. Because they did not feel involved in the planning and implementation of the promotion staff were not motivated to achieve better results.

The results for the second initiative saw OSA average 79 per cent across all 10 stores investigated with the best being 93 per cent, close to grocery store percentages, and the worst being 66 per cent. The retailer's database indicated OSA should have been around 90 per cent, thus there was a negative variance of 11 per cent. The final phase of this study involved interviewing the senior manager responsible for trading and OSA issues. She confirmed that the jeans product category required a constant in-store presence and that OSA was of importance to the retailer in that a trading team specifically monitors stock and sales for each store. They used forward-factor calculations to ensure that stores had at least two weeks' cover of stock and the use of separate product identification codes allowed the company to allocate more stock to larger stores that had greater stock turn. However, further questioning revealed that size analysis at store level was not carried out and so if a store had a particular strength in selling size 20 jeans they would still only receive what an average store would sell of this size. Despite having two weeks' cover of stock this retailer was failing to ensure it was allocated in the correct quantities for specific sizes and thus OOS was a frequent occurrence. Final questioning in this area uncovered that store teams were not specifically trained in the importance of OSA and the process of solving OOS issues was not officially communicated to store. Also, to cut costs due to the recession, the retailers no longer held store engagement days and store staff were therefore not trained on the importance of replenishing repro stock. This means that OSA was viewed from a process-driven headquarters perspective rather than from the shop floor.

Suggestions to improve in-store consumer service

Fernie and Grant (2014b) conceptualized an enhanced replenishment model for grocery and non-grocery retailers based on an ECR Europe model for the grocery sector that had seven levers: measurement, managerial attention, replenishment systems, in-store execution (merchandising), inventory accuracy, promotion management and ordering systems. Fernie and Grant's model is more holistic than the ECR Europe model as it includes three sets of antecedents they believe are required before the management levers can be implemented: *human resources* comprising management and staff commitment and appropriate incentive structures; *appropriate infrastructure* not just encompassing buildings and vehicles but also IT, centralized buying and the logistical network; and *inter-organizational collaboration* between retailers, suppliers and 3PL service providers. The empirical studies looked at previously confirm the applicability of these antecedents and, once they are sufficiently understood by management, an availability agenda using the ECR Europe seven levers blueprint can be put forward. The outcomes would be greater product OSA, consumer satisfaction and improved logistical productivity, which in turn should increase revenue and reduce costs. Some specific suggestions for these three antecedents follow.

Suggestions for human resources

There appears to be a need for a greater level of 'cross-training' across functional boundaries so that a retailer's human resources, including managers and in-store operational staff, may move towards a 'T-shaped' skills profile developed by Leonard-Barton (1995) and since adopted by logisticians (eg Mangan and Christopher, 2005; Kovács and Tatham, 2010). The theory here is that employees will not only have to develop specific logistics skills (ie the vertical bar of a 'T'), but also develop a wider understanding of related areas (the horizontal bar of a 'T'). For example, in-store retail replenishment employees should become familiar with tasks such as ordering, data, shelf fulfilment and inventory – the main in-store processes identified by Kotzab and Teller (2005) – as well as merchandising or dealing with supplier representatives in vendor-managed inventory (VMI) situations. Such skill enhancement suggests employees will move to becoming 'knowledge workers' (Drucker, 1993) who know more about their job than anyone else in the organization, are autonomous and project-oriented and who hold the tacit knowledge required for problem-solving, creativity, strategic flexibility and market responsiveness (Butcher, 2007).

Trautrims *et al* (2012) proposed a typology which categorized the four management interaction types found in retail in-store logistics operations according to the amount of interaction replenishment staff have with the systems and the impact they have on such systems. The first is an operations focus where retailers ask replenishment personnel for frequent interaction with replenishment systems to achieve data accuracy and to provide information for central decision making. However, as employees do not have much impact on decision making within the systems, the replenishment system should be designed in a centralized and standardized fashion for the operations focus retailer. A large department store fashion retailer like House of Fraser is an example for such a replenishment system. The second is a customer care focus where retailers aim to free store staff from basic tasks so they can properly advise and help customers; interaction with the customer and not the systems is at the centre of employees' attention. The replenishment system should be designed in such a way that the employees do not need to interact with it often, but can do so if required for customer orders. A luxury fashion retailer like Gucci is an example of such a replenishment system.

The third is a store-based focus where a retailer devolves a lot of decision making to store floor employees as local knowledge and judgement are essential for store operations. Store employees need to interact often with the systems and can adjust data and orders according to their store's specific needs. A fast-fashion retailer like Zara is an example for such a replenishment system. Finally, the fourth is an outlet offering focus where staff replenish to shelf what is delivered to the store and have little or no say in what these products are. Correspondingly, they cannot see which products are coming to the store or order products for customers. A pure discount retailer like TK Maxx is an example of such a replenishment system.

Suggestions for appropriate infrastructure

Quick response (QR) can be a very appropriate strategy to improve replenishment; however, it is a process and involves changes in job functions for both retailers and suppliers (Fiorito *et al*, 1995, 1998). Under QR a retailer agrees to provide the supplier with sales data searchable by stock-keeping unit such as colour, style and size. The supplier agrees to hold this data confidential and use it only as needed to fulfil the QR programme with the specific retailer. Both parties must reach agreement on these factors in advance of the merchandise being shipped. With full implementation of QR strategies, buying and merchandising roles in retailing will no longer involve many of the day-to-day aspects of re-ordering – an activity which previously required a significant proportion of buyers' and merchandisers' time and effort.

The ultimate use of QR in fashion will be when a consumer's clothing needs are provided electronically with a 'body scanner' and data transmitted to the supplier where the garment is immediately made to order. That process is already underway. Alvanon is the world's largest producer of the mannequin body forms used by clothing makers when creating sizes. Alvanon works with brands to expand the number of people it can dress by focusing on not only size numbers but also body shapes, and its clients include brands like Nike, Target, Levi's, J C Penney, The North Face, Lacoste and Hugo Boss. Developed in 2001, Alvanon's AlvaScan device is a booth where a fully clothed person steps in and a full-body laser scanner moves up and down to capture accurate measurement data in seconds, much like an airport security scanner. The data are transferred to a computer and used to create a 3-D virtual body, the starting point for making a mannequin. This technique can also be used to upload a consumer's body size and shape data to a supplier via EDI, and is now being rolled out to retail stores (Peñaloza, 2011).

However, this technique suggests an order fulfilment as opposed to replenishment and perhaps suggests a shift in how OSA will be viewed in future. Ody (2013) argued that many retail supply chains now seem to be focused on delivering goods to stores in response to individual orders instead of being structured towards maintaining inventory levels to meet anticipated demand. One systems supplier suggested to her that retailers are moving from replenishment to fulfilment and she concluded that, as consumers are happy to place online orders and receive the goods two or three days later, so a growing number of retailers seem to believe that consumers will be just as delighted to call back the next day to collect what is currently OOS.

Suggestions for inter-organizational collaboration

Grant (2005) and Hingley *et al* (2011) have argued for increased collaboration among retailers, suppliers and 3PL service providers. A 3PL that extends or enhances its services to its customers, including sharing assets and equity in the form of systems capability, strategy development and process reengineering skills, is termed a fourth-party logistics (4PL) service provider. The 4PL acts as a single interface between the customer and other, multiple logistics service providers. Ideally they will manage all aspects of the customer's supply chain, aiming to establish an inherent and comprehensive supply chain solution which combines process, technology and management, to provide added value for the customer, rather than just improve the efficiency of physical logistics operations as a 3PL would (Hingley *et al*, 2011).

An example of how such collaboration is working in the clothing sector is the work done by Clipper Logistics (2015) in partnership with George Clothing for ASDA, the UK supermarket that is wholly owned by Walmart. George Clothing, the first supermarket clothing brand, was founded in 1990 by George Davies and bought by ASDA in 1995. It has since grown to become the largest clothing retailer by volume in the UK and sells a wide range of fashionable, yet affordable, clothing and footwear for men, women and children in ASDA stores in the UK and online. The brand is also traded by Walmart internationally.

In 2009, George approached Clipper to create a tailor-made distribution solution and system specifically for the George brand, which consists mostly of imported products, to improve time-to-store from the port of entry. Clipper provided a brand new deconsolidation centre at Teesport in northeast England that operates on a port-centric basis (Mangan *et al*, 2008). There, Clipper receives stock from over 15 different global supplier locations. On arrival at this port of entry the stock is unloaded and processed in either hanging or boxed delivery, and is checked against the George purchase order for quantity and quality. The stock then goes through a process of de-boxing, processing and picking ready for transportation to its designated DC. Clipper offers a specialist returns management process which includes checking, quarantine and remedial re-work to meet the customer's exact needs, and also has a photo studio on-site to photograph articles of clothing on mannequins and upload them to the George website so consumers can view and browse the landed products.

Conclusions

In-store logistics and processes influence operational performance, product availability and consumer service and satisfaction at all retail stores, including fashion retailers. Nevertheless, retail supply chain thinking often stops at the delivery ramp of the store and forgets about in-store logistics processes. This last 50 yards has largely been ignored not only in the literature but also in practice.

This chapter began with an overview of a fashion retailer's national supply chain and then considered issues regarding store replenishment, in-store on-shelf availability (OSA) and out-of-stocks (OOS) in the context of a theoretically led and empirically tested framework provided by this book's authors. It finished with suggestions for fashion retailers to address the three important sets of antecedent in this framework: human resources, appropriate infrastructure and inter-organizational collaboration. The next chapter extends this discussion about national fashion retail supply chains into the online or internet arena.

References

Anon (2013) Staying ahead of the curve, *Logistics and Transport Focus*, **15** (10), pp 28–29

ABF (2015) Annual Report 2014, *Associated British Foods* [online] *http://www .abf.co.uk/investorrelations/*annual_report_2014 [accessed 25 July 2015]

Attaran, M (2012) Critical success factors and challenges of implementing RFI in supply chain management, *Journal of Supply Chain and Operations Management*, **10** (1), pp 144–67

Birtwistle, G, Siddiqui, N and Fiorito, S S (2003) Quick response: perceptions of UK fashion retailers, *International Journal of Retail & Distribution Management*, **31** (2), pp 118–28

Bruce, M, Daly, L and Towers, N (2004) Lean or agile: a solution for supply chain management in the textiles and clothing industry? *International Journal of Operations and Production Management*, **24** (2), pp 151–70

Brun, A and Castelli, C (2008) Supply chain strategy in the fashion industry: developing a portfolio model depending on product, retail channel and brand, *International Journal of Production Economics*, **116**, pp 169–81

Butcher, T (2007) Supply chain knowledge work: should we restructure the workforce for improved agility? *International Journal of Agile Systems and Management*, **2** (4), pp 376–92

Caniato, F, Caridi, M, Moretto, A, Sianesi, A and Spina, G (2014) Integrating international fashion retail into new product development, *International Journal of Production Economics*, **147** Part B, pp 294–306

Carey, A and Staniforth, J (2007) Improving availability at House of Fraser: availability and demand planning, Presentation at ECR UK Conference, 21 March, London

Clipper Logistics (2015), Asda, *Clipper* [online] http://www.clippergroup.co.uk/case-studies/asda/ [accessed 25 July 2015]

Corsten, D and Gruen, T (2003) Desperately seeking shelf availability: an examination of the extent, the causes, and the efforts to address retail out-of-stocks, *International Journal of Retail & Distribution Management,* **31** (12), pp 605–17

Davenport, T H and O'Dwyer, J (2011) Tap into the power of analytics, *Supply Chain Quarterly* [online] http://www.supplychainquarterly.com/print/201104analytics/ [accessed 25 July 2015]

Davey, J and Thomasson, E (2015) Insight: M&S breaks with tradition to get more agile on style, *Thomson Reuters EIKON*, 4 March [online] http://thomsonreuterseikon.com/ [accessed 25 July 2015]

Drucker, P (1993) *The Post-Capitalist Society*, HarperCollins, New York

Felsted, A (2012) M&S finds itself going out of fashion, *FT.com*, 13 July [online] http://www.ft.com/cms/s/0/92b04b4a-cc4f-11e1-9c96-00144feabdc0.html#axzz3RvWfMu9D [accessed 25 July 2015]

Ferdows, K, Lewis, M A and Machuca, J A D (2004) Rapid-fire fulfilment, *Harvard Business Review*, **82**, (11), pp 104–10

Fernie, J and Grant, D B (2008) On-shelf availability: the case of a UK grocery retailer, *International Journal of Logistics Management*, **19** (3), pp 293–308

Fernie, J and Grant, D B (2014a) Investigating on-shelf availability in the UK retail clothing sector, in T-M Choi (ed), *Fast Fashion Systems Theories and Applications*, CRC Press, London, pp 95–109

Fernie, J and Grant, D B (2014b) On-shelf availability in UK retailing, in J Fernie and L Sparks (eds) *Logistics and Retail Management: Emerging issues and challenges in the retail supply chain* (4th edn), Kogan Page, London, pp 179–204

Fernie, J and Sparks, L (2014) Retail logistics: changes and challenges, in J Fernie and L Sparks (eds) *Logistics and Retail Management: Emerging issues and challenges in the retail supply chain* (4th edn), Kogan Page, London, pp 1–33

Fiorito, S S, May, E G and Straughn, K (1995) Quick response in retailing: components and implementation, *International Journal of Retail & Distribution Management*, **23** (5), pp 12–21

Fiorito, S S, Giunipero, L C and Yan, H (1998) Retail buyers' perceptions of quick response systems, *International Journal of Retail & Distribution Management*, **26** (6), pp 237–46

Grant, D B (2005) The transaction-relationship dichotomy in logistics and supply chain management, *Supply Chain Forum: An International Journal*, **6** (2), pp 38–48

Grant, D B (2012) *Logistics Management*, Pearson Education Limited, Harlow

Grant, D B (2014) Using marketing and logistics to fulfil customer needs, in S Rinsler and D Waters (eds) *Global Logistics: New Directions in supply chain management* (7th edn), Kogan Page, London, pp 104–17

Grant, D B and Fernie, J (2008) Research note: exploring out-of-stock and on-shelf availability in non-grocery, high street retailing, *International Journal of Retail & Distribution Management*, **36** (8), pp 661–72

Grant, D B, Lambert, D M, Stock, J R and Ellram, L M (2006) *Fundamentals of Logistics Management: European edition*, McGraw-Hill Education, Maidenhead

Hingley, M, Lindgreen, A, Grant, D B and Kane, C (2011) Using fourth party logistics management to improve horizontal collaboration among grocery retailers, *Supply Chain Management: An International Journal*, **16** (5), pp 316–27

Johnson, G, Scholes, K and Whittington, R (2007) *Exploring Corporate Strategy* (8th edn), Pearson Education Limited, Harlow

Kotzab, H and Teller, C (2005) Development and empirical test of a grocery retail instore logistics model, *British Food Journal*, **107** (8), pp 594–605

Kovács, G and Tatham, P (2010) What is special about a humanitarian logistician? A survey of logistics skills and performance, *Supply Chain Forum: An International Journal*, **11** (3), pp 32–41

Leonard-Barton, D (1995), *Wellsprings of Knowledge: Building and sustaining the sources of innovation*, Harvard Business School Press, Cambridge, MA

Logistics Manager (2011) Hugo Boss steps up efficiency with RFID [online]http://www.logisticsmanager.com/2011/07/16430-hugo-boss-steps-up-efficiency-with-rfid/ [accessed 25 July 2015]

Macchion, L, Moretto, A, Caniato, F, Caridi, M, Danese, P and Vinelli, A (2015) Production and supply network strategies within the fashion industry, *International Journal of Production Economics* **163**, pp 173–88

Mangan, J and Christopher, M (2005) Management development and the supply chain manager of the future, *International Journal of Logistics Management*, **16** (2), pp 178–91

Mangan, J, Lalwani, C and Fynes, B (2008) Port-centric logistics, *The International Journal of Logistics Management*, **19** (1), pp 29–41

Marks & Spencer (2014) Press release: From transformation to delivery, 20 May, *Marks & Spencer* [online] http://corporate.marksandspencer.com/media/press -releases/2014/marks-and-spencer-group-plc-full-year-results-201314-52-weeks -ended-29-march-2014 [accessed 25 July 2015]

Matalan (2015) http://www.matalan.co.uk/

Mehrjoo, M and Pasek, Z J (2014) Impact of product variety on supply chain in fast fashion apparel industry, *Procedia CIRP*, **17**, pp 296–301

Meng, Q, Grant, D B and Fernie, J (2012) Improving on-shelf availability and out-of-stocks in non-food retail, *Supply Chain Forum: An International Journal*, **13** (4), pp 4–12

Moore, C and Fernie, J (2004) Retailing within an international context, in M Bruce, C Moore and G Birtwistle (eds) *International Retail Marketing: A case study approach*, Elsevier Butterworth-Heinemann, Oxford, pp 3–37

ND (2013) http://www.norbert-dentressangle.co.uk/

Next (2015) http://www.nextplc.co.uk/

O'Connor, M C Can RFID save brick-and-mortar retailers after all? *Fortune* [online] http://fortune.com/2014/04/16/can-rfid-save-brick-and-mortar-retailers -after-all/ [accessed 25 July 2015]

Ody, P (2013) Moving the goalposts, *Supply Chain Standard* [online]http://www .supplychainstandard.com/liChannelID/2/Articles/4455/Moving+the+goalposts .html [accessed 25 July 2015]

O'Reilly, K and Paper, D (2012) CRM and retail service quality: front-line employee perspectives, *International Journal of Retail & Distribution Management*, **40** (11), pp 865–81

Peñaloza, M (2011) From body scan to body form: sizing a clothing line, *NPR* [online]http://www.npr.org/2011/12/11/143004761/from-body-scan-to-body -form-sizing-a-clothing-line [accessed 25 July 2015]

Perry, P and Towers, N (2009) Determining the antecedents for a strategy of corporate social responsibility by small- and medium-sized enterprises in the UK fashion apparel industry, *Journal of Retailing and Consumer Services*, **16**, pp 377–85

Primark (2015) http://www.primark.com/en/homepage

Pookulangara, S and Shephard, A (2013) Slow fashion movement: understanding consumer perceptions – an exploratory study, *Journal of Retailing and Consumer Services*, **20** (2), pp 200–206

Ruddick, G (2014) Why are Marks & Spencer sales still falling? *Telegraph,* 3 November [online] http://www.telegraph.co.uk/finance/newsbysector/epic/ mks/11203400/Will-Marks-and-Spencer-be-able-to-beat-the-Christmas-blues .html [accessed 25 July 2015

Sandberg, E (2013) Understanding logistics-based competition in retail: a business model approach, *International Journal of Retail & Distribution Management*, **41** (3), pp 176–88

Scott, A J (1970) Location-allocation systems: a review, *Geographical Analysis*, **2** (2), pp 95–119

Trautrims, A, Grant, D B and Wong, C Y (2012) The interaction of human resources and managerial systems as they affect in-store replenishment operations, *Supply Chain Forum: An International Journal*, **13** (2), pp 56–66

Tyler, D, Heeley, J and Bhamra, T (2006) Supply chain influences on new product development in fashion clothing, *Journal of Fashion Marketing and Management: An International Journal*, **10** (3), pp 316–28

US Department of Transport (2015) Federal Highway Administration freight management and operations – appendix 2 economic framework [online]http://ops.fhwa.dot.gov/freight/freight_analysis/econ_methods/freight_cba_study/app_2.htm [accessed 25 July 2015]

Watson, M Z and Yan, R-N (2013) An exploratory study of the decision processes of fast versus slow fashion consumers, *Journal of Fashion Marketing and Management*, **17** (2), pp 141–59

Zinn, W and Liu, P C (2008) A comparison of actual and intended consumer behavior in response to retail stockouts, *Journal of Business Logistics*, **29** (2), pp 141–59

Online consumer service

07

Introduction

This chapter discusses online retail logistics as an extension to Chapter 6, which dealt with in-store supply chain issues. The concept of electronic commerce, or e-commerce, in business to business (B2B), business to consumer (B2C) and consumer to consumer (C2C) exchanges has been rapidly rising in importance for over 20 years (Fernie *et al*, 2014). B2B e-commerce is primarily concerned with electronic tendering, purchasing or procurement or data interchange (Grant, 2012) which were discussed in Chapter 5.

C2C platforms such as eBay and Gumtree reflect a growing trend in consumers willing to act as logistical intermediaries in buying and selling goods to one another. The top six most-visited UK e-commerce websites in the month of May 2014 (Statista, 2015a) were Amazon with 15.9 million, followed by eBay (15.2 million), Tesco (6.7 million), Argos (5.3 million), ASDA (3.9 million) and Gumtree (3.4 million). Some B2C retailers take part in these C2C platforms and will be discussed in this chapter where relevant.

However, online retailing is a topic worthy of its own chapter from a B2C perspective. The boundaries of this chapter are the logistics and SCM activities required to provide B2C online retail order fulfilment and return services to consumers. The chapter begins with an overview of the growth and characteristics of online retailing and generic retail online processes. Next, issues regarding online ordering, fulfilment and return services and their effect on logistical systems design and consumers are discussed. The chapter concludes with a summary of suggestions for retailers to improve their online processes and service.

The online fashion retail supply chain

The growth of online retailing against store retailing

Online retailing has grown significantly since the mid-1990s and there has been much debate as to whether physical retail stores, commonly referred to as 'bricks and mortar' will exist in fifty years' time or whether all retailing activity will take place online. Many cities in North America and Europe have seen a decline in city centre or 'high street' retailing. There are around 40,000 retail stores vacant across the UK, a fact that prompted the Government to appoint retail consultant Mary Portas in 2011 to lead a review into the future of the UK's high streets. The Government subsequently provided £2.3 million to fund 27 Portas Pilot Schemes to enable local councils, residents, retailers and other businesses to try out new ideas in local high streets to meet local circumstances (DCLG, 2013).

However, some criticized the Portas Review as a celebrity gimmick, as well as the Review's contention that high streets must shift their focus away from retail to community activities (Pagano, 2013). Bill Grimsey, former chief executive at the UK supermarket chain Iceland, conducted an independent review stemming from his frustrations with the Government over the Portas Review and Pilot Schemes, and pronounced the high street dead as most people know it (Mesure, 2013). Grimsey's review (2013) concluded that retail should be part of a total high street mix and provided 31 recommendations that support the report's belief that, going forward, there will 'be far fewer shops and technology will completely re-design the way we see and use our local high street [... and] we expect it to develop around multi-purpose community hubs... education, housing, leisure, arts and health will play a much bigger role' (2013, p 49).

Both reviews only peripherally discussed online retailing and missed the point that consumer behaviour is changing towards online retailing due to economic, lifestyle, demographic and other factors. Physical retail stores are no longer competing with online retailing due to this consumer choice (Dunn, 2013) and as a result it is predicted that an additional 50,000 shops and 400,000 jobs will disappear in the UK by 2018 (Pagano, 2013). However, while physical store retailing has its challenges others believe it will survive, albeit in a modified format, for example with new offerings to provide a different and more holistic shopping experience (Sharma, 2014), and remains a key contributor for revitalizing weak European economics (Dickinson, 2014).

One reason for the growth in online retailing is increased access and connectivity to the internet, which is the primary vehicle for online activity.

Europe is the world leader with 82.1 per cent of households having internet connectivity and access, followed by Russia and Eastern Europe at 60.1 per cent, the Americas at 60 per cent, the Middle East at 40.3 per cent and Asia at 39 per cent (Statista, 2015b). Online retail sales have been growing almost exponentially every year since the early 2000s. Total worldwide retail sales are expected to reach US $25.4 trillion in 2015 with online sales comprising US $1.6 trillion or just over 6 per cent of the total (eMarketer, 2014). The top five countries in online retail sales are expected to be China at US $563 billion, the US (US $306 billion), the UK (US $94 billion), Japan (US $79 billion) and Germany (US $73 billion).

Online retailing distribution

Figure 6.1 presented a generic national or domestic fashion supply chain. Figure 7.1 focuses on and expands the online aspects from Figure 6.1 to show a generic online supply chain for fashion goods. By necessity this chapter will focus on online ordering, fulfilment and returns, but it is important to also be aware of the following aspects of the online supply chain. Some online retailers distribute through their national or regional distributions centres but many have set up specific online fulfilment centres (OFCs)

FIGURE 7.1 A generic online fashion supply chain

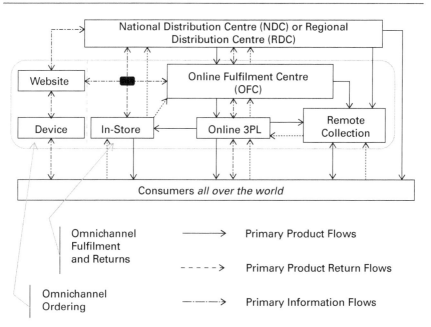

or 'dark stores' (Wood, 2012; The Logistics Business, 2015). While some retailers provide their own transport for fulfilment and delivery, most use third-party logistics (3PL) service providers and 3PLs will be the focus here. Consumers for online products can be all over the world; this chapter's focus will consider domestic or national order, fulfilment and returns. The key issues are similar to an international environment, apart from any transportation and tariff or tax issues found in international transactions. Finally, online retailers can either be pure players, ie they have no physical stores (such as Amazon and ASOS), or multi-channel, ie they distribute through multiple channels as described in Chapter 5.

The term used for satisfying individual online purchases is fulfilment, ie the order is fulfilled as opposed to a store's stock being replenished. This term will be used throughout the following sections to also mean transport and delivery by 3PLs. Another term regarding the online retail phenomenon has come into use since the mid-2000s: omnichannel (sometimes spelled omni-channel), which means that a consumer's entire online shopping experience, ie both sales and fulfilment, is seamlessly and consistently integrated across all channels of interaction, including in-store, digital media including computers, mobiles and tablets, social media, catalogues and call centres (Rigby, 2011; EY-TCGF, 2015). From a supply chain perspective, omnichannel also means there should be complete visibility across channels, along with a holistic, unified view of the path to purchase. The entire omnichannel environment is shown within the oval box in Figure 7.1 and is split between the omnichannel ordering and omnichannel fulfilment and return functions.

Omnichannel ordering

Mobile technology such as smartphones and tablets has dramatically affected consumer online buying habits. Mobile commerce, also called m-commerce, accounted for just 1 per cent of UK e-retail sales in 2010, but it was the source of 48 per cent of all retail website traffic, and accounted for 34 per cent of purchases in the £91 billion UK online retail market by 2014 (Smith, 2014).

Much of this traffic is generated by 'young millennial' shoppers – a cohort of people born between the early 1990s and the early 2000s (Hamilton, 2014). Young millennials are true digital natives (Prensky, 2001a, 2001b) who have grown up with iPads, smartphones, text messaging, Facebook, Twitter, YouTube and other online social platforms and have an innate affinity for and ease with technology. Young millennials crave 24/7 instant connectivity and as a social cohort they are the most demanding in terms of instant gratification. They want to buy and receive items as soon as possible, placing added pressure on retailers and their 3PL fulfilment partners to ensure this happens. Young millennials will have a big impact on the shopping landscape for years to come, with fulfilment a key part of this dynamic (Hamilton, 2014).

Xing and Grant (2006) developed an online fulfilment service quality model from the consumer's perspective as shown in Figure 7.2. The model was derived from Parasuraman, Zeithaml and Berry's original service quality model (1985) and, after consideration of other academic literature, suggested four important consumer criteria expectations of the online fulfilment experience: availability, timeliness, condition and return.

Availability refers to inventory capability, ie having inventory readily sourced to fulfil consumer orders. Key questions consumers have include: is the product in stock at the OFC at the point of order placement or, if not, does it need to be ordered, when it is going to be available or what kind of substitution can be made if possible? Consumers would turn away if products they want are out of stock and another website selling similar products is only a click away. Alternative offerings for substitution may be useful to retain consumers if used properly. Further, availability considers how a consumer would be able to track and trace their order; this ability to trace and track orders is important to consumers. Their perceived lack of control over delivery of their orders makes them more eager to know when to expect arrival of orders.

FIGURE 7.2 Online fulfilment service quality from the consumer's perspective (adapted from Xing and Grant, 2006)

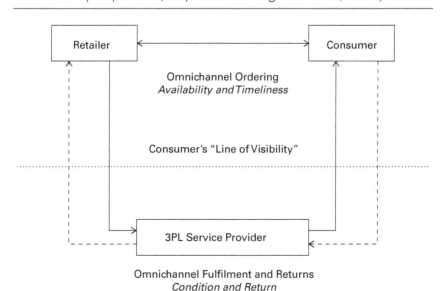

Retailer

Consumer

Omnichannel Ordering
Availability and Timeliness

Consumer's "Line of Visibility"

3PL Service Provider

Omnichannel Fulfilment and Returns
Condition and Return

Timeliness measures order cycle performance and, for the consumer, is the time elapsed between placing and receiving an order. Timeliness is also about how many choices the consumer has over the fulfilment date and time window; how quickly the consumer receives the order and whether the retailer's actual performance matches its promise when the order is confirmed. Reliable, on time and quick delivery is of central significance for the consumer as they are more likely to return products that arrive late, and this has an important bearing on repeat purchase and the profitability of the retailer. Offering consumers more choice while they are in the online buying process can be critical as a retailer's ability to meet a consumer's schedule is often a key factor in making a sale (ChainLink Research, 2013).

Condition is the form and composition of the delivered order and is about the accuracy and quality of the order. Nobody likes damaged or faulty products, which result in return or even cancellation of orders. The condition of products directly affects consumers' perception of delivery service quality.

Return refers to processes available to return products from the point of receipt or consumption to the retailer or supplier for possible repair, resale, recycling, etc. Return is about how many channel options consumers have to return the products, how promptly the products can be collected or replaced and how the retailer deals with damaged, unwanted or faulty products. Convenient and easy ways for returns serve as an important facilitator for consumers using online shopping.

The first two criteria, availability and timeliness, are visible to the consumer through the ordering platform. However, the last two criteria, condition and return are below the consumer's line of visibility and are the responsibility of the retailer and 3PL. Regardless, the nature of these four criteria suggest that a consumer's online purchasing behaviour tends to be more like a business-to-business logistics buyer instead of exhibiting usual hedonistic consumer behaviour patterns.

Xing et al (2010) tested this model in a survey of online consumers in a large UK city and found support for all criteria. They also asked survey respondents to compare their expectations of service with their perceptions of an actual online order experience. Pure players were perceived to have better service than multi-channel retailers, which was consistent with previous work that found late market entrant pure players exhibited superior timeliness and reliability relative to conventional and well-established retailers (Rabinovich and Bailey, 2004).

For example, in the mid-2000s the UK electrical retailers Dixons and Comet had nearly 1,400 UK stores between them (Leroux, 2014). In 2015, Comet no longer exists after going bankrupt in 2012 while Dixons has reshaped its portfolio to focus on 550 larger megastores that combine its Currys and PC World brands. Electrical retailers feel the pressure from online most keenly because their goods are overwhelmingly branded and therefore easy to price-check, and their prices are high enough to justify serious research.

However, there are signs that multi-channel retailers are turning the tide against pure-play rivals as they are now considering their bricks-and-mortar physical stores as assets as opposed to a liability. M-commerce is also expanding to include consumer experiences in bricks-and-mortar physical stores, particularly as to when and how they take delivery of goods. Consumers checking the price of a washing machine in a store on a smartphone may discover a lower price elsewhere, but being on site and knowing the availability and other retailer service features means the price gap will have to be much larger to induce them to buy from the competitor than if they were sitting at home. The arrival of m-commerce means that physical stores are now an integral part of online shopping. This situation is the opposite of the 'showrooming' behaviour disliked by bricks-and-mortar retailers where consumers seek out advice and demonstrations at a specialist store and then order the product online from another low-price competitor (Leroux, 2014).

M-commerce is also having a marketing effect on shopping experiences in physical stores. Apple introduced the iBeacons application (app) in 2014 which uses Bluetooth wireless sensors to detect when a compatible device has come within a certain range of an Apple store. It is like any other app to allow consumers to purchase products, but it also changes state when a consumer goes near the store to tell them about in-store events and makes it easy to book a technical support appointment. US retailers such as Macy's and Walmart have begun to experiment with iBeacons although UK retailers have not really embraced this technology yet. A further stage would use apps like iBeacons to give consumers more specific information and offers. For example, the technology could sense a consumer walking down the dairy aisle of a supermarket and could cross-reference the mobile shopping list with in-store offers. Banks, airports and department stores might also be able to use the technology to identify particularly loyal customers when they walk into a store and then single them out for special attention (Smith, 2014).

In summary, consumers today are equipped with the tools to make shopping via desktop, tablet and mobile a seamless and content-rich process from start to finish. Consumers also want to obtain their purchases quickly, ie products in stock and delivered promptly in good condition, at a time convenient to them. But, if the purchase fails for any reason consumers also want prompt and convenient satisfaction (Xing and Grant, 2006). This is particularly important for one of the fastest-growing market segments in modern society, the young millennials. However, product discovery and purchase are only one part of the online path (Hamilton, 2014). Retailers and their 3PL fulfilment partners must ensure they go the extra mile in the 'last mile' to provide consumers with the best fulfilment experience possible.

Omnichannel fulfilment

The rise of online retailing has brought many logistical and supply chain challenges, especially in the physical distribution to the final consumer or omnichannel fulfilment. In traditional bricks-and-mortar physical stores consumers choose products and take them home at any time they want, unless it is a large product that requires delivery such as furniture or large electrical appliances (Teller *et al*, 2006, 2012). However, consumers can always take away most fashion products at the time of in-store purchase.

Alternatively, online retail enables consumers to select products online and have them brought to their doorstep or elsewhere (Xing *et al*, 2011). In this context in-store replenishment switches to a fulfilment process and responsibility for that process switches from consumer to retailer. In the online environment, retailers undertake logistical operations such as order picking, packaging and delivery usually performed in-store by consumers (Kämäräinen and Punakivi, 2002). This final extension to the definition of logistics management from 'point of origin to point of consumption' (Grant, 2012), ie directly to the consumer's home and referred to as the 'last mile' process, means greater complexity now attaches to a retailer's distribution system. This has major strategic implications for a retailer as the efficient management of fulfilment in the last mile can reduce costs, enhance profitability and thus provide a competitive advantage for the retailer. The following case study on the pure player Zappos.com shows how they established an efficient but effective fulfilment system through the use of automation and information technologies.

CASE STUDY   Zappos.com: Leveraging a service philosophy into competitive advantage

The US pure-play shoe retailer Zappos.com was founded in 1999 and claims to have the largest selection of shoes anywhere in the world, either online or elsewhere, with over 1,000 brands and almost 3 million

pairs of shoes. As well as selection, Zappos prides itself on its unique 'wow' philosophy of service that includes 365-day free returns, 24/7 operations, 110 per cent price protection, and free overnight delivery. The Zappos website also has features that are fast becoming the norm in online retail: website search options, views of every product from every angle, and 'live' inventory information. Zappos' service philosophy provides it with a significant competitive advantage over rivals and consists of two main components: fast fulfilment and customer service.

With its logistical partners, London-based Arup Consulting and FKI Logistex, Zappos designed a fast and optimized order fulfilment system in 2005 after outgrowing its existing fulfilment centre. Zappos took on a new 832,000-square-foot (or 75,000 square metre) facility in Kentucky that contains an automated fulfilment system. Zappos made a rapid order cycle time its highest priority and specified that the system be able to process an order in under an hour. FKI customized a high-speed UniSort XV sortation system and reconfigured conveyors to cut travel time through the system from 35 to 5 minutes. Average fulfilment cycle time, ie time from receiving an order to despatch, is about five hours but they have the capability to process an order in under an hour.

This ability to do fast fulfilment allows Zappos to offer free next-day delivery to consumers for any orders received up until 4:00 pm and also ensures that any order received by 8:00 pm is on a vehicle for next-day shipping. When a consumer places an online order, it is picked from static racking and placed on a conveyor where it is taken to a single- or multi-pack area. Completed packages are routed to automatic labelling and then sorted to an appropriate shipping lane and placed directly on a vehicle. Zappos uses UPS air and ground services for deliveries and by 2008 they were one of its top three overnight shippers.

From a customer service perspective, another fulfilment centre feature is a photo lab. An FKI Accuzone conveyor takes the first of every new stock-keeping unit (SKU) to the lab to have photos taken and uploaded immediately to the website for consumers to see. Zappos also uses a loyalty business model and relationship marketing to keep in touch with its consumers. The primary sources of its rapid growth have been repeat customers and numerous word-of-mouth recommendations. Over 75 per cent of its customers are repeat buyers. About 95 per cent of consumer interactions are through the website while the remaining orders and questions are handled 24/7 by the 400 staff at the call centre in its Las Vegas headquarters. On average Zappos answers 5,000 calls a month and 1,200 e-mails a week, except in the holiday season when call frequency increases significantly. Call centre staff don't have scripts and there is no time limit on calls – the longest call reported is almost ten-and-a-half hours.

Zappos deals with excess or obsolete inventory by ensuring that it does not overbuy in order to reduce the amount of slow-moving inventory to be dealt with. However, it has three strategies for doing so:

1 limited discounts on the Zappos.com website so as not to dilute its brand, affect sales of new stocks, or lose money on its thin margins;

2 sell excess inventory in outlet stores; and

3 sell to a different consumer base through a discount website – Zappos acquired the online discount shoe company 6pm.com in 2007 to give it this vehicle.

Zappos' success with its service philosophy saw it reach US $1 billion in sales in 2008 and as a result in July 2009 Amazon purchased Zappos for around US $1.1 billion in a stock and cash deal, allowing Zappos to continue to operate as an independent entity. In 2012 Amazon took over all of the Kentucky fulfilment centre's operations.

SOURCES Whittaker (2008), McCarthy (2009), Hoyt et al (2009), Zappos.com (2015).

There are two primary methods for online fulfilment: picking in an existing retail store or using OFCs. Logistics and fulfilment operations under both scenarios are expensive to carry out (Esper et al, 2003; Grant et al, 2006), entail operational difficulties (Fernie et al, 2014), and are more environmentally unfriendly (McKinnon and Edwards, 2014).

OFCs or dark stores have evolved as online distribution centres (DCs) and leverage the efficiencies expected in modern DC operations. No longer are they modelled on a generic layout of a traditional store but can introduce productivity drivers like product zoning, pick-face profiling, efficient pick routes and a degree of automation such as 'goods-to-person pick stations' that are not possible in a traditional store environment.

Dark stores can also be situated in less expensive locations outside of prime/high rental areas with better on-site access for local delivery vans and to the road networks that service their catchment area. Another benefit is that picking costs are reduced. For example, the cost of a store-picked grocery order is around £18–£20, whereas if a dark store is used the cost comes down to around £12, making dark stores a less costly and more appealing prospect (The Logistics Business, 2015).

Many retailers and 3PLs offering fulfilment use a rigid methodology based on fixed delivery schedules and delivery time windows (ChainLink

Research, 2013). During final online checkout a few scheduling choices are offered to consumers, generally with long delivery windows, based on a static model using a set of assumptions about what demand might be for a given territory. This approach is limited because delivery services require consumers to be at home to receive a delivery, and so consumers ideally want a precise delivery time. Hence, 'online shopping cart abandonment' occurs frequently at the checkout payment point when consumers realize they are not going to get the product when they want it.

The greatest logistical challenges providing online fulfilment are faced by grocery retailers who must typically pick an order of 60–80 products across three temperature regimes – ambient, chilled and frozen – from a total range of up to 25,000 products within 12–24 hours for delivery to consumers within one- to two-hour time slots (Grant et al, 2006). Online shopping thus imposes new logistical requirements for grocery retailers. First, it is substantially increasing the volume of products that must be handled, creating the need for new OFCs and larger vehicle fleets if the retailer is providing their own fulfilment. Second, online grocery retailers are serving consumers from different socio-economic backgrounds and since they live in different neighbourhoods the geographical pattern of fulfilment is challenging. Third, as noted above all online consumers typically have high logistical expectations, demanding rapid and reliable fulfilment at convenient times (Xing and Grant, 2006).

Online shopping for non-grocery products requires less logistical effort. Catalogue mail-order companies have had long experience of delivering a broad range of merchandise to the home, while some major retailers in Europe have traditionally made home delivery a key element in their service offering (Teller et al, 2006). The distribution of non-grocery products, however, normally exhibits the following different characteristics (Fernie et al, 2010):

1 Non-grocery online retailers generally supply directly to the home from the point of production or a central OFC.

2 Each order comprises a small number of products (often just one) and order picking is centralized at a national or regional level.

3 A large proportion of orders are channelled through 'hub-and-spoke' networks of large parcel carriers or mail-order companies such as DPD, UPS, Yodel and the Royal Mail in UK.

4 Each order must be individually packaged at the OFC in these types of delivery networks. This not only increases the volume of packaging in the supply chain, it also takes up more space on vehicles in both the forward and reverse channels.

5 There is a large flow of returned products, which requires a major reverse logistics operation comprising the retrieval, checking, repackaging and redistribution of returned merchandise, and there have been considerable efforts made in rapid 'refurbishment' of returned products to ensure they are quickly available for online re-sale.

In making the final delivery to the home, companies must strike an acceptable and profitable balance between customer convenience, distribution cost and security. Most customers would like deliveries to be made at a precise time, with 100 per cent reliability. This would minimize waiting time and the inconvenience of having to stay at home to receive the order. However, few customers are willing to pay the high cost of time-definite delivery and in fact demand free delivery and return (Hamilton, 2014).

The business case for omnichannel retailing

Retailers will have to select the optimum distribution channel to succeed financially with omnichannel fulfilment, whether it is by consumers ordering in-store and the retailer delivering to home or consumers ordering online and the retailer or 3PL fulfilling from any store or OFC location. Each option has a different cost structure that retailers need to understand.

In the United States, the ARC Advisory Group and *DC Velocity* conducted a study of 177 retail executives regarding their efforts for omnichannel fulfilment (Banker and Cooke, 2013). What emerged from the study was evidence of a wide gap in the cost accounting capabilities of OFCs versus stores. While most respondents could pinpoint the costs associated with various activities at the OFC, few had a clear picture of the corresponding costs for store fulfilment. For example, 78 per cent of respondents said they knew the cost of picking individual items by stock-keeping unit (SKU) or product class in their OFC. However, only 38 per cent could pin down the corresponding costs for the back room of a store and only 29 per cent said they understood the expenses associated with picking individual items in the front of the store. Additionally, 70 per cent said they could break out their transportation costs by SKU or product class for deliveries from an OFC but, only 57 per cent had that same level of understanding for shipments from a store.

As for how retailers are filling their online orders, the study found that stores are playing a significant and growing role. Thirty-five per cent of retailers fill online orders from in-store stock and 56 per cent of those retail respondents who are not currently filling online orders from in-store stock plan to begin doing so within the next few years.

While retailers may be shifting more of their e-commerce fulfilment activities to the stores, it is not clear if they have the proper groundwork in place, particularly where inventory accuracy is concerned. Today, cycle count accuracy levels at DCs and OFCs that use warehouse management systems (WMS) software in conjunction with automatic identification technology exceeds 99 per cent (Grant, 2012). Accuracy at stores however, is far short of that mark, as discussed in Chapter 6.

The Banker and Cooke (2013) study suggested that one reason for poor in-store inventory accuracy rates was the respondents' failure to make use of point-of-sale (POS) information. When asked what types of auto ID technology they used to ensure inventory accuracy only 46 per cent said they used POS data to update their inventory systems. The majority of respondents, 62 per cent, relied on traditional bar-code scanning on the store floor or in the back room for inventory updating. Only 8 per cent were using RFID for this purpose. At the other end of the scale, 20 per cent were not doing anything in this regard or did not know if their company used any type of automatic identification in conjunction with inventory system updates. The failure to take advantage of modern tracking technologies and a lack of real-time visibility of store-level inventory could result in high consumer dissatisfaction rates for retailers who offer consumers the option to order online and then pick up their orders at the store.

The study also examined how quickly retailers were getting merchandise ordered online and shipped from their stores into customers' hands. Six per cent of respondents guarantee delivery in four hours and 21 per cent guarantee same-day delivery from a store location. However, 34 per cent of respondents said a store-originated shipment would arrive the next day, another 21 per cent said they guaranteed two-day shipping and the remaining 17 per cent said they were unable to commit to a delivery time of less than three days. Eighty per cent rely on parcel carriers for the delivery portion of fulfilment. Fifty-one per cent are doing drop shipping to 3PL partners, while 43 per cent use 3PL services for the entire journey.

Banker and Cooke (2013) concluded that for retailers to succeed in omnichannel distribution they will have to adopt many established upstream distribution practices within their store operations. Retailers will not fare well if they rely solely on buffer inventory in their stores and long lead times for customer delivery. Transformations in store operations will be necessary to ensure retailers' ability to profitably compete in an environment where consumers are becoming ever more demanding.

The issue here is the lack of understanding of supply chain efficiency, and logistics metrics and data mean that, while the system is busy moving goods and materials rapidly around in real time, the value and profitability equations are proving almost impossible to determine. One of the challenges is that many retailers do not know if the various channels they are using are making money and do not understand the 'cost to serve' consumers who want free delivery and free returns (McClelland, 2014; Davies, 2015).

Setting up an online service also requires a high initial investment but takes off rather slowly, and may cannibalize other channels. Competition in the online environment also may decrease prices and affect margins or prompt channel conflict. As a result, it remains unclear whether the online channel itself provides strong performance and whether this performance contributes to the overall performance of the retailer or its 3PL partners, especially parcel carriers.

Logistical design considerations for omnichannel fulfilment

Retail stores are the final logistical link to consumers in bricks-and-mortar retail supply chains and online retailing thus requires different logistics tasks from the retailer. Traditional retailers need to redesign their distribution systems to operate in this new multi-channel format. Some retailers, such as those who sell furniture or white goods, already have home delivery systems in place and have been able to easily adapt their systems to accommodate online sales. However, many small retailers or those who sell physically smaller products may have little or no home delivery experience. Their distribution systems are only geared to shifting pallets of goods from warehouse to store shelves. For them, online retailing and home delivery is a new area and a challenge in learning how to add such capabilities to their existing business model.

Yet, channel performance evaluation is crucial for designing an appropriate multi-channel distribution strategy in terms of optimal channel mix, channel design, level of channel independence and resource allocation across channels. Information about channel performance also helps determine appropriate pricing, assortment and service level decisions (Wolk and Skiera; 2009, Davies, 2015).

Research into online grocery cost relationships between the width of home delivery time windows and transport costs noted that savings of 40–60 per cent are possible where 3PLs can fulfil at any time during a 24-hour day (Punakivi and Tanskanen, 2002). However, such time flexibility can only be achieved where a system of unattended delivery is available, as failed home deliveries and appointments are costing retailers and 3PLs £53 billion a year according to a survey reported in *Logistics Manager* (Anon, 2013a).

Over 31 per cent of all delivery and service appointments fail and the main factor is a lack of notification or communication of arrival times. The primary reason of consumers not being at home had the most impact on retailers, utilities, telecommunications and postal service firms with an estimated cost of £238 per individual failed delivery or service attempt. This cost was attributed to associated increases in administration and business process costs (25 per cent), a lack of capacity utilization (16 per cent), and call centre overburden (10 per cent). The failure of two UK parcel carriers in the last year, City Link in December 2014 and the Dutch-owned Whistl (formerly TNT) in May 2015 demonstrate how important but precarious costs are to parcel delivery and the impact of non-delivery (Davies, 2015). That situation may be about to change in the UK. Hewitson and Bridge (2015) noted that Amazon Prime subscribers in London can pay a fee of £6.99 to receive goods within one hour and that John Lewis will start charging £2 for click-and-collect orders under the value of £30. One solution is simply leaving the consignment outside the house or apartment, preferably in a concealed location, which is known as unsecured delivery. This eliminates the need for a return journey and can be convenient for customers, but obviously exposes the order to the risk of theft or damage. However, consumers are more interested in a secured delivery to mitigate this risk. When encountering a failed delivery attempt, a 3PL can ensure a secured delivery by:

1 returning for a second, pre-arranged delivery;

2 giving the delivery driver internal and secure access to the home or an outbuilding;

3 placing the order at a home-based reception or drop box;

4 leaving it at the delivery depot or a local collection point for pick-up by the consumer; or

5 delivering the order to a local agency which stores it and delivers it when the customer is at home (McKinnon and Tallam, 2003).

To date, there has been very limited investment in home access or reception facilities. Investment in such facilities at an individual home can only be justified where the consumer makes regular use of online fulfilment. The volume of non-food products being fulfilled is still too low to make such an investment worthwhile for the average household (Fernie *et al*, 2014).

Due to this, collection and delivery points strategically located in or around retail outlets, transport terminals and petrol stations to provide 'click and collect' for consumers offer the best prospects for commercial viability (Dunn, 2013) and are proving popular with consumers as an estimated 30 million people use them in the UK (Butler, 2014). Click and collect provides a balance between the conflicting demands of consumer convenience, delivery efficiency and security and can also integrate flows of B2C and B2B orders to achieve an adequate level of throughput, especially for grocery retailers (Fernie *et al*, 2014).

Sainsbury's and Tesco opened collection points at some London Underground station parking lots in 2014, though both pulled out of their deals with Transport for London in June 2015 (Hickey, 2015). However, ASDA has opened click-and-collect facilities in locations separate from their stores and Tesco is rolling out standalone click-and-collect sites in the car parks of its larger hypermarkets. This method is popular in France where lower population densities make home delivery prohibitively expensive, and the grocery market there is dominated by click-and-collect drive-through stores or 'drives' with Auchan and E. Leclerc leading the way (Leroux, 2014).

From a fashion retailer perspective, Network Rail announced plans in mid-2014 to provide click-and-collect stores at 300 rail stations in the UK in a joint venture business called Doddle (Butler, 2014). Doddle is open to any retailer, parcel carrier or shipper to use for shipping out products or accepting returns. Doddle has 30 outlets in station locations that provide very high levels of footfall, for example London Waterloo, which has footfall levels of around 100 million people a year. Consumers receive text messages or e-mails to notify them of the arrival of parcels, as happens with other parcel services; however, some Doddle outlets even feature changing rooms for consumers to confirm whether they wish to keep or return products. Consumers can pay a one-time fess of £1.95 per collection but 7,000 Doddle 'members' pay £5.00 per month for unlimited collections (Hickey, 2015). Retailers already on board to use Doddle include ASOS, New Look, TM Lewin and Amazon (Butler, 2014).

And yet, from an environmentally sustainable perspective click and collect can also represent a 'half-way house' solution. A failed delivery attempt, a redirection to a click-and-collect site and a consumer driving to pick up the order, ie not collecting it en route in a normal journey, entails three distinct travel activities that increase greenhouse gas emissions, use more fuel and add to congestion. Issues regarding sustainability are further discussed in Chapter 9.

The online purchase of physical products involves different handling and movement involving more substantial packing, picking, dispatching, delivering, collecting and returning. From a consumer's perspective a product purchased online cannot be utilized unless it is delivered to them at the right place, at the right time and in the right condition. An important question is who should undertake that activity in the online channel – the retailer or the 3PL service provider. The key benefit that 3PLs provide to retailers is functional expertise. However, they may not truly understand the retailer/consumer relationship and the consumer's need for order fulfilment. Further, are they able to assist the retailer in their marketing efforts to online consumers and add value to the retail offering given their 'invisible' nature in the fulfilment process as shown in Figure 7.2 (Xing and Grant, 2006)?

Outsourcing brings online retailers several benefits. By contracting out OFCs or deliveries, retailers may be able to obtain cost savings not attainable internally. This is especially important for pure players as they can avoid a very significant initial fixed cost and concentrate on marketing (Xing *et al*, 2011). However, as suggested by Rabinovich and Bailey (2004), outsourcing may also impose new expenses such as monitoring and controlling the level of third-party service to consumers. Problems may occur and the integration between retailers and 3PLs is not always as smooth as expected, while control over outsourced activities can prove to be crucial. Retailers need to weigh both the benefits and risks carefully when they choose LSPs.

The findings from research interviews with retailers, 3PLs and other experts indicate that multi-channel retailers are considered to still be learning what customer service needs and delivery standards are in this environment (Xing *et al*, 2011). Pure players already understand such needs and standards as they comprise the core competitive criteria for them; if a pure-play retailer doesn't understand them, consumers will not return. The interviewees also considered pure-play retailers to have superior information technology and software systems that enable them to better advise consumers regarding product availability and the delivery process. However, respondents also considered delivery standards provided by both 3PLs and other fulfilment specialists such as parcel carriers are still lacking and would benefit from being tightened up and providing more options to consumers. Interviewees considered that consumer dissatisfaction with product condition and returns boiled down to retailers needing to provide better packaging – able to withstand more than the outbound trip – and a better collection and return process. Finally, the need to provide good service at the right cost emerged from the interviews and must be considered in all improvement decisions.

To address these shortcomings retailers, 3PLs and others in the fulfilment process should undertake collaborative operations and marketing to better serve consumers, reduce costs and become more profitable. Retailers, 3PLs and others, and consumers are the main stakeholders in the online retail process and all need to communicate more and look for mutual understanding and solutions. Inefficiency of home delivery stems mainly from the interfaces of these concerned stakeholders and thus a solution focus needs to define responsibility areas and improve communication.

The rapid rise of omnichannel has had an enormous impact on returns management. The sophistication of the front-end buying experience across different platforms has resulted in equally high customer expectation about the returns process. Between 25 to 50 per cent of products sold online are returned, with almost 45 per cent of clothing and footwear products being returned, representing a value of £1.2 billion in 2013 (Clipper Logistics, 2015).

In the retail sector a returned item is handled differently depending on the type and condition of the product, and the relationship between the retailer and the manufacturer/vendor. If the item is in good condition, with no apparent damage, it will often go back to the shelf. However, if the manufacturer desires to keep strict quality control and high standards, the item will not return to the retail shelf until the manufacturer inspects the product. This may be a necessary step for products with high risk of liability, such as fashion clothing (Ruiz-Benitez and Muriel, 2004). The following case study describes how the Boomerang™ returns service offered by Clipper Logistics enables fashion retailers such as ASOS to maintain such control over their online product return flows.

CASE STUDY   Clipper Logistics: A 'boomerang' service for returns

The UK-based and global online fashion retailer ASOS offers over 60,000 branded and own-label product lines across womenswear, menswear, footwear, accessories, jewellery and beauty, with approximately 1,500 new product lines being introduced each week. With 6.5 million active users, ASOS. com is the world's most visited fashion website per day by 18–34 year olds, and ships to customers in 241 countries and territories from its 1.1 million-square-foot (or about 11.8 million square metre) global fulfilment centre in Barnsley,

Yorkshire. ASOS sells clothing in 190 countries worldwide with 64 per cent of sales coming from outside the UK. ASOS' 2014 annual report reported sales of £976 million for the fiscal year ending 31 August and had distribution expenses of £147 million, or 15 per cent of sales.

In 2013 ASOS awarded the management of the Barnsley facility to Norbert Dentressangle, the French-based third-party logistics (3PL) service provider for three years in a logistics deal worth over £100 million, one of Europe's largest. However, ASOS also selected the Yorkshire-based 3PL Clipper Logistics to provide a returns management service that will see Clipper accept and process millions of items of returned clothing every year from ASOS customers across the UK and Europe. After collection at Clipper's central European returns warehouse in Germany, the ASOS returns operation will be carried out at the existing Clipper shared-user site in Selby, Yorkshire, which is a little over 30 miles or about 50 kilometres from Barnsley.

Clipper has developed a sophisticated returns service named Boomerang, which attracted ASOS. Boomerang handles, reprocesses and repackages returns, identifies faults and rectifies them and reworks items. For other clients, Clipper also disposes of items not fit for conventional resale via other portals, such as Genesis-UK, its eBay store dedicated to its retail customers.

The Boomerang process uses original retailer sales data to match the returned goods to the consumer's account, quality-check the product and provide data to the retailer's parent system in real time. This technology provides the retailer with the critical information needed to allow credit processing as well as real-time stock status and visibility information. Boomerang retains and tracks all the pertinent data relating to each individual item right through the process, which allows the retailer to return stock, repair it, warranty return to the manufacturer, or pass items on for secondary channel sale, disposal or recycling. Boomerang can also be quickly configured to match the data interfaces the retailer requires, allowing specific policies and quality standards to be incorporated and managed throughout the process, and allowing retailers to generate bespoke reporting that provides strategic information on their customer.

Besides these process features, Boomerang also provides several logistical and operational benefits for retailers:

1 stock is confirmed as returned once it arrives at the German facility;

2 stock is processed, checked and returned to inventory quickly by systematically sending it to Clipper's UK warehouse for cross-docking and consolidating back to the retailer or supplier;

3 only good stock is returned to UK, reducing the cost of moving damaged stock around;

4 the central returns process leverages Clipper's European infrastructure to reduce lead times and improve customer service; and

5 backhaul consolidation reduces the cost of transportation.

SOURCES Anon. (2013b); ASOS (2015); Clipper Logistics (2015).

Suggestions to improve online fulfilment service

Online shopping is a hugely competitive sector and with the consumer now savvier – and with greater expectations – maintaining a presence in the e-commerce market can be challenging. The foregoing sections have addressed many of the challenges and issues in omnichannel logistical activities for retailers of all kinds, including fashion retailers. The following is a summary of the key points as suggestions for retailers to consider:

- Recognize that convenience and timeliness in all aspects of the ordering and fulfilment process is the driving force behind why people shop online. This means providing a website with clear pointers on browsing, reviewing the basket, making payment and delivery options is an essential first step to address these important needs to prevent 'clickthroughs' to competitors' websites and to build a consumer's confidence and trust in the retailer.

- Provide a range of fulfilment options that the consumer can pick and choose to ensure a flexible and tailored service. While some consumers require delivery in a matter of hours, others are happy to pay a lesser delivery charge if it means waiting a couple of days.

- Develop a strong online operations team and internal planning and organization so the different areas of the business operate smoothly. Systems and processes are central to achieving this, as seen with Zappos.com, from ordering through fulfilment and returns, and should be reviewed on a regular basis to ensure they remain relevant.

- Deliver excellent customer service. Consumers will have queries about a product or service and responding to these queries as quickly as possible will provide differentiation to competitors. This also provides an opportunity to engage with consumers; they recognize and appreciate great customer service and will often praise a positive experience via social media or review websites.

- Maintain a dialogue with the consumer throughout the whole e-commerce process. Consumers don't like to be left in a vacuum and it is important to reduce uncertainty from their perspective by giving them information.

In summary, a great consumer experience is only as good as the weakest link – even those links that the retailer may not be directly responsible for such as the payment gateway, 3PL or parcel carrier. Poor customer service from the lack of 'searchability' on the website through an awkward payment process and inflexible fulfilment options to lack of communication can either discourage a consumer before they make a purchase or mean they don't make another purchase in the future (Lobel, 2014).

Conclusions

The omnichannel environment for online retailing is rapidly growing and has many complexities, particularly for the last mile in the fulfilment process. Consumers are also very discerning with high expectations for great customer service that include prompt and accurate processes. This chapter began with an overview of the online retail phenomenon and next considered issues pertaining to the online supply chain, particularly omnichannel ordering, fulfilment and returns. It finished with a summary of suggestions for retailers to consider to enter the online market or enhance their current online offerings.

References

Anon. (2013a) £53 billion cost of failed deliveries, *Logistics Manager* [online] http://www.logisticsmanager.com/2013/03/20208-53-billion-cost-of-failed -deliveries/ [accessed 25 July 2015]

Anon. (2013b) Norbert Dentressangle wins logistics contract with ASOS, *Logistics & Transport Focus*, **15** (10) p 30

ASOS (2015) Annual report and accounts [online] http://www.asosplc.com/ ~/media/Files/A/ASOS/results-archive/ASOS_Report_2014%20FINAL.pdf [accessed 25 July 2015]

Banker, S and Cooke, J A (2013) Stores: the weak link in omnichannel distribution, *DCVelocity*, August [online] http://www.dcvelocity.com/articles/20130805 -stores-the-weak-link-in-omnichannel-distribution/ [accessed 25 July 2015]

Butler (2014) Network Rail plans 300 pick-up points for online shoppers, *Guardian*, 19 June, p 29

ChainLink Research (2013) Home delivery for retailers: more sales, less cost [online]http://www.ChainLinkResearch.com/ [accessed 25 July 2015]

Clipper Logistics (2015) Boomerang: the future of returns management [online] http://www.clippergroup.co.uk/services/boomerang-the-future-of-returns -management/ [accessed 25 July 2015]

DCLG (2013), The future of high streets: progress since the Portas review, July, *Department for Communities and Local Government* [online] https://www.gov .uk/government/uploads/system/uploads/attachment_data/file/211536/Future _of_High_Street_-_Progress_Since_the_Portas_Review_-revised.pdf [accessed 25 July 2015]

Davies, M (2015) Online: time to focus on cost to serve, *Supply Chain Standard* [online]http://www.supplychainstandard.com/2015/01/online-time-to-focus-on -cost-to-serve/ [accessed 25 July 2015]

Dickinson, H (2014) Retail can drive UK economy forward, *Raconteur Future of Retail*, supplement in *The Times*, 24 June, p 15

Dunn, C (2013) Delivery the key to growth of online retail, *Guardian*, 18 April, p 28

eMarketer (2014) Retail sales will top $22 trillion this year [online] *http://www .emarketer.com/Article/Retail-Sales-Worldwide-Will-Top-22-Trillion-This -Year/1011765* [accessed 25 July 2015]

Esper, T L, Jensen, T D, Turnipseed, F L and Burton, S (2003) The last mile: an examination of effects of online retail delivery strategies on consumers, *Journal of Business Logistics*, **24** (2), pp 177–203

EY-TCGF (2015) Re-engineering the supply chain for the omni-channel of tomorrow [online] http://www.ey.com/Publication/vwLUAssets/EY-re-engineering-the -supply-chain-for-the-omni-channel-of-tomorrow/$FILE/EY-re-engineering-the -supply-chain-for-the-omni-channel-of-tomorrow.pdf [accessed 25 July 2015]

Fernie, J, Fernie, S and McKinnon, A C (2014) The development of e-tail logistics, in J Fernie and L Sparks (eds) *Logistics and Retail Management: Emerging issues and challenges in the retail supply chain* (4th edn) Kogan Page, London, pp 205–35

Fernie, J, Sparks, L and McKinnon, A C (2010) Retail logistics in the UK: past, present and future, *International Journal of Retail & Distribution Management*, **38** (11/12), pp 894–914

Grant, D B, Kotzab, H and Xing, Y (2006) Success@tesco.com: Erfolg im online-lebensmittelhandel oder 'wie macht das der Tesco?' in P Schnedlitz, R Buber, T Reutterer, A Schuh and C Teller (eds), *Innovationen in Marketing und Handel,* Linde, Vienna pp 203–13

Grant, D B (2012) *Logistics Management*, Pearson Education Limited, Harlow

Grimsey, B (2013) The Grimsey Review, *Vanishing High Street* [online] http://www
.vanishinghighstreet.com/wp-content/uploads/2013/09/GrimseyReview04.092
.pdf [accessed 25 July 2015]

Hamilton, A (2014) Online fulfilment: what millennial shoppers want, use and
value, *Retail Week Reports*, December

Hewitson, J and Bridge, M (2015) Why the courier business may not deliver the
goods, *The Times*, 4 July, p 62

Hickey, S (2015) Click all the right boxes or online shopping collections, *Guardian*,
20 June, p 49

Hoyt, D, Lee, H and Marks, M (2009) Zappos.com: developing a supply chain to
deliver wow! Stanford Graduate School of Business Case GS-65 [online] https://
www.gsb.stanford.edu/faculty-research/case-studies/zapposcom-developing
-supply-chain-deliver-wow [accessed 25 July 2015]

Kämäräinen, V and Punakivi, M (2002) Developing cost-effective operations for
the e-grocery supply chain, *International Journal of Logistics: Research and
Applications*, **5** (3), pp 286–98

Leroux, M (2014) Trials and tribulations of real and virtual worlds, *Raconteur
Future of Retail*, supplement in *The Times*, 24 June, pp 12–13

Lobel, B (2014) Shipping and logistics: how best to create an outstanding e-commerce
experience for customers, *Small Business* [online] http://www.smallbusiness.co.uk/
how-to-hub/2462692/shipping-and-logistics-how-best-to-create-an-outstanding
-ecommerce-experience-for-customers.thtml [accessed 25 July 2015]

McCarthy, C (2009) Amazon to snap up Zappos, *cnet* [online] http://www.cnet
.com/news/amazon-to-snap-up-zappos/ [accessed 25 July 2015]

McClelland, J (2014) Revolution with fries and a shake, *Raconteur Future of
Retail*, supplement in *The Times*, 24 June, pp 8–9

McKinnon, A C and Edwards, J (2014) The greening of retail logistics, in J Fernie
and L Sparks (eds), *Logistics and Retail Management: Emerging issues and
challenges in the retail supply chain* (4th edn) Kogan Page, London, pp 237–56

McKinnon, A C and Tallam, D (2003) Unattended delivery to the home: an
assessment of the security implications, *International Journal of Retail &
Distribution Management*, **31** (1), pp 30–41

Mesure, S (2013) The high street of the future is like nothing we know,
Independent on Sunday, 1 September, pp 10–11

Pagano, M (2013) Look to the past for high street's future, *Independent on Sunday*,
23 June, p 74

Parasuraman, A, Zeithaml V A and Berry, L L (1985) A concept model of service
quality and its implications for future research, *Journal of Marketing*, **49** Fall,
pp 41–50

Prensky, M (2001a) Digital natives, digital immigrants part 1, *On the Horizon*, **9**
(5), pp 1–6

Prensky, M (2001b) Digital natives, digital immigrants part 2: do they really think
differently? *On the Horizon*, **9** (6), pp 1–6

Punakivi, M and Tanskanen, K (2002) Increasing the cost efficiency of e-fulfilment using shared reception boxes, *International Journal of Retail & Distribution Management*, **30** (10), pp 498–507

Rabinovich, E and Bailey, J P (2004) Physical distribution service quality in Internet retailing: service pricing, transaction attributes, and firm attributes, *Journal of Operations Management*, **21**, pp 651–72

Rigby, D (2011) The future of shopping, *Harvard Business Review*, **89** (12), pp 65–76

Ruiz-Benitez, R and Muriel, A (2004) Consumer returns in a decentralized supply chain, *International Journal of Production Economics*, **147**, pp 573–92

Sharma, R (2014) Physical stores won't go away, but they must change to keep customers, *Wall Street Journal Europe*, 28–30 November, p 11

Smith, E (2014) Shopping on the move with mobiles and tablets, *Raconteur Future of Retail*, supplement in *The Times*, 24 June, p 10

Statista (2015a) Commerce websites ranked by visitors in the UK in May 2014 [online] http://www.statista.com/statistics/286489/uk-visitors-to-mass -merchandiser-websites/ [accessed 25 July 2015]

Statista (2015b) Percentage of households with internet access worldwide in 2015, by region [online] http://www.statista.com/statistics/249830/households-with -internet-access-worldwide-by-region/ [accessed 25 July 2015]

Teller, C, Kotzab, H and Grant, D B (2006) The consumer direct services revolution in food retailing: an exploratory investigation, *Managing Service Quality*, **16** [1], pp 78–96

Teller, C, Kotzab, H and Grant, D B (2012) The relevance of shopper logistics for consumers of store-based retail formats, *Journal of Retailing and Consumer Services*, **19**, pp 59–66

The Logistics Business (2015) Shedding light on the dark store [online] http://www .logistics.co.uk/Shedding-Light-On-The-Dark-Store [accessed 25 July 2015]

Whittaker, N (2008) Fast fulfilment, *Supply Chain Standard*, **16** (2), pp 24–26

Wolk, A and Skiera, B (2009) Antecedents and consequences of Internet channel performance, *Journal of Retailing and Consumer Services*, **16**, pp 163–73

Wood, Z (2012) Supermarket dark stores where pickers and packers lighten the load for shoppers, *Guardian*, 1 December, p 43

Xing, Y and Grant, D B (2006) Developing a framework for measuring physical distribution service quality of multi-channel and pure player Internet retailers, *International Journal of Retail & Distribution Management*, **34** (4/5), pp 278–89

Xing, Y, Grant, D B, McKinnon, A C and Fernie, J (2010) Physical distribution service quality in online retailing, *International Journal of Physical Distribution & Logistics Management*, **40** (5), pp 415–32

Xing, Y, Grant, D B, McKinnon, A C and Fernie, J (2011) The interface between retailers and logistics service providers in the online market, *European Journal of Marketing*, **45** (3), pp 334–57

Zappos.com (2015) http://www.zappos.com/

Luxury fashion and supply chain management

08

Introduction

This chapter is different from the other chapters of the book because it focuses upon one sector – the luxury fashion goods sector. Why? As explained in Chapter 2, it has been one of the fastest growth sectors in the fashion industry even during the economic recession of the late 2000s/early 2010s. However there is considerable debate about what a luxury fashion brand is, how it has achieved global recognition and at what cost to its original *raison d'être*. Marie-Claude Sicard, a Parisian professor, wrote a controversial book, *Luxury Lies and Marketing*, published in 2013. As the title implies this is a critique of modern luxury branding, especially French brands with their distortion of history and arrogance at marketing, and notably the Court Society heritage which underpins the basis of their marketing.

The growth of luxury companies to becoming some of the world's largest and most valued brands is a relatively recent phenomenon and has been driven by the development of new products and markets. In the Interbrand 2014 list of the world's most valuable brands, nine appeared in the top 100 brands; they were Louis Vuitton (19), Gucci, (41), Hermès, (46), Cartier, (58), Prada, (70), Tiffany & Co, (71), Burberry, (73), Ralph Lauren, (83) and Hugo Boss (97). The BRIC (Brazil, Russia, India and China) markets have been the main catalyst for growth of these brands in the 21st century as more millionaires enter the market for luxury goods. And these millionaires tend to be younger than their European and US counterparts. A whole new generation (of mainly Asian) consumers also desire accessible luxury and spend a higher proportion of their incomes on such items than their western contemporaries.

This growth has changed the way that luxury companies view their supply chains. Expansion into new products and markets has resulted in the development of new relationships with suppliers and a major shift from the domestically produced hand-crafted items that were targeted at a very rich but narrow customer base, to a wider and global audience. To compete, luxury companies have embraced similar supply chain principles as their fast-fashion counterparts. Thus offshore sourcing and a shift to full-package suppliers to produce their diffusion lines has become established practice.

This chapter will first of all define what luxury and luxury branding entails. The growth and evolution of luxury brands will then be discussed prior to detailing the supply chain implications of such growth as indicated above. The sector will be viewed within the context of SCM principles outlined in Chapters 2, 3 and 4. The phenomenal success of the British brand, Burberry, will be the focus of a case study and examples of French and Italian luxury brands will also be used to highlight trends in the sector.

Definitions of luxury and luxury branding

The concept of luxury has its roots in the early Greek and Roman civilizations with most researchers attributing the term 'luxury' as deriving from the Latin *Luxus* which means 'soft or extravagant living, sumptuous, opulence' (Dubois *et al*, 2005; Brun and Castelli, 2013). Subsequently the term was associated with *Lux,* the Latin for light, and tended to be associated with the massive wealth of royalty and the Church. It was this Court Society that shaped lavish living and used fashion to establish class structures of the time. It was Louis XIV's minister, Colbert, however, who had the vision to see the export potential of luxury goods, something that was to become a reality during the Industrial Revolution as quality products could be manufactured in greater volumes for markets seeking 'Made in Country of Origin (COO)' branded goods.

The current industry of luxury goods, therefore, has its origins in 19th-century Europe and remained essentially a niche business until the trend of 'massification' and the democratization of luxury with globalization and product range extensions towards accessible luxury items (Brun and Castelli, 2013). The concept of luxury is complex and has been debated extensively in literature (see Fionda-Douglas, 2012; Brun and Castelli, 2013). Similar problems ensue when trying to reach agreement on a definition of a luxury brand, so whereas the luxury guru Kapferer (with Bastien, 2009b) claims that the traditional principles of marketing have to be abandoned with luxury marketing, Sicard (2013) states that this is nonsense and notes that many of these brands have bought in people from Procter & Gamble and other FMCG groups to sharpen up their approach to marketing.

Luxury can be conceptualized from either a consumer perspective (Gutsatz, 1996; Dubois *et al*, 2001; Vickers and Renand, 2003; Vigneron and Johnson, 1999, 2004) or from a product/brand point of view (Alleres, 2003; Jackson, 2001; Nueno and Quelch, 1998). With reference to a consumer perspective, luxury is defined in terms of its symbolic function for status, its psychological values (symbolic and hedonic) and the consumption experience that reflects the person's self-concept and satisfies his/her need for self-expression and the increase of esteem (Vigneron and Johnson, 1999, 2004). In this context, Dubois and Duquesne (1993) argued that luxury goods are purchased for what they symbolize, thereby expressing the consumer's values. From the product/brand perspective, luxury brands are defined in terms of the nature and characteristics of the concept of luxury. Numerous concepts have been developed, each of them proposing only slightly different characteristics. Among those aspects that were identified by several authors are a strong brand identity (Alleres, 2003; Okonkwo, 2009; Phau and Prendergast, 2000), high quality (Dubois *et al*, 2001; Okonkwo, 2009; Phau and Prendergast, 2000), high price (Dubois *et al*, 2001; Hagtvedt and Patrick, 2009; Moore and Birtwistle, 2005), heritage (Alleres, 2003; Beverland, 2004; Moore and Birtwistle, 2005), rarity (Berthon *et al*, 2009; Dubois and Paternault, 1995; Nueno and Quelch, 1998), craftsmanship (Dubois *et al*, 2001; Kapferer, 2012; Nueno and Quelch, 1998) and controlled distribution (Keller, 2009; Moore and Birtwistle, 2005; Okonkwo, 2009).

Several authors have attempted to bring together these different aspects to identify key dimensions of a luxury brand or critical success factors (CSFs) of luxury. Brun and Castelli (2013) identify the following factors:

a) consistently delivering premium quality in all products in the line and across the whole supply chain;

b) a heritage of craftsmanship ensuring the manufacture of high-quality objects;

c) exclusivity through scarcity production and selective distribution;

d) a marketing approach that provides an enhanced customer shopping experience;

e) a global brand reputation;

f) a recognizable style and design;

g) an association with a country of origin;

h) establishing uniqueness;

i) superior technical performance through product innovation;

j) creation of a lifestyle that consumers can share.

Fionda and Moore (2009) in their study of luxury fashion brands in the UK found nine interrelated attributes crucial to the creation of a luxury fashion brand. These were:

1 clear brand identity;

2 marketing communications;

3 product integrity;

4 brand signature;

5 premium price;

6 exclusivity;

7 heritage;

8 luxury environment and experience; and

9 culture.

Even though the framework was created for luxury fashion brands, the authors emphasize that the proposed model is also applicable to generic luxury brands. The differences stem from specific characteristics that only fashion brands place an emphasis on, namely the development of innovative and new products every season, a renowned fashion designer working as the creative director, flagship stores and fashion shows held in the fashion metropolises of New York, Milan, Paris and London (Fionda and Moore, 2009). Figure 8.1 shows the framework.

The 'new' luxury

Brun and Castelli (2013) identify this as the modern oxymoron of accessible luxury. No longer are goods necessarily rare or exclusive to be classified as luxury, especially as fashion brands extend into newer segments with wider distribution networks. In the past, elite culture, distinction and class differentiation formed the basis of the rules of luxury brand management (Kapferer, 2012). Now luxury is no longer the preserve of the elite but is available to households who previously would consider luxury brands out of their reach (Silverstein and Fiske, 2003a). The luxury market has been described as becoming a mass market, (Yeoman and McMahon-Beattie, 2006) leading to

FIGURE 8.1 Dimensions of a luxury fashion brand

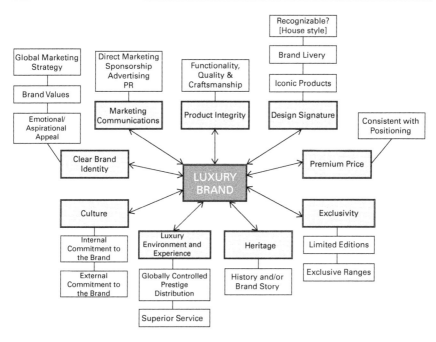

SOURCE After Fionda and Moore (2009)

'the democratization of luxury' (Kapferer and Bastien, 2009a). As indicated earlier, much of this demand is fuelled by the wealth created in the newer emerging markets where foreign luxury brands are seen as an indulgence in relation to their lifestyle constructs (Kapferer, 2012).

The new luxury has led authors to classify this sector (Silverstein and Fiske, 2003b) thereby re-classifying luxury brands. For example Brun and Castelli (2013) quote the threefold classification produced by D'Arpizio (2007). It is as follows:

1 Absolute luxury brands characterized by elitism, heritage and uniqueness; example is Hermès.

2 Aspirational luxury brands that achieve their status by being recognizable and distinctive; examples are Gucci and Louis Vuitton.

3 Accessible luxury brands that are characterized by affordability, status and membership; examples are Coach and Burberry.

We will now turn our attention to how brands such as those identified above have achieved such prominence in the global market.

The evolution of the luxury brand

It has been alluded to in earlier sections that the luxury brand was an elitist, made-to-order product for a very niche, rich audience throughout much of its history. These brands, however, were already global by the 1960s and Stan Hollander, in his seminal work *Multinational Retailing* (1970) coined the phrase 'London, New York, Paris syndrome' to indicate the presence of these brands and the fashion shows of the time in these capital cities. This narrow focus began to change as fashion designers replicated their one-off designs as ready-to-wear collections with distribution in up-market department stores. It is interesting to note that early penetration into the Chinese market occurred in five-star luxury hotels because of the dearth of appropriate department stores to display stock.

The growth and spread of the luxury brand since the 1990s can be attributed to a range of factors but the main ones were:

- the shift to accessories and new product lines;
- distribution to a wider customer base;
- the geographical expansion of the main companies;
- access to capital.

By the 1990s many family-owned firms, especially those based in the United States (Ralph Lauren, Donna Karen and Tommy Hilfiger) became public listed companies in order to have access to external capital to expand their business (Moore *et al*, 2000). In Europe considerable consolidation has taken place since the 1990s. The market is now dominated by three major conglomerates, two of which are based in France. They are LVMH, Kering (formerly PPR) and Richemont, based in Switzerland. The latter group has a strong portfolio of jewellery brands, Kering is more focused upon fashion brands and LVMH has a strong portfolio of luxury wines and spirits in addition to its famous luxury fashion brands. Moore and Birtwistle (2005) discuss the advantages of being part of a large conglomerate in that small niche brands or those that require rejuvenation can benefit from capital investment and central group synergies in marketing, product development and intra-group supplies of product. The authors consider these synergies as 'parenting advantage' and used Gucci as a case study along with brands in the group such as Yves Saint Laurent (now Saint Laurent, Paris).

The pyramid brand model tends to be the one espoused by European brands to explain the 'new luxury' since the 1990s (see Figure 8.2 and the Burberry case study). These brands lead with their main fashion shows or

FIGURE 8.2 The Pyramid Brand Model

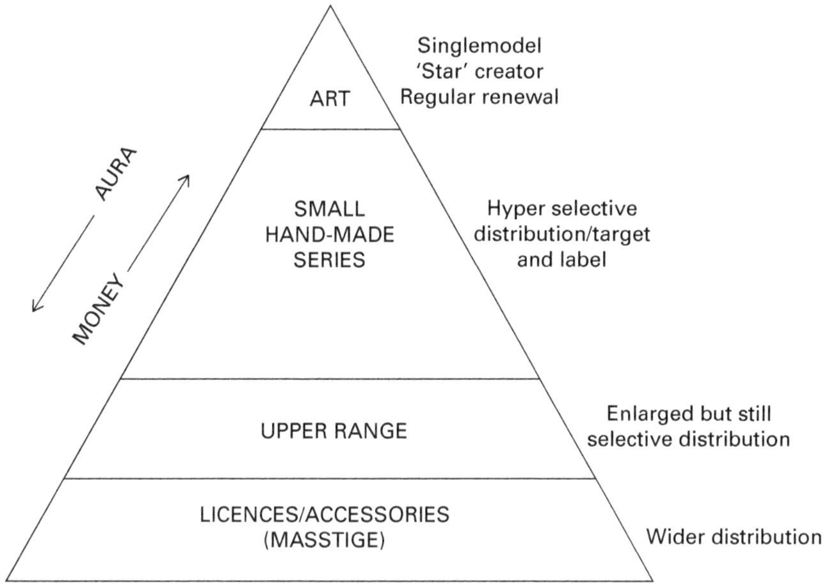

SOURCE Kapferer and Bastien (2009a)

expensive creations that are likely to be seen at the Oscar film awards early in the year. These couture lines are the focus for the whole collection (small hand-made series in Figure 8.2). They are hand-made to order and are produced in limited quantities with exclusive distribution. The ready-to-wear (RTW) lines are 'off-the-peg' creations, expensive and distributed through upscale department stores and flagship stores (upper range in Figure 8.2). Finally the diffusion lines/accessories are branded to the middle market and tend to be mass-produced for widespread distribution. Each market is segmented to allow trading up (or down) and is branded with the company name and a brand extension. So Giorgio Armani has Giorgio Armani Couture, Giorgio Armani – Le Collezione and Emporio Armani to reflect each price point and distribution channel (Moore *et al*, 2000).

Sicard (2013) argues that the pyramid model is a distinctive French creation with the creator at the top of the pyramid down to products that have no real association with the brand at the bottom. However, the price points remain high. By contrast she argues that the new luxury brands from the United States and to some extent Italy (dismissed by the French as not luxury brands) have more care and attention devoted to them across all product categories rather than only part of the portfolio. She argues that this is the galaxy model, which is a flatter, less hierarchical model comprising a number of orbiting planets. The value of the brand is the same wherever it finds expression and therefore there is a narrowing of price points between couture and prêt à porter. She compares Donna Karan and Saint Laurent to show the much wider price points of the French luxury house compared to its US counterpart.

Fernie (2012) used an Ansoff grid to explain the evolution of luxury fashion brands (see Figure 8.3). Currently most of the main Italian and French brands (and Burberry) are increasing their market penetration in China and moving into Tier 2 and 3 cities as the main coastal Tier 1 cities reach market saturation. The fact that China has become the market with most potential in the 21st century with growth rates of 20–35 per cent per annum until the 2010s shows how market development has evolved. The main European fashion houses targeted the United States in the 1960s and 1970s, Japan in the 1980s/1990s and now China. Other new market developments have occurred in the last decade, however, with the rise of online and off-price channels that account for around 8 per cent of sales in total. All major luxury brands have moved into new products and services, building upon their brand reputation for craftsmanship and heritage of their traditional core product – for example Louis Vuitton handbags and the Burberry trench coat. Armani has the most extensive product range of all the luxury brands

FIGURE 8.3 Alternative directions of growth for the luxury fashion brand

| | Product | |
	Present	New
Present	**Market penetration** Concentrate investment in specific markets	**Product development** Extend merchandise range
New	**Market development** International and online expansion	**Diversification** • related • unrelated Move into hotels

(Market axis on left; Product axis on top)

SOURCE Fernie (2012)

and is one of five Italian fashion brands that have diversified into hotels. Even then it can be argued that Versace, Armani and Missoni have engaged in new product development in that their Casa collections are represented in their hotels. Nevertheless nearly all of these fashion companies have entered into joint ventures or licensing agreements with international hotel chains or property development companies to develop this business. The locations of these hotels mirror Hollander's 'fashion capitals' of internationalization, adding Tokyo and Shanghai to the original fashion show sites.

Gaining control of marketing channels

A critical success factor for luxury fashion companies is the ability to control the manufacture and distribution of their products. Burberry (see case study) and Gucci (Moore and Birtwistle, 2005; Tokatli, 2012) are the luxury brands most quoted as having lost their way because of their loss of control of manufacturing and retail distribution through a flawed licensing and franchising strategy. Indeed, Moore and Birtwistle, (2005) noted that the third generation of the Gucci family spent most of their time feuding and selling the right of the Gucci name, so that by 1979 the Gucci Accessories Collection comprised more than 20,000 product lines. Domenico De Sole and Tom Ford were brought in as CEO and Creative Director respectively in 1995 and began the turnaround in repositioning the Gucci brand. Gucci then terminated or bought back 100 licenses, reducing the number of lines to 7,000. International expansion had been realized through franchising agreements but from 1996 Gucci began a buy-back strategy to take over control through direct store openings.

This strategy was later replicated by Burberry. With Rose Marie Bravo as CEO and Christopher Bailey as creative director, the repositioned brand was targeted at company-owned stores, distribution rights were bought back in specific markets and stockists that did not fit in with the luxury brand image were delisted (see case study). Other smaller British companies have tried to rejuvenate iconic but tired British brands albeit with less success. For example the former Marks & Spencer executive Kim Winser repositioned the Scottish luxury brand Pringle to move it away from a golf sweater brand found in scattered outlets and bring it back to being a desirable upscale brand with selective distribution. She then moved to Aquascutum, another brand with associations with the military and trench coats. But after she failed in a management buy-out the company has struggled, going into administration in 2012 before being bought by its Asian licensee.

CASE STUDY Burberry

*Founded in 1856, Burberry today remains quintessentially British,
with outerwear at its core. Digital luxury positioning and the
optimization across innovative mediums of the trench coat, trademark
check and Equestrian Knight Device heritage icons, make the brand
purer, more compelling and more relevant globally, across genders and
generations. (Burberry Annual Report, 2013/14 p 15.)*

Burberry is a British retailing success story. In 2000 when the company was
implementing its re-positioning strategy it had sales of £226 million and profits
of £18.5 million; by 2014 it had sales of £2.33 billion and profits of £461 million.
There has also been a diversification of product offering in that in 2000,
33 per cent of revenues came from womenswear, 30 per cent from menswear
and 25 per cent from accessories. By 2014, accessories accounted for
36 per cent of sales, womenswear 30 per cent, menswear 23 per cent, beauty
7 per cent and children's wear 4 per cent.

The catalyst for this impressive growth goes back to 1997 and the
appointment of Rose Marie Bravo, the CEO, who radically re-aligned the
company's business model. At that time, profits were falling, mainly because of
the decline in the Japanese economy, a major market for the company. Of more
concern was the decline of the iconic brand whose image was tarnished partly
through a host of indiscriminate licensing and distribution agreements that had
accrued during the company's international expansion. The new management
team sought to reposition the Burberry brand as a distinctive luxury brand with
a clear design, sourcing, marketing and distribution strategy. The new approach
to brand management began in the late 1990s/early 2000s with a new logo, name
(dropping the 's' to become Burberry), and the use of supermodels to portray the
young, new all-British ethos of the brand. (Moore and Birtwistle, 2004).

The new design director (and now CEO) was Christopher Bailey who had
gained experience from another iconic brand (Gucci) that had repositioned its
offering in the market place in the 1990s. Bailey launched the Prorsum collection
and provided creative direction to the Burberry London range. The diffusion
offering and accessories range gave Burberry the chance to gain leverage of the
brand to different segments of the market (see Figure 8.2). The pyramid model is
still utilized today and in Burberry's 2013/14 report it noted that Burberry Prorsum
accounted for 5 per cent of sales, Burberry London 45 per cent and Burberry
Brit 50 per cent. Moore and Birtwistle (2004) used the pyramid model to explain
the growth of Burberry. However, it should be noted that the Thomas Burberry

line was discontinued in 2010. The Blue and Black labels were targeted for the Japanese market and sold by Sanyo Shokai, their Japanese licensee, but this licence was allowed to expire in June 2015 as Burberry focused on a company-owned store network. Now the diffusion lines are mainly branded as Burberry Brit. When Angela Ahrendts became CEO in 2006 she continued the work of her US predecessor by eliminating excessive brand extensions to focus on core product offerings leading with the Prorsum fashion shows and re-focusing all design, especially for outerwear, in London.

One of the key issues for Burberry at the time of repositioning was the loss of control over licensing and distribution of the brand. Burberry began a process that has continued to the present time (see the Sanyo Shokai example noted above) of buying back distribution rights and reviewing licensing agreements. Burberry, like most major luxury brands, seeks to have greater control over its distribution channels and hence the shift to company-owned stores between 2005 and 2015. In the 2013/14 annual report, Burberry Group Chairman Sir John Peace commented on investment in flagship markets, noting that 25 cities account for the majority of retail sales. The flagship store has been a major market entry strategy for luxury brands, especially in emerging markets such as China (Moore *et al*, 2010).

Burberry's success can be attributed to the returning to its roots with the emphasis on the trench coat. It was Thomas Burberry who initially sold outerwear in 1856 but the company then developed a waterproof fabric 'gabardine' which was suited for military needs. The 'trench' coat was lined with the iconic Burberry check and became popular with explorers and subsequently film stars. The trench coat, and the Prorsum range of the 2000s became the focus of the British heritage brand storytelling. By 2009 Burberry had embraced social media using its Art of the Trench site to help build a community of followers and by 2014 the site had recorded 24 million page views from over 200 countries. Burberry uses all elements of digital marketing from iPads in shops to runway shows online. The company partners with other high-tech brands such as Apple and Google to share product marketing in social media. It is the most followed luxury brand on Facebook with 17 million fans, its Twitter following is 3 million and Instagram around 1.4 million (Annual Report, 2013/14). Although the company discusses the integration of digital and traditional sales platforms, it does not disaggregate its online sales from overall retail sales in its reporting of results. It is clear from the evidence available that many of the sales are click and collect with the possible exception of the US market where online growth is strongest. Burberry also comments that all inventory for off and online will be pooled in China so that customers can access stock from stores or distribution centres.

Ahrendts left the company in 2014, with Bailey succeeding her. In her time as CEO Ahrendts not only focused upon creating a global brand image, she also reconfigured the supply chain. Under Bravo most of the core lines were manufactured in England, the United States and Italy with the diffusion lines sourced from offshore markets in low-cost locations or under licence as was the case in Japan. By 2005, however, Stacey Cartwright, the new chief financial officer, had undertaken an overhaul of IT systems and began to reduce inefficiencies in the Burberry supply chain. As Burberry centrally handled the purchase of fabric for quality control reasons, the raw material then had to be distributed to the factories. In Wales it was decided to close the factory that produced polo shirts and move production to China. This caused quite an adverse media reaction primarily because Burberry had been repositioning itself as quintessentially British.

To be fair to Ahrendts she closed down the US factory and others in Europe that were making outerwear to concentrate production in Castleford in Yorkshire to re-emphasize the 'Made in Britain' credentials of their core product and to review the sourcing of other product lines. In 2006 Burberry recruited Andy Janowski from Gap to be the vice president responsible for sourcing and his management team began to review the procurement model. Burberry had been responsible for fabric procurement as mentioned earlier and suppliers in Europe were therefore applying the cut, make and trim model. By abandoning this approach and building relationships with full-package manufacturers Burberry empowered suppliers to procure raw materials under its specifications and also 'eliminate the need for the retailer to spend money on procurement or worry about late deliveries' (Tokatli, 2012, p 69). The net result of these changes was that 15 per cent of all Burberry products (primarily the trench coat) were made in the UK with the remainder being sourced from full-package manufacturers in Italy, Turkey, Eastern Europe, North Africa and China.

In its annual reports, Burberry has a section, Burberry Beyond, which deals with how it implements CSR. Burberry does tend to perform well in relation to its peers on CSR issues although it is rather vague on the outcomes of audits, only reporting the number of audits, supplier visits and hotline training visits. This hotline allows workers to cite grievances if a supplier abuses the ethical code of conduct espoused in their ethical trading policy. Burberry stresses that most of its products are made in Europe, mainly Italy and it did terminate its relationship with a Chinese supplier of handbags in 2012 because the workforce worked excessive hours, thereby breaching the company's code of conduct. On other CSR issues Burberry does report its efforts on how it is reducing CO_2 across the supply chain and monitors progress on its 2012–17 targets. It also records volunteering hours and community donations.

The examples we have discussed concern the repositioning of iconic luxury brands that had lost their image through a flawed distribution/licensing strategy. It should be noted, however, that some of the classical French brands have tended to retain control over the manufacture of their products and their distribution to the market. Both Louis Vuitton and Hermès manufacture primarily in workshops in France, stressing the craftsmanship and quality of their products. They also maintain strong control over distribution through their own company stores.

Supply chain management in luxury fashion

With the growth of luxury brands through internationalization and product extensions, the supply chain has become more complex, offering challenges for management. Brun and Castelli (2014) have identified these challenges in Table 8.1 in relation to recent trends in the luxury business.

TABLE 8.1   The supply chain management challenges facing the luxury business

Recent trends in the luxury business	SCM challenges
Success in recent years was based on building brand image and on extending product range: • Loss of 'material' competitive advantages • Risk of diluting brand exclusivity into accessible lines	Back to basics – market orientation, product quality, service level, mastering core competences – to regain the ability to deliver the promises made by the brand
Consumers are now more literate as regards quality in product/ services and accept they will pay a premium price when their requirements are satisfied	Guaranteeing adequate quality even though (part of) the production process is outsourced
Fashion effect: product life cycle is every day shorter	Flexible and responsive supply chains

(Continued)

TABLE 8.1 (*Continued*)

Recent trends in the luxury business	SCM challenges
Rising attention to operations and SCM, with a number of companies currently restructuring their supply chains (Prada, Bulgari, Versace, Ferragamo...)	SCM is now one of the top priorities in management's agenda, operations are more stressed
The soaring of scale and bargaining power of major retail buyers in the market, the advent of own brands' retail networks, globalization of the luxury consumers	Attention to distribution and retail
Wide use of outsourcing of manufacturing processes, off-shoring of manufacturing activities and sourcing on a global scale	Need to control and coordinate a large and geographically scattered network of actors
New and aggressive players are now entering the market	Need to create a sustainable competitive advantage, leveraging the capability of all the 'partners' within the supply network
Different requirements depending on the type of luxury (eg accessible lines require availability, exclusive segments require superior service)	Need to develop a differentiated approach

This table summarizes much of our discussion on the increasing scale and complexity of luxury companies' portfolios. It also notes the shift to offshore sourcing and outsourcing in order to compete in global markets. The degree to which companies have outsourced and offshore sourced is largely dependent upon the extent of product proliferation and the development of diffusion brands. So Burberry has a high degree of diffusion as identified in its pyramid model compared with a company such as Hermès. Brun and Castelli (2014) have tried to classify the luxury business into typologies of supply chain models. This approach builds upon the work of Fisher (1997) discussed in the Lean, Agile, Leagile section of Chapter 3. This means Louis Vuitton handbags that can only be produced in small quantities require a different approach to the more mass-production requirements of a Burberry polo shirt.

Earlier work by Brun and Castelli (2008) can be used to highlight this approach. Using the example of Fratelli Rossetti, a luxury shoe manufacturer, they show how it continues to have a vertically integrated supply chain for its core heritage product (men's shoes) but has outsourced production of other elements of its developing portfolio. However, unlike some luxury clothing brands that have offshore outsourcing, when Fratelli Rossetti extended the brand into women's shoes, it decided to outsource to manufacturers in the same Italian industrial district. This allowed the company to control the design, material selection and distribution but outsource the manufacturing phases thereby retaining the 'Made in Italy' label. When the company further expanded into a sports diffusion brand (Flexa), country of origin was of less concern so these shoes were designed in Italy but manufactured in Romania. As with other fashion companies, Fratelli Rossetti designs and distributes leather accessories with production outsourced to specialist companies. Figure 8.4 illustrates the supply chain configuration of Fratelli Rossetti and also shows the retail channels through which the company's products are sold. It is worth noting that the DOS (direct operated stores) mono-brand outlets are company owned and staff are trained to communicate the brand image by selling the full product range.

FIGURE 8.4 Supply Chain Configuration of Fratelli Rossetti

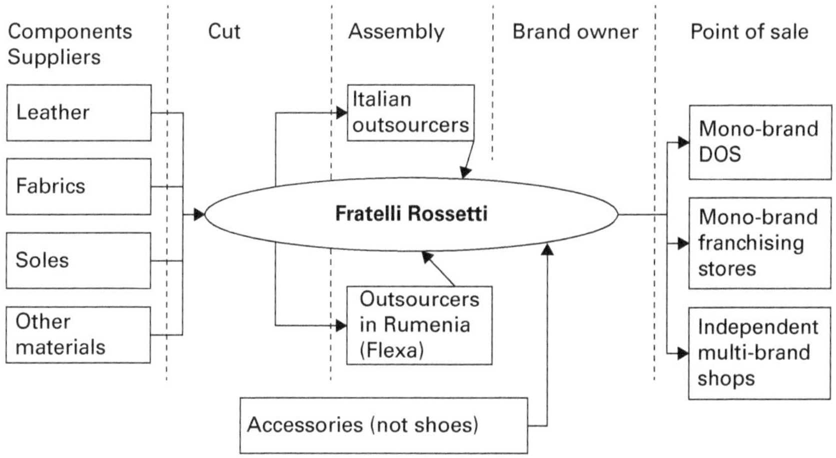

SOURCE Brun and Castelli (2014)

CSR and luxury fashion brands

One of the most controversial issues in relation to the supply chain strategies of luxury companies has been their attitude to CSR. The root of this concern goes back to two reports published in 2007 and 2011 that strongly criticized the luxury sector's record on CSR and accused it of lagging behind other sectors of the fashion industry. To some extent we touched upon these issues in Chapters 2 and 4. For example, in our discussion on slow fashion in Chapter 2, the link to heritage craftsmanship implied that luxury companies would be in the vanguard of this movement. However, the best examples offered were of fast-fashion retailers, notably H&M (see Figure 2.1). In Chapter 4, which focused upon CSR, the best practice examples again tended to be fast fashion or outdoor clothing specialists.

A report by Bendell and Kleanthous (2007) for the World Wildlife Fund (WWF) UK ranked the 10 largest publicly traded companies on a range of environmental, social and governance performance indicators, with most companies scoring no better than C+ (L'Oréal, Hermès, LVMH) and Tods shoes scoring an F. In the 2011 report by Moore on behalf of the Ethical Consumer Research Association, 15 companies were ranked according to ethical criteria incorporating animal rights, human rights, social and environmental performance. Once again the rankings exhibited low scores with Calvin Klein and Tommy Hilfiger coming out best with 7.5 out of 20 compared with Louis Vuitton, Kenzo and others at 3.5.

The problem with these reports is the value judgements that they make during a time of economic recession. The tone of the reports suggests an inherent bias against the rich and the management of luxury companies at a time of increasing global inequality. And of course some of the raw materials in the luxury products (furs, leather, diamonds and gold) trigger hostility from animal rights and human rights campaigners. The Moore (2011) report also berates the companies for not completing their questionnaire. Our case study company Burberry only declined when it found that it was the only company willing to participate. Luxury companies are well known for being coy with external communications. Secrecy in terms of new products has always been a part of the mystique of the brand.

Kapferer (2010) has discussed the challenges of sustainable luxury in the wake of criticism from the initial Bendell and Kleanthous 2007 report. He notes that some companies such as L'Oréal do not pursue a luxury strategy in that their main distribution outlets are mass-market supermarkets. As we discussed in Chapter 4, most concerns with regard to workers' rights emanate from the offshore sourcing of production in Asia by high street fashion chains. Kapferer argues that this delocalization is the result of mass production of general fashion brands and not true luxury brands. This is indeed the case with French brands such as Hermès and Louis Vuitton. These companies have most of their production in France and have been opening new factories and creating new apprenticeships to continue the craft tradition. These products are durable and made to last unlike the disposable goods associated with fast fashion.

Luxury products use the best quality materials so unlike their fast-fashion counterparts they do not use recycled materials in their manufacture. Kapferer (2010) uses the case of Lacoste to show how the best polo shirt in the world, the L.12.12, is sourced from Peruvian Pima cotton which is of exceptional quality. He argues that Lacoste could buy sustainable cotton from a variety of suppliers but this would not give the same consistency of quality and performance as Pima cotton. This point was confirmed by research from Achabou and Dekhill (2013) who undertook empirical research on consumers of French luxury clothing and confirmed that the use of recycled materials in such products affects consumer preferences negatively.

During the 2010s the luxury sector has markedly improved its CSR reporting and it would be interesting to know how public-listed companies would perform now in an industry-wide audit. In the late 2000s and in 2010 the reports cited above and Kapferer's article did draw attention to companies with strong CSR credentials. For example Tiffany & Co was acknowledged to be a sustainability leader in the jewellery sector. Tiffany developed policies in the 1990s that became mainstream in the new millennium and it has been producing annual CSR reports that monitor social and environmental impacts of its operations. It was one of the first companies to support the Kimberley Process Certification Scheme (KPCS) which ensures the traceability of precious metals from suppliers and deals with certified mines and countries that have signed up to KPCS. In essence KPCS was an effort to avoid sourcing diamonds from rebel organizations that promulgated civil strife in many African countries. These 'blood diamonds' gained further media coverage with the release of Edward Zwick's film, *Blood Diamond*, in 2006. For a company that is dependent upon the mining of raw materials for its continued existence, it is interesting that Tiffany strongly opposes the proposal to mine gold and copper at Alaska's Bristol Bay because of the environmental consequences, mainly on salmon fisheries, of such a scheme.

Gucci was another company praised for its initiatives building upon its 2004 voluntary certification process of its entire production cycle. Since then it has developed sustainable products, mainly in eyewear and the launch of bags that are 100 per cent traceable and certified as zero deforestation from Amazon leather. Gucci is part of the conglomerate Kering which has an ambitious five-year social and environmental plan for its key luxury brands. The group has set targets on carbon emissions, waste and water, sourcing, paper and packaging. It also intends to eliminate all hazardous materials from its production by 2020.

One of the main reasons for the increased information on CSR in the luxury sector relates to legislation in France, namely the Grenelle 2 Act which came into law in April 2012. Grenelle 2 requires all large publicly listed companies on the French stock exchange to incorporate information on the social and environmental consequences of their activities into their annual reports in addition to their societal commitments for sustainable development. As many of the world's famous luxury brands are French or owned by Kering or LVMH, a wealth of information is now forthcoming in their annual reports. For example the reports of LVMH and Hermès have detailed appendices on water and energy consumption and CO_2 emissions of their operations in addition to detail on employees, local community support and responsible partnerships. Hermès in particular provides considerable information on their production sites, most of which are located in France, and the environmental/social impact of their factories on local communities.

Conclusions

The luxury sector is a dynamic one, exhibiting considerable growth since the 1990s. Some of the world's top brands in terms of value and brand equity are in the luxury sector. This enhanced brand status and growth can be attributed to the internationalization and extension of the luxury brand. However, this expansion did bring difficulties to some brands and has led to supply chain challenges for most companies.

We used the pyramid model to explain how brands have developed from iconic, heritage, hand-crafted products to diffusion brands. Our case study, Burberry, was used to illustrate such developments from the Prorsum couture brand to Burberry London (ready to wear) to Burberry Brit (diffusion brand). Burberry and Gucci are well-documented cases of success stories of companies that have repositioned their brands as a result of a flawed licensing and franchising strategy causing a loss of control of product distribution. All of the key players on the international stage have strong control over the production and distribution of their brands so that international growth is mainly through a company-operated network where possible.

The segmentation of the luxury market as illustrated by the pyramid model has meant that luxury brands have become more accessible to the mainstream fashion consumer. However the degree of segmentation influences the extent to which companies have moved from a highly integrated in-house supply chain model to one that is more common to other fashion sectors, namely the offshore sourcing/outsourcing model. The Burberry case has shown that the company not only overhauled its brand image over time but also its supply chain. This has meant a focus of UK production on outerwear, primarily the trench coat, with other product lines being sourced from full-package suppliers in lower cost regions.

It is often this shift in production that has caused most angst in the media about CSR issues – usually workers' rights issues. However, in luxury most of the adverse comment on companies relates to raw material sourcing of precious metals, leather and furs. Critical comment has been made on 'blood diamonds', environmental degradation and animal rights issues. One criticism levelled at luxury companies has been their lack of transparency at reporting on their CSR activities. But in our last section we showed that French companies are now obligated by law to publish detailed information on the social and environmental consequences of their operations. As most of the world's most prominent luxury brands are French or owned by French companies this criticism is no longer valid, as highlighted by the detailed information contained within Hermès' annual reports.

References

Achabou, M A and Dekhill, S (2013) Luxury and sustainable development: is there a match? *Journal of Business Research*, **66** (10), pp 1896–903

Alleres (2003) Cited in Bruce, M and Kratz, C (2007) Competitive marketing strategies in luxury fashion companies, in T Hines and M Bruce (eds) *Fashion Marketing: Contemporary issues*, (2nd edn) Elsevier/Butterworth-Heinemann, New York

Bendell, J and Kleanthous, A (2007) *Deeper Luxury: quality and style when the world matters*, WWF/UK, Woking

Berthon, P, Pitt, L, Parent, M and Berthon, J P (2009) Aesthetics and ephemerality: observing and preserving the luxury brand, *California Management Review*, **52** (1), pp 45–66

Beverland, M (2004) Uncovering 'theories in use': building wine brands, *European Journal of Marketing*, **38** (3/4), pp 446–66

Brun, A and Castelli, C M (2008) Supply chain strategy in the fashion industry: developing a portfolio model depending on product, retail channel and brand, *International Journal of Production Economics*, **116** (2), pp 169–81

Brun, A and Castelli, C M (2013) The nature of luxury: a consumer perspective, *International Journal of Retail & Distribution Management*, **41** (11/12), pp 823–47

Brun, A and Castelli, C M (2014) Supply chain strategy in the fashion and luxury industry, Chapter 6 in J Fernie and L Sparks (eds) *Logistics and Retail Management* (4th edn), Kogan Page, London

D'Arpizio, C (2007) Monitor Altagamma 2007 on luxury markets [online] www.altagamma.it [accessed 25 July 2015]

Dubois, B and Duquesne, P (1993) The market for luxury goods: income versus culture, *European Journal of Marketing*, **27** (1), pp 35–45

Dubois, B and Paternault, C (1995) Understanding the world of international luxury brands: the dream formula, *Journal of Advertising Research*, **35** (4), pp 69–77

Dubois, B, Laurent, G and Czellar, S (2001) Consumer rapport to luxury: analyzing complex and ambivalent attitudes, *Working Paper 736*, HEC School of Management, Jouy-en-Josas

Dubois, B, Laurent, G and Czellar, S (2005) Consumer segments based on attitudes to luxury, *Marketing Letters*, **16** (2), pp 115–28

Fernie, J (2012) The evolution of the luxury fashion brand, Keynote address at The International Workshop on Luxury, Retail, Operations and Supply Chain Management, Milan, December

Fionda-Douglas, A (2012) British luxury fashion brand repositioning: motivations, strategy and processes, Unpublished PhD thesis, Heriot-Watt University, Edinburgh

Fionda, A M and Moore, C M (2009) The anatomy of the luxury fashion brand, *Journal of Brand Management*, **16** (5/6), pp 347–63

Fisher, M (1997) What is the right supply chain for your product? *Harvard Business Review*, **75** (2), pp 105–17

Gutsatz, M (1996) Le Luxe Représentations et Compétences, *Décisions Marketing*, **9**, pp 25–33

Hagtvedt, H and Patrick, V M (2009) The broad embrace of luxury: hedonic potential as a driver of brand extendibility, *Journal of Consumer Psychology*, **19** (4), pp 608–18

Hollander, S (1970) *Multinational Retailing*, Michigan State University Press, East Lancing

Interbrand (2014) The Best Global Brands [online] www.bestglobalbrands.com /2014/rankings [accessed 21 May 2015]

Jackson, T (2001) International Herald Tribune Fashion 2001 – a conference review, *The Journal of Fashion Marketing*, **6** (4)

Kapferer, J-N and Bastien, V (2009a) *The Luxury Strategy: Break the rules of marketing to build luxury brands,* Kogan Page, London

Kapferer, J-N and Bastien, V (2009b) The specificity of luxury management: turning marketing upside down, *Journal of Brand Management*, **16** (5/6), pp 311–22

Kapferer, J-N (2010) All that glitters is not green; the challenge of sustainable luxury, *European Business Review*, November/December, pp 40–44

Kapferer, J-N (2012) Abundant rarity: the key to luxury growth, *Business Horizons*, **55** (5) pp 453–62

Keller, K L (2009) Managing the growth trade-off: challenges and opportunities in luxury branding. *Journal of Brand Management*, **16** (5/6), pp 290–301

Moore, B (2011*) Style over Substance: Why ethics are not in fashion for designer labels*, Ethical Consumer Research Association, Manchester

Moore, C M and Birtwistle, G (2004) The Burberry business model: creating an International luxury fashion brand, *International Journal of Retail & Distribution Management,* **32** (8), pp 412–22

Moore, C M and Birtwistle, G (2005) The nature of parenting advantage in luxury fashion retailing: the case of Gucci group NV, *International Journal of Retail & Distribution Management*, **33** (4), pp 256–70

Moore, C M, Fernie, J and Burt, S (2000) Brands without boundaries: the internationalisation of the designer retailer's brand *European Journal of Marketing*, **34** (8), pp 919–37

Moore, C M, Docherty, A-M and Doyle, S A (2010) Flagship stores as a market entry strategy method: the perspectives of luxury fashion retailing, *European Journal of Marketing*, **44** (1/2) pp 139–61

Nueno, J L and Quelch, J A (1998) The mass marketing of luxury, *Business Horizons*, **41** (6), pp 61–69

Okonkwo, U (2009) The luxury brand strategy challenge, *Journal of Brand Management*, **16** (5/6), pp 287–89

Phau, I and Prendergast, G (2000) Conceptualizing the country of origin of brand *Journal of Marketing Communications*, **6** (3), pp 159–70

Sicard, M-C (2013) *Luxury, Lies and Marketing: Shattering the illusion of the luxury brand,* Palgrave Macmillan, Basingstoke

Silverstein, M and Fiske, N (2003a) Luxury for the masses *Harvard Business Review*, **81** (4), pp 48–57

Silverstein, M and Fiske, N (2003b) *Trading Up: The new American luxury,* Penguin Group, New York

Tokatli, N (2012) Old firms, new tricks and the quest for profits: Burberry's journey from success to failure and back to success again, *Journal of Economic Geography*, **12** (1), pp 55–77

Vickers, J S and Renand, F (2003) The marketing of luxury goods: an exploratory study – three conceptual dimensions, *The Marketing Review*, **3** (4), pp 459–78

Vigneron, F and Johnson, L W (1999) A review and a conceptual framework of prestige-seeking consumer behavior, *Academy of Marketing Science Review*, **99** (1), pp 1–15

Vigneron, F and Johnson, L W (2004) Measuring perceptions of brand luxury, *Journal of Brand Management*, **11** (6), pp 484–506

Yeoman, I and McMahon-Beattie, U (2006) Luxury markets and premium pricing, *Journal of Revenue and Premium Pricing*, **4** (4), pp 319–28

Sustainable fashion retailing and logistics

09

Introduction

This chapter discusses issues of environmental sustainability in fashion retailing and related logistics and SCM activities. Environmental sustainability is one element in John Elkington's (1994) 'triple bottom line' of profit, people and planet. Chapter 4 discussed the people element in the context of corporate and social responsibility (CSR) and other chapters have considered aspects related to the profit element. Hence, this chapter is focused on the planet element and begins by discussing concepts of sustainability in general and environmental sustainability related to logistics and SCM. Next, concepts of sustainability management and the use of environmental management systems (EMS) provide guidance for both fashion firms, ie suppliers, producers and manufacturers, and fashion retailers in developing their sustainability strategies. Finally, sustainability issues directly affecting the fashion retail sector are presented.

Concepts of sustainability

Sustainability was set out by the 1987 Brundtland Commission Report entitled *Our Common Future* as development that meets the needs of the present without compromising the ability of future generations to meet their own needs (Grant *et al*, 2015).

There are several theoretical motivations that underlie corporate and sustainable strategy and the two major motivations (Grant, 2012) are presented here. One is transaction cost economics (TCE) which contains four key concepts of bounded rationality, opportunism, asset specificity and informational asymmetry. Essentially, TCE describes the firm in organizational terms, or as a governance structure where decision makers respond to economic factors or transaction costs within the firm that affect both the structure of the firm and the structure of the industry within which it operates (Williamson, 1999). The increasing division of labour in a supply chain is determined by governance mechanisms and has been recognized as a means of competitiveness through terms such as 'strategic sourcing' or 'outsourcing' which was discussed in Chapter 5.

TCE, and the means of creating and developing resources and capabilities, can be applied to achieve supply chain improvement as the level of analysis moves away from the firm towards inter-organizational relationships. This wider context of logistics and the supply chain, and in particular the adaptability of organizing economic activities under different economic conditions was investigated by Williamson, and he focused on how TCE should be operationalized, emphasizing the efficient alignment of transactions with alternative modes of governance. This cost-benefit view of governance and relationships supports the concepts of lean and agile logistics and supply chains presented in Chapter 5.

Another theoretical motivation is the resource-based view of the firm (RBV) developed in the late 1950s by Penrose (2009), who defined a firm as a collection of resources where growth is limited by its resource endowment. As the nature and range of these resources vary from firm to firm, so do the respective resource constraints. RBV suggests that a firm's resources and its capability to convert these resources to provide sustainable competitive advantage are the keys to superior performance. In general, resources are referred to as physical, financial, individual and organizational capital for a firm and are necessary inputs for producing the final product or service, forming the basis for a firm's profitability. They may be considered both tangible assets such as plants and equipment and intangible assets such as brand names and technological know-how. Resources can also be traded, but few resources are productive by themselves. They only 'add value' when they are converted into a final product or service.

The two motivations of TCE and RBV, while appearing dissimilar, come together in the triple bottom line (TBL) model of profits or economic performance, people or social performance, and planet or environmental performance developed by Elkington (1994) and presented in Figure 9.1. The TBL posits that firms should focus not just on maximizing

FIGURE 9.1 The 'triple bottom line' of sustainability

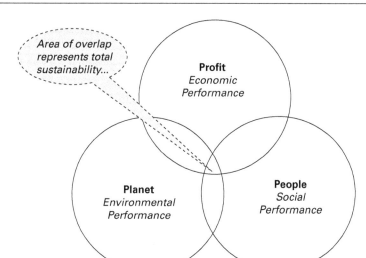

shareholder wealth or economic value but also on the environmental and social value that they may add – or possibly destroy – in order to achieve long-term environmental security and egalitarian living standards for all human beings. The overlap of these three elements in the Venn diagram represents true and total sustainability from an economic, ecological and human perspective.

Profit or economic performance is the bottom line shared by all commerce and features implicitly in Chapters 2, 3, 5 and 6–8. People or social performance pertains to fair and beneficial business practices towards labour and the community and region in which a firm conducts its business and is more of a corporate social responsibility (CSR) concern as addressed in Chapter 4. Planet or environmental performance refers to sustainable environmental practices and is the focus of this chapter, particularly as it effects logistics and supply chain activities. A firm that totally addresses the TBL endeavours to benefit the natural order as much as possible or at the least do no harm and curtail environmental impact. Therefore, the TBL concept requires that a firm's responsibility should be to all stakeholders rather than only to its shareholders.

Markley and Davis (2007) compared the TBL to what Hart (1995) proposed as a natural resource-based view (NRBV) of the firm to determine strategic directions for firms seeking sustainability as a competitive advantage. The NRBV incorporates resources in the natural environment in a three-part framework of pollution prevention, product stewardship and sustainable development. Such resources must also possess certain properties: they must be valuable and non-substitutable, tacit or inferred, socially complex or rare (Hart, 1995). Markley and Davis (2007) argued that both TBL and NRBV emphasize the importance of stakeholder value on sustainable competitive advantage; thus their research looked more specifically at the correlations between the company stakeholders of customers, employees and general society and the relationships these have with financial outcomes. According to both TBL and NRBV concepts, firms employing a stronger focus on creating sustainable supply chains that emphasize lower negative interactions with society and the environment, in addition to employing higher codes of ethics, should have stronger ratings on scales of sustainability measures, customer and employee satisfaction, CSR and profitability measures.

Carter and Rogers (2008: 368) defined sustainable supply chain management (SSCM) as:

> the strategic, transparent integration and achievement of an organization's social, environmental, and economic goals in the systemic coordination of key interorganizational business processes for improving the long-term economic performance of the individual company and its supply chains.

Their definition is based on the TBL as well as four supporting facets: risk management, transparency, organizational culture and strategy.

Risk management must go beyond managing short-term profits within an operational plan and also manage risk factors in the firm's products, waste and worker and public safety through contingency planning and managing supply disruptions and outbound supply chains. Transparency not only includes reporting to stakeholders but also actively engaging them and supplier operations. Organizational culture for sustainability must be deeply ingrained and respect organizational citizenship, values and ethics. Lastly, sustainability must form part of an integrated corporate strategy. These four facets are not intended to be entirely mutually exclusive and interrelationships will exist among them.

Thus a firm's sustainable, environmental or 'green' agenda and strategy will need to contain elements of the TBL and possibly other facets within whichever strategic motivation a firm has: TCE, RBV or perhaps even NRBV. However, it is also clear that an additional 'green' aspect, ie the colour of money, should emerge from achieving cost reductions through energy and emissions savings. Thus, like any other strategic business decision a firm will make, a sustainable or environmental agenda will be subject to its own cost-benefit trade-offs.

But how can a firm calculate all true and total costs and benefits? Some form of performance measurement is required to fit into the three strategic plans and to do so firms can adopt an environmental management system (EMS). Types of EMS are discussed later in this chapter.

Sustainability in logistics and SCM

Environmental issues have been an area of growing attention for businesses. For example, transportation, production, storage and the disposal of hazardous materials are frequently regulated and controlled on a global scale while in Europe firms are increasingly required to remove and dispose of packaging materials used for their products. These issues complicate logistics and SCM activities, increasing costs and limiting options, and form the backbone to three main 'themes' in sustainable logistics and SCM (Abukhader and Jönson, 2004):

1 reverse logistics;

2 emissions assessment; and

3 the 'greening' of logistical and supply chain activities.

Reverse logistics and product recovery or returns

Reverse logistics is not particularly new and the return, recovery and recycling of products have been practised for decades. Reverse logistics has been defined (Rogers and Tibben-Lembke, 1998: 2) as:

> ...the process of planning, implementing, and controlling the efficient, cost-effective flow of raw materials, in-process inventory, finished goods and related information from the point of consumption to the point of origin for the purpose of recapturing value or proper disposal.

Note that this definition is very similar to the definition of logistics discussed in Chapter 5, with only the latter part changed. Reverse logistics encompasses all activities in the definition, but the difference is that reverse logistics activities occur in the opposite direction, ie against the one-way flow towards the consumer or the point of consumption. Further, reverse logistics includes processing returned goods due to damage, seasonal inventory, restock, salvage, recalls or changes in the consumer's need or desire for the goods.

There are four primary questions regarding reverse logistics from a strategic perspective:

1 What types of materials may be returned, recovered or recycled?
2 How are responsibilities defined in a reverse logistics supply chain?
3 What is reasonably possible to return, recover or recycle?
4 How are economic value and ecological value determined?

There are also some key differences between new product and reverse logistics supply chains (Rogers and Tibben-Lembke, 1998) including the following:

1 Uncertainty in the recovery process regarding reverse product quality or condition, quantity and timing.
2 Return forecasting, which is an even more difficult task than demand forecasting.
3 Uncertainty in consumer behaviour as the consumer has to initiate the return of products as opposed to simply disposing of them, the consumer has to accept and purchase recovered and refurbished products, and the price offered and value placed by the consumer on returning or recycling goods is not always clear.
4 The number of collection points is greater and uncertain in location or viability and there may be delayed pick-up of products as time is not critical.
5 Products being returned often have poor packaging and small consignment sizes, and the clarity of information, traceability and visibility may be poor.
6 Inspection and separation of products are necessary and are very labour-intensive and costly.

Once fashion goods are sold to consumers, and are not returned due to a change in the consumer's preferences, the responsibility for the final journey of these goods passes from the retailer to the consumer.

Emissions assessment

Both transportation and storage activities are users of energy, for example fuel and electricity, and the use of energy produces carbon dioxide (CO_2) emissions as a result. The World Economic Forum (2009) estimated that logistics activities account for 2,800 mega-tonnes of CO_2 emissions annually, or about 6 per cent of the total 50,000 mega-tonnes produced by human activity. Thus it is not surprising that firms are beginning to assess the energy consumption of their supply chains as a way to reduce their overall CO_2 emissions.

As an example in transportation, vehicle engines are becoming more efficient in terms of fuel use and emissions and there are ongoing efforts to consider alternative fuels such as biodiesel or bioethanol, hydrogen, natural gas or liquid petroleum gas and electricity. However, these developments are still in their infancy and also have their own environmental impacts. For example, the growth of crops for biofuels requires the use of arable land, which displaces the growing of crops for food.

Concerning warehousing, the World Business Council for Sustainable Development (2007) noted that buildings account for 40 per cent of world-wide energy use. Initiatives to increase the efficiency of building in using energy and reducing emissions have been developed by the Leadership in Energy and Environmental Design certification programme (LEED) in the United States and the Building Research Establishment Environmental Assessment Method (BREEAM) in the UK (Grant *et al*, 2015).

The 'greening' of logistical activities and supply chains

The 'greening' of logistical and supply chain activities means ensuring these activities are environmentally friendly and not wasteful. The World Economic Forum (WEF) (2009) argued that a collaborative responsibility for 'greening' the supply chain resides with three groups: logistics and transport service providers, shippers and buyers, and government and non-government policy makers. In this context fashion retailers may be considered as shippers and buyers who purchase services from logistics and transport service providers, and who are subject to policies from the policy makers. The WEF provided several recommendations for shippers and buyers, ie retailers, to 'green' such activities:

- *Transportation, vehicles and infrastructure networks*. Shippers and buyers should build environmental performance indicators into the contracting process with logistics service providers, work with consumers to better support their understanding of carbon footprints and labelling where appropriate, and make recycling easier and more resource efficient, support efforts to make mode switches across supply chains and begin to 'de-speed' the supply chain.

- *Green buildings*. Shippers and buyers should improve existing facilities through retrofitting green technologies, work towards industry-wide commitments to boost investment into new building technologies and develop new offerings around recycling and waste management.

- *Sourcing, product and packaging design*. Shippers and buyers should determine how much carbon is designed into a product through raw material selection, the carbon intensity of the production process, the length and speed of the supply chain and the carbon characteristics of the use phase. Shippers and buyers should also agree to additional standards and targets around lighter weight packaging, the elimination of excess packaging and the modularization of transit packaging materials. They should also develop sustainable sourcing policies that consider the CO_2 impact of primary production, manufacturing and rework activities, and integrate the impact of CO_2 emissions into the business's case for near-shoring production.

- *Administrative issues*. Shippers and buyers should develop CO_2-offsetting solutions for own operations and work with policy makers to develop universal CO_2 measurement and reporting standards, build an open carbon trading system, review tax regimes to remove counter-productive incentives and support efforts to move towards further carbon labelling.

Sustainability management and management systems

Mollenkopf (2006) presented a framework for creating a sustainable supply chain and considered that product development and stewardship are key factors impacting all stages of logistics and SCM. Hence a retailer's product development process needs to design appropriately for the environment. A better understanding of the life cycle of the product is critical in terms of when it reaches end of use or end of life as well as the costs and environmental impacts of the product at each stage.

A sustainable supply chain must also consider both upstream and downstream firms. Supplier requirements and codes of conduct can be employed to ensure that suppliers and customers behave in socially and environmentally responsible ways. Further, sustainability is also about ensuring the source of the product. Traceability and chain of custody capabilities are necessary to ensure this is the case, and this must be demonstrable to customers.

Many fashion retailers are now using design for the environment pro-grammes so that the environmental impact of their products during design and production as well as end of life will be minimized. For example, H&M has implemented a sustainable programme, Conscious Action, in which eco-material is used and promoted, sustainable manufacturing is adopted in countries with a high sustainable consciousness, green distribution approaches with less energy use and fewer emissions are used and 'green' retailing and consumer education are promoted (Shen, 2014).

Abukhader and Jönson (2004) noted that there was little use of life-cycle assessment (LCA) in logistics and SCM at the time of their article, and that there was little consideration of environmental impacts beyond cost-benefit analysis. LCA is one of a set of environmental management systems (EMS) first mentioned at the beginning of this chapter. Besides LCA, two other major EMS are the International Organization for Standardization's ISO 14001 and the European Union's eco-management and audit scheme known as EMAS.

There are a number of factors to consider when designing, implementing and evaluating an EMS. The most important is that no single approach is suitable for every firm; each firm has its own management systems and environmental impacts, organizational culture and structure. Further, the approach selected must also be responsive to all possible audiences such as management, employees, shareholders and the public. Many of the systems proposed by regulatory bodies are based on a plan-do-check-act framework. The planning stage is to set the targets and objectives and to detail how these will be attained through assigning individual responsibility. Implementing or 'doing' the system means providing the necessary resources to accomplish the objectives which have been set. Actions for checking and correcting areas which require attention include monitoring and measurement to determine how well the organization is achieving its stated environmental goals. Finally, there needs to be a periodic review of the actions to ensure progress is as expected; the results from these reviews should also be documented as a log for continuous improvement (Murphy, 2013).

ISO 14001 (ISO, 2015) is intended to provide firms with the elements of an EMS that can be integrated with other management requirements and help firms achieve environmental and economic goals. ISO 14001 specifies requirements for an EMS to enable a firm to develop and implement a policy and objectives which take into account legal requirements and information about significant environmental aspects, and is also intended to apply to all types and sizes of firms and to accommodate diverse geographical, cultural and social conditions.

EMAS (EMAS, 2015) is the second most popular EMS standard in Europe. Structurally the ISO 14001 and EMAS standards are very similar, but there are some fundamental differences between them (Murphy, 2013). For example, EMAS firms must be compliant to relevant environmental rules and regulations to guarantee their certification while although ISO 14001 states that a commitment to compliance is required in the policy, compliance is not essential to keep their certification.

Further, evaluation of the EMAS standard is guaranteed by obligatory three-yearly audits where all cycles are checked and a statement is made public. ISO 14001 audits check for environmental system performance against internal benchmarks, with no penalties for lack of improvement, and the frequency is left to the discretion of the individual firm. These differences are perhaps the reason that the number of ISO 14001 certifications in UK is far greater (14,346 in 2010) than EMAS registrants (289 in 2012). ISO 14001 appears to be the least demanding of the two standards and hence more favourable to firms on an effort and cost basis.

The LCA is an all-encompassing method proposed for environmental performance measurement and is a 'cradle-to-grave' approach for assessing industrial systems and supply chains (Curran, 2006). The approach begins with the gathering of raw materials from the earth to create products for consumption and evaluates all stages of a product's life cycle from the perspective that they are interdependent, meaning that one stage leads to the next. LCA also enables the estimation of cumulative environmental impacts resulting from all stages in the product life cycle, often including impacts not considered in more traditional analyses, for example raw material extraction, material transportation and ultimate product disposal. By including these impacts throughout the product life cycle, LCA provides a comprehensive and holistic view of the environmental aspects of the product or process and a more accurate picture of the true environmental trade-offs in product and process selection (Grant, 2012).

LCA has four phases: goal and scope definition, ie can a firm do a true cradle-to-grave analysis; inventory analysis at each node in the industrial system or supply chain; the impact assessment at each stage; and interpretation of the findings. These phases are not simply followed in a single sequence: LCA is an iterative process in which subsequent iterations can achieve increasing levels of detail or lead to changes in the first phase prompted by the results of the last phase. LCA has proved to be a valuable tool to document and analyse environmental considerations of product and service systems that need to inform decision making for sustainability, and ISO 14040 provides a general framework for LCA.

Thus the situation surrounding EMS in general and LCA in particular has improved since Abukhader and Jönson's article in 2004, and the following case study describes Levi Strauss & Company's use of LCA to investigate and mitigate the impact on the environment of a pair of blue jeans.

CASE STUDY   The sustainability of blue jeans

At the height of the California gold rush in 1853 the first pairs of Levi Strauss & Company (LS&Co.) denim jeans were manufactured. Since their introduction, Levi's denim blue jeans and shirts have moved beyond ordinary work clothes. After a boom in jeans use by the youth culture of the 1950s–1960s, Levi Strauss has become a global entity and symbolizes global culture. Levi's jeans are now sold in all six populated continents and are produced in many different countries.

LS&Co. enacted several programmes in 2006 to address the company's internal and external environmental impacts throughout their product line. These included programmes looking at environmental compliance, supplier codes of conduct and global effluent guidelines, as well as their organic cotton initiative, which established what they claimed to be a more environmentally friendly line of products coined as their *Eco* brand. Around the time these programmes were created, LS&Co. also began to conduct research on several of their products according to a cradle-to-grave methodology, where the full life span of a product was analysed and the overall sustainability of that product was then determined through the assessment.

This methodology, a derivative of a life-cycle assessment (LCA), is useful in sustainability analysis because it treats the wide array of systems in creating the product as an aggregate system, which is useful for addressing the inherent complexity involved in synthesizing, distributing and dismantling a consumer good. LS&Co.'s research led to a report on their findings, posted on their corporate website in 2009, as *A Product Lifecycle Approach to Sustainability.*

In LS&Co.'s LCA, the life cycle of a pair of Levis® 501® jeans from cradle-to-grave is a collection of seven independent 'product systems'. These systems are, in respective order: (1) cotton production; (2) fabric production; (3) garment manufacturing; (4) transportation and distribution; (5) consumer use; (6) recycling, which may go back to step (2); or (7) waste stream in a landfill.

The LS&Co. methodology includes measures of:

- the contribution to climate change through the carbon dioxide equivalent for all greenhouse gas emissions attributable to the product;

- the energy consumed to produce a product;

- the percentage of total energy use from renewable resources to produce a product;

- the water consumed to produce a product;

- the area of land occupied to produce a product;

- the percentage of fibres grown under a recognized cultivation programme to address areas of sustainability, ie qualified sustainably grown or QSG;

- the primary solid waste generated during spinning, dyeing, weaving, cut/sew and finishing a product;

- the efficiency of primary material use, ie materials that end up in the product;

- the percentage of materials used from post-consumer recycled sources, ie recycled content;

- a measure of the land transformed from its original state as a result of product production; and

- eutrophication, which is a measure of the discharge of harmful nutrients to freshwater bodies that cause algal growth as a result of product production.

LS&Co. determined that for the entire cradle-to-grave life cycle the overall climate change impact from one pair of Levis® 501® jeans was highest in step 5, consumer use through washing, at 58 per cent of total impact or 18.6 kilograms of carbon dioxide equivalent ($KgCO_2e$). The next highest amount was step 2, fabric production, at 21 per cent or 6.6 $KgCO_2e$. Only in water consumption (45 per cent or 1,575 litres of water used) was consumer use behind step 1, cotton production (49 per cent or 1,704 litres used).

These findings are consistent with general theory behind LCA, where use or operations provide the majority of climate change impact. To mitigate this impact, LS&Co. noted that their denim jeans are hearty and hence consumers don't need to wash their jeans after every wearing. If consumers washed their jeans once a month versus once a week they could decrease their impact on climate change by 48 per cent to 9.7 $KgCO_2e$ and amount of water used by 35 per cent to 1,024 litres. LS&Co. also noted that the type of washing machine used and the wash water temperature can make a difference. For example, a top-loading washing machine on cold water wash and drying by line only produces 1.9 $KgCO_2e$ versus the worst-case 18.6 $KgCO_2e$ on a warm water wash and machine dry cycle. Conversely, a side-loading washing machine produces 1.1 and 14.2 $KgCO_2e$ respectively.

SOURCES Camp, Clark, Duane and Haight (2010); Levi Strauss and Co. (2004); Levi Strauss and Co. (2009); Levi Strauss and Co. (2010).

Once a firm selects a framework or technique to include sustainability into its corporate strategy, eg a TBL, EMS or LCA approach, it will then need to assess such matters as the economic viability, technological feasibility and environmental sustainability of that strategy. The consideration of these relationships gives rise to assessing whether the strategy or strategic option fulfils what Elliott (2013) terms the '10-tenets of sustainable management' which would enable firms to assess, manage and solve an environmental issue in a holistic manner but within what is possible in the real world. The basis of Elliott's '10-tenets' are described in Table 9.1.

Not every one of them needs to be adhered to, nor indeed is it possible to do so in some cases, but the approach demonstrates the need for a multidisciplinary approach to environmental management and 'may also require some disciplines to move out of their comfort zone. [If any firm, including a retailer uses this approach then it should be able to] deliver societal benefits and achieve and manage [environmental and] socio-economic connectivity' (Elliott, 2013: 4). Afterwards, a governance framework can then be adopted to encompass environmental and economic valuation for communication and management decisions thus giving a sustainable management framework.

In summary, to ensure environmental sustainability in its logistical and supply chain activities, a fashion retailer will need to adopt whatever EMS meets the strategic needs of the firm and its stakeholders, and works in conjunction with the other two aspects of the TBL, profit and people. It could then consider using the '10-tenets' to ensure all stakeholder views are met. This is important for them to do as all aspects of sustainability in the fashion sector are very visible in 2015, and are now perceived as being overdue for attention by firms and governments.

Naomi Klein's book *No Logo* was published in 2000 and was one of the first to document 'sweatshop' and 'child labour' practices by sportswear and fashion retailers in foreign markets. However, conditions only marginally

TABLE 9.1 The 10-tenets for sustainable management (adapted form Elliott, 2013)

Ecologically sustainable: Measures will ensure that the ecosystem features and functioning and the fundamental and final ecosystem services are safeguarded.

Technologically feasible: The methods, techniques and equipment for ecosystem and society/infrastructure protection are available.

Economically viable: A cost-benefit assessment of the environmental management indicates (economic/financial) viability and sustainability.

Socially desirable/tolerable: Environmental management measures are as required or at least are understood and tolerated by society as being required; that society regards the protection as necessary.

Legally permissible: There are regional, national or international agreements and/or statutes which will enable and/or force the management measures to be performed.

Administratively achievable: The statutory bodies such as governmental departments, environmental protection and conservation bodies are in place and functioning to enable successful and sustainable management.

Politically expedient: The management approaches and philosophies are consistent with the prevailing political climate and have the support of political leaders.

Ethically defensible (morally correct): The management approaches to tackle the causes of problems and find solutions requires the ethics and morals of any such solutions to be considered.

Culturally inclusive: All management actions have to be accepted or tolerated by society and an increasing stakeholder input for decision making requires that some cultural considerations may take precedence.

Effectively communicable: Scientists and researchers need to better communicate their science and projected results of any management action to stakeholders to allow better decision making.

changed until the collapse of a garment factory at Rana Plaza, Dhaka, Bangladesh in April 2013, killing 1,138 garment workers, spurred major retailers such as Primark, Zara owner Inditex, Mango, Denmark's Mascot, Canada's Loblaw, Walmart and Benetton into paying into a compensation fund for victims in February 2015 (Butler, 2015).

Sustainability in the fashion retail sector

As sustainability in fashion supply chains becomes more important, Caniato *et al* (2011) examined the fashion supply chain's state of the art in drivers, practices and measured sustainability performance among larger multinational firms they labelled green international brands (GIBs) and small manufacturers upstream in the supply chain they labelled alternative firms (SAFs). They found GIBs focus on product design and retailing, relying on external manufacturers for the production activities. Thus product design practices are highly relevant for GIBs, whereas internal processes have a low potential impact on environmental performance. At the same time, supply chain practices for GIBs are crucial as suppliers' environmental performance is by far the main determinant of their final products' environmental footprint, so inbound supply chains have not been radically redesigned to better respond to environmental criteria. Instead, GIBs have made incremental changes affecting suppliers (eg training, incentives, supplier selection and extension of codes of conduct). The outbound supply chain has not been completely revised either as the majority of GIBs still adhere to traditional channels; the most significant recent innovations involve adoption of the internet as an additional channel.

On the other hand, the primary driver for SAFs has been the need to find new ways to compete and market their products. They are primarily suppliers to international brand-owning companies and subject to pressure to reduce costs. Their recent choices to sell products directly to final consumers have pushed them to focus on particular market segments where consumers are usually concerned about environmental sustainability issues. Thus SAFs have started investing in green practices instead of focusing on cost reduction. SAFs have always been manufacturers and directly control the main phases of the production process. As a result, process design has a strong impact on environmental performance and SAFs are investing a lot on greener processes (eg sun drying and natural dyeing). They also use green criteria to select their suppliers and try to foster sustainability through their inbound supply chain by sourcing either locally or in a fair-trade context, but the more radical change is the complete redesign of the outbound supply chain with the goal of excluding distributors and retailers to reach consumers directly. While not a sustainable approach by itself this choice makes it possible for SAFs to increasingly invest in environmental sustainability. Hence, the key takeaway from Caniato *et al*'s (2011) study is that one size doesn't fit all fashion firms and retailers, and that firm size has implications for how they approach sustainability.

In a 2009 research study, The Forum for the Future, a London-based not-for-profit sustainable development corporation, found two important underlying factors influencing how a retailer approaches sustainability: the specific business environment and the retailer's perceptions of their own marketplace power. The business environment includes:

- Store formats: hypermarkets may be more sustainability efficient at a store level while smaller, urban stores may have a smaller consumer transport footprint due to their proximity to consumers which results in fewer vehicle journeys to the store.
- Regulatory environment: high regulatory standards appear to be drivers of better firm behaviour.
- Business culture: German retailers for example prefer to design and deliver sustainability initiatives internally without much fanfare while UK retailers have ambitious overall sustainability targets and annual progress reports.

Regarding a retailer's marketplace power perception, the study found a continuum from contributors to leaders. At one end contributors do not lead the consumer or try to influence their behaviour. Contributors instead focus on information provision and work behind the scenes with private label suppliers to reduce environmental impacts. At the other end, leaders are more willing to lead the consumer and work on both direct and indirect impacts, eg they engage suppliers across brand and private label to improve sustainability impacts including a holistic approach to logistics across the supply chain.

The study sample was skewed towards food retailers, but two major trends identified by all participants are not dissimilar to others discussed in preceding sections: the effect of CO_2 including carbon footprinting and labelling, and issues of packaging, waste and recycling.

The Forum for the Future also investigated sustainability in fashion (2007) and identified eight key issues affecting making clothing more sustainable:

1 fashion consumption, ie the increasing number of fashion items that are purchased and then disposed of, particularly in fast-fashion contexts;
2 the intensity of cotton production requiring lots of energy, water and pesticides;
3 working conditions across the supply chain from cotton production to sweatshops;
4 energy consumed when washing clothes, which contributes to climate change;

5 toxic chemicals in the working environment that damage workers' health and the local environment;

6 unsustainable man-made fibres taking longer to degrade in landfill sites;

7 fashion miles that produce CO_2 emissions as fabric and clothing are transported around the world;

8 animal welfare to ensure good standards are upheld during leather and wool production, and avoiding fur.

These issues are seen in Figure 9.2 across the fashion supply chain from point of origin to point of consumption (see Chapter 5 for a discussion of this logistical concept). There are two areas in this supply chain where retailers can have a *direct* impact on environmentally sustainable logistics and SCM: the retail setting itself, eg stores and storage, and transport. Retailers can really only have an *indirect* impact on the other four areas in the shaded boxes – materials, fabric and garment production, usage and disposal – through exercising influence on suppliers and informing consumers.

FIGURE 9.2 Sustainability issues in the fashion supply chain (adapted from Forum for the Future, 2007)

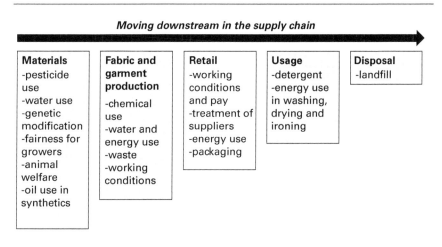

Moving downstream in the supply chain

Materials	Fabric and garment production	Retail	Usage	Disposal
-pesticide use		-working conditions and pay	-detergent	-landfill
-water use	-chemical use	-treatment of suppliers	-energy use in washing, drying and ironing	
-genetic modification	-water and energy use	-energy use		
-fairness for growers	-waste	-packaging		
-animal welfare	-working conditions			
-oil use in synthetics				

Transport
-CO_2 emissions and waste
-congestion

Transport across the entire supply chain

However, as noted in the case of Levi Strauss & Co., some firms may be able to exercise such influence through a more vertically integrated supply chain that they control or by ensuring sources of supply and production adhere to their environmental standards. The desire and ability to exercise influence over consumers regarding sustainability is another matter. Turker and Altuntas (2014), investigating CSR statements in fashion firm and retailer annual reports, noted that many of these statements pay significant attention to reporting their sustainable logistical and supply chain activities and focus on integrating suppliers into their systems, but pay little attention to consumer issues regarding sustainability. Barnes and Lea-Greenwood (2006) noted that power in the fashion sector has shifted towards consumers from retailers and hence their desire, or not, for sustainable products is important to both fashion firms and retailers.

Chan and Wong (2012) investigated consumers' eco-fashion consumption patterns, where eco-fashion is the type of clothing designed and manufactured to maximize benefits to people and society while minimizing adverse environmental impacts. Eco-fashion goods are produced by taking account of their environmental impacts, ie biodegradable or recycled materials (such as organically grown cotton and corn fibre) and environmentally responsible production processes (such as use of natural dyes). Recent studies informing Chan and Wong's work noted that fashion consumers' sustainable consumption decisions are highly complicated: they are less likely to purchase eco-fashion despite positive attitudes towards environmental protection and thus there is an attitude-behaviour gap between their environmental protection interests and ethical consumption.

Chan and Wong determined that eco-fashion consumption can be a key contributor to sustainable development in fashion supply chains by driving demand for eco-fashion goods. They suggested that while fashion companies and retailers are increasingly urged by stakeholders, such as government, customers and consumers, and public groups, to mitigate environmental impacts and build a sustainable fashion supply chain, it is important for them to devise marketing plans to promote eco-fashion consumption to facilitate that development.

The Forum for the Future's work on sustainable fashion provided six suggestions to address 'some overarching "unsustainable" aspects of the clothing industry' (2007: 12) in order to achieve a more holistically sustainable supply chain and which are also supported by academic research and theory discussed in this chapter:

1 *Raising awareness amongst key industry players.* A breadth of sustainability issues that need to be addressed among all

stakeholders, including consumers. Thus engagement with all stakeholders is a necessity.

2 *Transparent supply chains are a must.* Fashion firms and retailers must be able to trace the origins of their stock and ensure they have high standards of sustainability. That way, all stakeholders can be assured that sustainability does exist and that 'greenwashing' is not evident.

3 *International standards need to be developed and enforced.* While fashion firms and retailers typically resist regulation, standards help create a level playing field so that fashion firms and retailers can differentiate on other issues, eg fabrics used, design and responsible practice. Adoption of a suitable EMS is therefore crucial here.

4 *Training and support is needed along the supply chain.* As well as fair prices and terms of trade, suppliers need support, time, encouragement and incentives to convert to sustainable practices. Power plays a role here. Walmart was criticized for dominant retailer power (Mottner and Smith, 2009) whereby small suppliers operate in a dependency model where they have lower gross margins and operating income but higher turnover. However, Walmart has undertaken to rejuvenate its reputation (Hemphill, 2005) by holding stakeholder surveys and responding to them with a concerted non-market strategy involving complementary social, political and legal components.

5 *Empowering consumers is a priority driving demand for sustainable clothing.* As noted in the Levi Strauss & Co. case study, most of the climate change impact of an item of clothing tends to be in its use: washing, ironing and tumble-drying. Raising awareness to change behaviour will make a big impact.

6 *Designers are crucial to making sustainable fashion work.* They play a key role in promoting sustainable solutions for clothing and making ethical fashion appeal to the mainstream consumer, particularly for GIBs by ensuring clothing is desirable, functional and stylish. Hence they need to be involved in sustainability decision making right from the outset.

Summary

Logistics and SCM have a major impact on the global economy nowadays. However, while increased globalization, increased outsourcing and deeper relationships, more use of technology, lean and agile supply chain processes, and a one-way flow in the supply chain as discussed in Chapter 5 have assisted logistics and SCM activities, they have also been detrimental from a sustainability perspective. Reverse logistics or product recovery, emissions of CO_2 gases, use or misuse of fuel and other natural resources, pollution, and increased levels of waste from production and packaging are just some of these problems in fashion supply chains.

This chapter has discussed several recurring themes regarding sustainable logistics and SCM. First, the importance of sustainability in this sector is becoming increasingly important and needs to form part of logistics and supply chain strategies by fashion firms and retailers. Second, retailers can only exercise direct influence over their own internal operations. They can only exercise indirect influence over raw material producers, suppliers and manufacturers further upstream in their supply chain. However, this may become easier as such fashion firms also become more aware and interested in sustainability. Third, retailers' influence over consumers is still limited and more needs to be done to ensure consumers are also cognisant of sustainability issues and practise what they believe. Better and more involved communication with consumers will help in this task. Finally, fashion firms and retailers should utilize an appropriate EMS and related concepts such as LCA and the '10-tenets' to properly map and monitor their strategic sustainability efforts.

References

Abukhader, S M and Jönson, G (2004) Logistics and the environment: is it an Established Subject? *International Journal of Logistics: Research and Applications*, 7 (2), pp 137–49

Barnes, L and Lea-Greenwood, G (2006) Fast fashioning the supply chain: shaping the research agenda, *Journal of Fashion Marketing and Management*, 10 (3), pp 259–71

Butler, S (2015) Benetton agrees to contribute to Rana Plaza compensation fund, *Guardian*, 20 February [online] http://www.theguardian.com/business/2015/feb/20/benetton-agrees-contribute-rana-plaza-compensation-fund [accessed 25 July 2015]

Camp, S, Clark, G, Duane, L and Haight, A (2010) Life cycle analysis and sustainability report, *University of Vermont* [online] http://www.uvm.edu/~shali/Levi.pdf [accessed 25 July 2015]

Caniato, F, Caridi, M, Crippa, L and Moretto, A (2011) Environmental sustainability in fashion supply chains: an exploratory case study, *International Journal of Production Economics*, **135**, pp 659–70

Carter, C R and Rogers, D S (2008) A framework of sustainable supply chain management theory, *International Journal of Physical Distribution & Logistics Management*, **38**, (5), pp 360–87

Chan, T-Y and Wong, C W Y (2012) The consumption side of the sustainable fashion supply chain, *Journal of Fashion Marketing and Management*, **16**, (2), pp 193–215

Curran, M A (2006) Life cycle assessment: principles and practice, *EPA/600/R-06/060*, US Environmental Protection Agency, Cincinnati

Elkington, J (1994) Towards the sustainable corporation: win-win-win business strategies for sustainable development, *California Management Review*, **36**, (2), pp 90–100

Elliott, M (2013) The 10-tenets for integrated, successful and sustainable marine management, *Marine Pollution Bulletin*, **74** (1), pp 1–5

EMAS (2015) About EMAS [online] http://ec.europa.eu/environment/emas/about/index_en.htm [accessed 25 July 2015]

Forum for the Future (2007) Fashioning sustainability: a review of the sustainability impacts of the clothing industry [online] http://www.forumforthefuture.org.uk [accessed 25 July 2015]

Forum for the Future (2009) Sustainability: trends in European retail [online] http://www.forumforthefuture.org.uk [accessed 25 July 2015]

Grant, D B (2012) *Logistics Management*, Pearson Education Limited, Harlow

Grant, D B, Trautrims, A and Wong, C Y (2015) *Sustainable Logistics and Supply Chain Management (Revised Edition)*, Kogan Page, London

Hart, S (1995) A natural-resource-based view of the firm, *Academy of Management Review*, **20** (4), pp 986–1014

Hemphill, T A (2005) Rejuvenating WalMart's reputation, *Business Horizons*, **48**, pp 11–21

ISO (2015) ISO 14000 – Environmental management [online] http://www.iso.org/iso/home/standards/management-standards/iso14000.htm [accessed 25 July 2015]

Klein, N (2000) *No Logo*, Flamingo, London

Levi Strauss and Co. (2004) Timeline [online] http://www.levistrauss.com/sites/default/files/librarydocument/2010/4/LSCo_Heritage_Timeline.pdf [accessed 25 July 2015]

Levi Strauss & Co. (2009) A product life cycle approach to sustainability [online] http://www.levistrauss.com/sites/default/files/librarydocument/2010/4/Product_Lifecycle_Assessment.pdf [accessed 25 July 2015]

Levi Strauss and Co. (2010) Life cycle of a jean [online] http://www.levistrauss.com/sustainability/product/life-cycle-jean [accessed 25 July 2015]

Markley, M J and Davis, L (2007) Exploring future competitive advantage through sustainable supply chains, *International Journal of Physical Distribution & Logistics Management*, **37** (9), pp 763–74

Mollenkopf, D (2006) Environmental sustainability: exploring the case for environmentally sustainable supply chains, *CSCMP Explores*, **3**, Fall/Winter, CSCMP, Lombard, IL

Mottner, S and Smith, S (2009) WalMart: supplier performance and market power, *Journal of Business Research*, **62**, pp 535–41

Murphy, E (2013) Key success factors for achieving green supply chain performance: a study of UK ISO 14001 certified manufacturers, University of Hull PhD thesis, Hull, UK [online] https://hydra.hull.ac.uk/resources/hull:8412 [accessed 25 July 2015]

Penrose, E (2009) *The Theory of the Growth of the Firm* (4th edn) Oxford University Press, Oxford

Rogers, D S and Tibben-Lembke, R S (1998) *Going Backwards: Reverse trends and practices,* Reverse Logistics Executive Council, University of Nevada-Reno

Shen, B (2014) Sustainable fashion supply chain: lessons from H&M, *Sustainability*, **6**, pp 6236–49

Turker, D and Altuntas, C (2014) Sustainable supply chain management in the fast fashion industry: an analysis of corporate reports, *European Management Journal*, **32**, pp 837–49

Williamson, O E (1999) *The Mechanisms of Governance*, Oxford University Press Inc., New York

World Business Council for Sustainable Development (2007) Energy efficiency in buildings: business realities and opportunities [online] http://www.wbcsd.org [accessed 25 July 2015]

World Economic Forum (2009) *Supply Chain Decarbonization: The role of logistics and transport in reducing supply chain carbon emissions*, World Economic Forum, Geneva

INDEX

NB: page numbers in *italic* indicate figures or tables